Living Deeply *is the accumulated wisdom of many of our greatest living teachers, all adepts in the goal of personal transformation. This is one of the finest collections of gentle, penetrating insights available. Highly recommended.*

—Larry Dossey, MD, author of *The Extraordinary Healing Power of Ordinary Things*

Living Deeply *provides us with some of the most significant insights into spiritual transformation that I have ever read. Based on interviews with spiritual teachers, leading scientific researchers, religion scholars, important public intellectuals, and major writers, this volume is a remarkable example of an integrative approach to a topic of immense importance. It is marvelous to look through the different windows of transformation that are so richly described and interpreted both spiritually and scientifically.* Living Deeply *is a major accomplishment that will hopefully become a classic in an emerging field. It is truly a brilliant synthesis. I think* Living Deeply *will change lives and change the world for the better.*

—Stephen G. Post, Ph.D., professor of bioethics at Case Western Reserve University School of Medicine

living DEEPLY

The Art & Science of Transformation in Everyday Life

Marilyn Mandala Schlitz, Ph.D.
Cassandra Vieten, Ph.D.
Tina Amorok, Psy.D.

New Harbinger Publications, Inc.

Publisher's Note

This publication is designed to provide accurate and authoritative information in regard to the subject matter covered. It is sold with the understanding that the publisher is not engaged in rendering psychological, financial, legal, or other professional services. If expert assistance or counseling is needed, the services of a competent professional should be sought.

A copublication of New Harbinger Publications and Noetic Books

Distributed in Canada by Raincoast Books

Copyright © 2007 by Marilyn Mandala Schlitz, Cassandra Vieten, and Tina Amorok
New Harbinger Publications, Inc.
5674 Shattuck Avenue
Oakland, CA 94609
www.newharbinger.com

Cover and text design by Amy Shoup
Acquired by Catharine Sutker
Edited by Amy Johnson

Library of Congress Cataloging-in-Publication Data

Schlitz, Marilyn.
  Living deeply : the art and science of transformation in everyday life
/ Marilyn Mandala Schlitz, Cassandra Vieten, and Tina A. Amorok.
    p. cm.
  Includes bibliographical references.
  ISBN-13: 978-1-57224-533-4 (pbk. : alk. paper)
  ISBN-10: 1-57224-533-6 (pbk. : alk. paper)
  1. Consciousness. 2. Attention. 3. Change (Psychology) 4.
Spirituality. I. Vieten, Cassandra. II. Amorok, Tina. III. Title.
BF311.S3825 2007
158.1--dc22
                                    2007041232

10   09   08

10   9   8   7   6   5   4   3   2

Contents

Living Deeply:
The Fate of the Earth

—*Robert Thurman, Ph.D.*

As you savor the thoughtful messages in *Living Deeply*, consider this simple meditation. You are in a space capsule with Edgar Mitchell, the Apollo 14 astronaut. You're there in the vastness of outer space. You see all the stars shining majestically, unobscured by lights from any cities. You look down and see something that looks like a round, opalescent, glistening, shining jewel. You can see the blue of the oceans, the white of the clouds, the brown streaks of the deserts, the gray mountaintops, and the green of the jungles and forests. And of course, you're with Edgar, so you're hoping you're going to get back safely to this jewel called Earth.

You're having a vision of the unity of life on this planet. You may also be aware simultaneously that there are infinite numbers of such jewels in the universe. But this is yours—your home. It is also the home of six billion other human beings and many trillions of other life forms. As you look, you feel a wonderful sense of oneness and togetherness with all of those beings living on this thin, delicate film on the surface of molten rock under a thin layer of air—like the fuzz on a peach.

As you look down at this jewel, you have a little tinge of sorrow about the foolish people who are destroying the basis of life on this planet. It doesn't frighten you too much, though, for you realize that there must be some degree of wisdom, generosity, love, and compassion to match the beauty of Mother Earth, Mother Gaia.

From this perspective of deep space, you may then do what the Tibetans call *offering the mandala*. By *mandala* they mean the whole of the protected zone wherein life, mind, and spirit can thrive. You notice that there is an element in you that is possessive about this planet. In a way, even your own mind has a little element of what those foolish people who try to conquer and exploit life have in them. You may become aware that sometimes you, too, feel like you own the place. And yet you realize, from that capsule in deep space, that no one owns it. You can then imagine that you pick up the entire planet very gently in your hands—and you give it away. If you believe in angels, you give it to them. If you believe in deities, you give it to them. If you don't believe in all of that, you just give it to the enlightened beings. You give it away to wisdom. You detach yourself from a sense of ownership, and as you do this, you realize that you are a guest. And you realize that this ultimate generosity is the basis of true happiness.

This subtle shift in awareness is what *Living Deeply* is all about. By transforming our consciousness, we participate in the transformation of the world. Each of us has the capacity to shift from a dominator world-view to one in which we realize life is a precious gift; we understand what a privilege it is to be alive. Through hours of research and deep inquiry with masters from many world traditions, and surveys with everyday folks like you and me, Marilyn Schlitz, Cassandra Vieten, and Tina Amorok offer us a map to an expanded model of reality. As these noetic scientists explore the interface of Western science and Eastern "inner science," they offer insights essential to meeting the challenges of a twenty-first-century planet that out-of-control humans are pushing toward destruction. Through their findings based on a decade of serious research, heard through the voices of many wisdom teachers, the authors help us recognize more fully that our life is totally interwoven with every other person and with all other species on our beloved planet.

This book reveals that a sense of unity and connection is part of most world traditions. It certainly is very much a part of Buddhist philosophy, which I describe as "engaged realism." Buddha's discovery, so long ago, was that suffering comes out of ignorance of the true nature of reality, and from this ignorance arises an attachment to the control and domination of the Earth and the life that inhabits it. While we may be drawn to worldly delights, the Buddha observed that people's core needs are more basic, dealing with the meaning of life, sickness, old age, death, and suffering.

Buddha was not a religious prophet, but he was not an atheist either. He actually was said to have met the Hindu god Brahma during his transformative experience. In a state of meditation, he traveled with his subtle body-mind into the heavens. He came into the throne room, and Brahma was there with all the other little godlings. And Buddha said, "Oh great Brahma, I hear you are the world creator. Since you created it, you must know how it works. I am determined to discover how the world works, so please tell me." At first dismissive of Buddha, Brahma later called to him on his way out of heaven. "I can't let you leave without giving you a proper answer," he said. "You see, the thing is, I didn't really create it, and therefore I don't know how it works. I'm just the biggest shot around here. But these godlings think I did create it and they think I know how it works and they feel secure in my protection. If I had said to you in front of them, 'I don't know what's going on,' they would have had an identity crisis, and we're a little short of shrinks here in heaven. But you're going to be a Buddha in a future life, and you will know how it works and in that time you have to do two things. One, come and tell me. I'm a quick study; I am "God," after all. And two, tell the human beings that when things go terribly wrong for them—when their children die, they have a terrible accident, there's a disaster or a catastrophe—tell them it's not my fault. I'm not in total control. I do my best for them. But it's all our mutual karma. It's our entire mutual collective situation that draws these difficulties down upon us."

So Buddha did meet God, but he didn't get a "message from God" like the ones that lead many religious founders to rush out and say "Believe in this or that or the other and then we'll save you from suffering." Buddha did not say that to people. In fact, he did not say that believing in anything would save you. He said, "Eureka! There's a way you can be saved from suffering, but that way is that you have to understand yourself and you have to understand your reality."

Now just the fact that he had a vision of life doesn't prove he was right. Even though hundreds of millions of people over the millennia have thought he was right, he may have been wrong. So the Buddha founded an educational movement rather than a religion. His vision was to bring out our own wisdom rather than to assert the truth. He taught in dialogic form, like Socrates and Confucius. He talked with people, questioning them, getting them to think critically, helping them to see through their own delusions, and encouraging them to come up with a deeper insight into the nature of things.

In that sense, Buddha was a scientist—a noetic scientist. He understood that the most important factor in the quality of life for a human being is how the person's mind is managed. From this perspective, transforming our consciousness is the most important work we can ever do. And today, as I travel with His Holiness, the Dalai Lama, he always tells us that we should not think that the solution is to all become Buddhists, but rather that we should explore for ourselves ways of training and educating the mind, developing the emotions, becoming aware of ourselves, managing our negative habits, and detoxifying ourselves from our mental toxins.

This can be done, he tells us, if you are a Christian or a Jew or a Muslim or a Hindu or a secular humanist or something else. The goal is to free our minds from suffering by understanding who we really are. What the Buddha discovered is that the nature of reality is bliss. Of course, he didn't say we have to believe that, but he encouraged us to investigate for ourselves, and he reported that this is what he himself discovered. Not from a place of fanatic, fundamentalist spirituality, but from a place grounded in a deep respect for the mystery of life and a consciousness that sees the connections rather than the appearance of separation.

What is needed today is an expansion of the noetic sciences—the kind of sciences that allow us to understand our inner being. As we explore the nature of consciousness, we can see that the root cause of the destruction of this planet is the toxins of our mind, especially delusion, hatred, and greed. Hatred produces war, greed produces industrial overproduction and pollution, and delusion makes us want to do all of that but keeps us miserable anyway. Noetic sciences should be a national and even international priority, allowing each of us to be the scientist of our own experience, our own way of knowing and being in the world.

As we turn our attention inward, we begin to discover, just as the many people interviewed for this book express so elegantly, that we are not the center of the universe and that we do not control the nature of reality. Contrary to what we hear from the materialist domains of science, which emphasize reductionism and an objective detachment from the world outside ourselves, we are not really separate from each other or from the world in which we live. Through a process of consciousness transformation, whether sudden or gradual, you can become more and more aware of the ways in which you are interconnected with all other beings. When you realize this, the struggle is over. The joy of others becomes your joy. You become compassionate about the suffering of others because it's your suffering. Realizing your interconnectedness is like going into a cold stream on a warm summer day. You put that toe in and you say, "Oh, I didn't need to come swimming here. I think I'll go back. I'll go back into my air conditioning. I don't need to jump in there. I might have a heart attack!" But then you jump in anyway, and it changes your whole day, your whole life, and you love it. As each of us jumps into this stream, we are contributing to the healing of ourselves, our fellow humans, and all the living beings that make up this precious planet we call home. As a kind British lady I know once said, "Think globally. Act joyfully." This is indeed the art and science of living deeply.

Enjoy this book, so wisely and lovingly put together by its authors, which provides you with an inspiring vision of what you will find, to your lasting delight, when you use your chosen method to take a really good look into your mind, your world, and your interconnectedness with all life. It is my pleasure and privilege to congratulate the authors for their accomplishment, and to welcome you to the real world to which this book is an open door.

—Robert A. F. Thurman
Jey Tsong Khapa Professor of Indo-Tibetan
Buddhist Studies, Columbia University
President, Tibet House US
Author of *Inner Revolution, Infinite Life,* and
The Tibetan Book of the Dead
September 18, 2007

Preface

—*Richard Gunther*

I was in a Gestalt session at the Esalen Institute, sitting in a circle with other seekers, when I suddenly felt an urge to leave the group and walk onto the adjoining balcony of Fritz Perls's house, a circular dwelling that overlooks the dramatic Big Sur coastline. As I left the group and stepped onto this balcony, I walked into a world of unbelievable beauty. It was a brilliant day, the sun reflecting off the surf that broke on the rocks below. The shoreline extended south for miles, rock, sand, and waves, with the occasional seal. It was a breathtaking vista, completed by mountains just beyond the coast. I felt like the whole scene was smiling at me, awaiting my arrival, and I was flooded with contentment and the joy of feeling whole, of *being blessed*. It was as though I had walked through a sci-fi energy screen into a new world. The sun, the sea, and the mountains had always been external objects that I could describe by intensity (the sun), by scale (the mountains), and by color (the sea), but on that magic day these descriptions were merely linear, not true reflections of all I was experiencing. For the first time ever, external physical elements had become a part of my internal world.

I am not a religious person, I am a very successful, highly rational businessman, but at that moment I experienced a profound spiritual awakening, an awareness that I was in a markedly altered state of being, a different reality. My awakening was this: *we are all part of a single entity.* I was part of all others and all others were part of me. I soared into this new awareness, losing all sense of myself as an individual. *There is no me alone, only a universal us.* Is this what it means to be truly human? I wondered. To feel—to know—that all reality is totally connected? Since all matter is a form of energy in motion, could there be a collective consciousness at the molecular level that stems from some sort of subatomic connection? I only knew that I had never felt this breadth and depth in my life before. I was certain, with no question in my mind, that I had had a fleeting glimpse of a new, wonderful level of existence.

What had caused this awareness, this opening, to suddenly explode in me? Would this enhanced level of being become permanent, or would it disappear as soon as I left the balcony? And if it did fade, what could I do to revive the profundity? That experience was almost forty years ago, and while the dramatic peak of those moments has dimmed, the life-changing insight has remained. I realized then that I had been living my life in a narrow arc of reality. I was worker, husband, father, and citizen, and that was the circle of my days. I learned from those moments of insight that I was, in my soul, a highly spiritual person—I needed the shock of this opening to accept that truth.

This great realization has vitally affected my life. Today, some forty years later, I am open to thoughts and moments of beauty and love in ways that I wasn't in my early life. I joyfully participate in the world of service. I speculate on spiritual questions and the mysteries of God and the universe. I am amazed by the majesty of the heavens at night and wonder at the magic of existence. I still live a full life as husband, father (and now grandfather), businessman, and social entrepreneur, but now I am also often awed by the marvel of being alive.

Why did this awakening happen at this particular time, and were there unique conditions that precipitated the event? The environment at Esalen was certainly wonderfully supportive, and the setting full of physical beauty. However, is it possible that what I experienced was a glimpse of the next natural maturational stage of a self-reflective person? A person whose vision has broadened and deepened to include a sense of wonder, awe, and mystery buried during an earlier, more combative stage of life?

Psychologist Erik Erikson (1982) describes the individual's growth process as comprised of eight stages. Stage eight, the final stage, he describes as "elder adulthood," a stage marked by a tension between integrity and despair. But is there perhaps a ninth stage? A stage in which an individual sees himself as part of a greater whole? A stage in which an individual outgrows the sole focus on self? With the enhanced vision of this stage could come the opportunity to explore a different path in life, to see yourself as a citizen in a wondrous new world, to become an active participant in this broader scene and invest yourself in the effort to create a more aware and compassionate world. In this stage, our expanded consciousness can lead us into the world of service as our next work in the world.

In my Jewish tradition there is a Hebrew phrase *Tikkun Olam*, which translates into English as "the repair of the world." It is to this path—to the work of repairing the world—that my Esalen enlightenment has led me. I offer this question: is transformation a necessary part of the human process for those who move along this path, either through choice or through some mystery of creation?

You may be wondering if this new insight has helped me through rough times. My wonderful twelve-year-old granddaughter Eva, a black belt in tae kwon do, was representing California in the Junior Olympics when she stepped out to cross a public street and was hit and killed by a drunk driver. This most remarkable young woman was lost forever. I was crushed, devastated. How could this have happened? She had so much to offer—why her? I have never known such pain, for Eva and the life she will never have, for our children whose lives are shattered, for my wife and me.

Over the years since that tragedy I have gradually climbed out of the deep blackness of despair, still with no answer for my "why?" questions. But just as my joyous experience at Esalen opened my eyes to a broader awareness of reality, so, too, did this tragedy broaden my understanding of the complexities, anguishes, and unknowns in life. This broadened understanding has given me more compassion for the pain I see everywhere—for friends who are sick, some dying; for the millions of people starving around the world; for the one-third of the world's population that suffers from crushing poverty. As I have seen our children, Eva's parents, battle back to life, I have been filled with admiration and gratitude for the strength of the human spirit. This insight has not only deepened my sensitivity and compassion, it has led me into my principal public service activity. I serve in the field of microenterprise, helping where I can to fight the battle against worldwide poverty.

I still cry when I think of Eva. Some nights I still try to reach my heart out to her heart. Is her energy out there somewhere for me to contact? Who knows what the next step will be when I move beyond this life. Maybe my spirit will contact her spirit, somewhere, someday. I believe that the transformations that I have experienced, both joyous and tragic, have awakened me to the great mysteries that exist—and for this awakening I am most grateful.

The purpose of *Living Deeply* is to make these transformative shifts in awareness available to all who seek them. *Living Deeply* is written by three scholars who have reached out to the great transformative teachers of our time and collected their accumulated wisdom in this volume. The authors and I share the belief that all human beings are born with innate capacities for compassion, joy, and service; unfortunately, living in our complex, torn world frequently buries these birth gifts. It is my hope that *Living Deeply* will, for many, open the door to a life that is wider, deeper, and more fulfilling than they had ever imagined possible. May it be so.

—Richard Gunther

Acknowledgments

This book is the result of indirect contributions from more people than we can possibly mention, including the membership, staff, and board of the Institute of Noetic Sciences (IONS).

In terms of direct contributions, we are grateful to Richard Gunther, whose vision and generosity initiated and sustained this study of transformation. We appreciate Peter Baumann, Bruce McEver, and the Clements Foundation, whose support and keen insight helped shape our study to have the broadest possible impact. We are also indebted to Jeremy Tarcher, who planted the seeds of this book, and to George Zimmer, for standing by us through thick and thin.

We are grateful beyond measure to our administrative team at IONS, without whom none of this would have happened. To Jenny Mathews and Charlene Farrell, you are dear and shining lights. We thank Kelly Durkin for lugging equipment all over creation to film in every kind of inhospitable condition, and her assistants Ladd McPartland and Jose Vergelin for their skillful filming of our interviews. We thank, as well, Orly Ben Yosef for graciously filming our early interviews. Our gratitude also goes to Kathleen

Erickson Freeman, Olivia Hansen, and Arianna Husband for all the various ways they encouraged us, and to Matthew Gilbert, editor of the IONS magazine, *Shift*, who collaborated with Catharine Sutker and the wonderful team at New Harbinger Publications to create a Noetic Books/New Harbinger partnership.

We wholeheartedly thank the over 900 research participants who contributed their time and effort to complete our surveys and interviews. These individuals not only spent valuable minutes and hours of their lives helping us, they opened their hearts and told us their stories. We thank them for so generously trusting us with their deepest hopes and fears, and their most intimate experiences of joy and pain, in our quest to make positive transformation possible for everyone who seeks it. We also give thanks and a huge cheer to the team of research interns and volunteers who spent many hundreds of hours coding videotapes line by line, transcribing interviews, conducting thematic analyses, brainstorming, and—after diving into this ocean of data—resurfacing with buried treasures to share with us. It takes a village to raise a research program of this size! Their generosity, commitment, sense of humor, and wisdom make them coinvestigators on this collaborative effort. Our core team of interns included: Alicia Bright, Damian Bundschuh, Nathalie Daneau, Michelle Fontaine, Brandon Houston, Nancy Lund, Lee Lusted, Tatsuo Okaya, Frank Pascoe, Claire Russell, and Judy Scheffel. Research volunteers included: Lynn Abraham, Emily Banelis, Ray Benton, Jackie Bitowt, Tobias Bodine, Deborah Breitbach, Patricia Brooks, Gary Buck, Nick Cederland, Shana Chrystie, Adrienne Citron, Carey Clark, Cathy Coleman, Ameko Crain, Patricia Danaher, Karen Dawson, Rita de los Santos, Ann Delvin, Adam Dolezal, Cardum Dottin, Jerry Duke, Ted Esser IV, Lynn Gardener, Stephanie Goodman, Gail Hayssen, Amy Helm, Celeste Jackson, Eli Jacobson, Jennifer Jandak, Linda Kaplan, Kathleen Kendrick, Stephen Kenny, Susan Knight, Kevin Kohley, Rebecca Kraeg, Judith McBride, Rainbow Moon, Kerry Needs, Serena Philips, Sherri Phillips, Brian Pilecki, Linda Ratto, Jennifer Regoli, Linda Roebuck, Billie Rogers, Sunny Sabini, Joan Sadler, Jasmine Scott, Mary Murray Shelton, Doug Slakey, Susan Steele, Serena Sterling, Karin Swann, Elizabeth Valenti, Connie Venhaus, Jean Vieten, Pat Vieten, Claudia Welss, and Ben Young.

We also thank Adam Cohen, who collaborated on the survey research, and others who collaborated and consulted on this project, including John

Astin, Susanne Brown, Khadijah Chadly, Scott Churchill, Ken Corr, Charles Grob, Solomon Katz, Dacher Keltner, Margaret Kemeny, Moira Killoran, Joan Koss-Chioino, Jeffrey Kripal, Michael McCullough, James O'Dea, John Phalen, Dean Radin, Belvie Rooks, Roger Walsh, Howie Whitehouse, Richard Wiseman, and many others. We thank Ladd McPartland for compiling the tonglen meditation in chapter 7. We thank our families at home—Giovanni, Skyler, David, and Indigo—for putting up with us through long days, late nights, and obsessive talk about transformation! And in the same spirit we thank our friends. You have all kept the hearth fires lit, warming our homes and hearts and helping us grow both ourselves and this work.

We wholeheartedly thank the teachers and practitioners who participated in our 1998 and 1999 focus groups: Alise Agar; Angeles Arrien, Ph.D.; Dean Elias, Ph.D.; Dick Gunther; Richard Heckler, Ph.D.; Stella Humphreys; Tom Hurley; Michael Hutton; Don Johnson, Ph.D.; Brooks Jordan; Moira Killoran, Ph.D.; Ann Krantz, Ph.D.; Bokara Legendre; Sharon Lehrer; George Leonard; Joel Levey, Ph.D.; Michelle Levey, MA; David Lukoff, Ph.D.; Karen Malik, MA; Ted Mallon; Frank Ostaseski; Margaret Paloma Pavel, Ph.D.; Yvonne Rand; Celeste Smeland; Jeremy Taylor, D.Min.; Luisah Teish; and Kevin Townley.

And finally, we are especially grateful to the teachers, masters, and scholars of transformative traditions, listed at the back of the book, who participated in our 2002-2007 research interviews. Our time with you was transformative in itself. The research findings you will encounter in this book rest upon the wisdom and generosity of these teachers. In the midst of so many demands on their time and energy, these transformative leaders, without fail, gave us their thoughtful attention, again and again naming the unnameable, speaking the unspeakable, and bringing the ineffable down to earth in terms that we could understand—and always with a sparkle in their eyes! Words cannot express our gratitude for their wisdom and unfailing support, both in this project and in their work in the world. In particular we honor the memory of Wink Franklin, Gilbert Walking Bull, and Rhea White, all of whom left their physical form before this work reached publication. We hope this book carries your wisdom into the world in an honorable manner.

Introduction

If you're like most people, your life has become increasingly complex and fast paced. As you rush from one event or task to another, you're most likely being bombarded by "weapons of mass distraction" that tip you off course even as you dutifully struggle to maintain your balance. Between the ringing of your cell phone, e-mail, kids' soccer games, business trips, 514 television stations (not to mention the TiVo recordings waiting for you), and taking care of all the basics, you may find yourself just skimming the surface of your life. It's easy to end up zipping from one thing to another, replacing truly renewing activities with more numbing pleasures. These many demands on your time can force you to make tough choices. You may find yourself prioritizing obligations that cannot be avoided and relegating joyful, meaning-making pursuits to the end of your to-do list. As a result, much of the time you may feel stressed, depleted, or overwhelmed.

Alternatively, you may feel a sense of restlessness, boredom, or meaninglessness. You may be someone who's now living "under the radar," no longer engaged by the pursuits that once brought you a sense of meaning and joy. You may feel disconnected from the world or have trouble finding your place in it. Perhaps you want to break out into a richer and fuller life, but you haven't yet figured out how.

Or, maybe you have reached a place of relative balance and abundance in your life, and now you want to integrate your insights and transformations more fully into your relationships, your work, and your creative pursuits. Perhaps you envision that when you live from a place of greater depth, the roots and fruits of your life will generate the kind of sustenance that touches others. You may want to create a life that will allow you to contribute to the well-being of your community in ways that are in line with your talents, affinities, inner resources, and most authentic nature.

Regardless of which of these drives you can relate to the most (it may be a little bit of each), you can probably identify a desire within yourself to live more deeply. If so, you are not alone. As psychologist and leader in mind/body medicine Jon Kabat-Zinn told us:

> [There is] *a huge and rising hunger on the part of just about everybody for authentic experience and reconnecting with what's deepest and best in ourselves in an ever accelerating and complex world.* (2004)

The good news: opportunities to transform your life in ways both small and large are available to you in every moment of every day—there are an infinite number of doorways into living deeply. The possibly daunting news: living deeply may require nothing less than a complete transformation of the way you view the world and your place in it.

LIVING DEEPLY

As you'll read, our decade of research on transformation has found that dramatic and lasting change for the better springs from *radically shifting your perspective of who you are*. Great external changes often come out of this shift in perspective. You may well find that as meaning and purpose become more clear to you, things that are out of alignment in your life gradually (and sometimes quickly) fall away. But the most fundamental change is within you; it is a profound shift in your perspective, where you direct your attention and your intention.

This most essential change, the one from which all other changes spring, is a change in your worldview and your perception of what's possible. Transforming your consciousness may be the most important thing you can do for yourself and the world.

Ultimately, this book is a kind of map of the transformative terrain. While we aren't able to traverse the entire terrain by ourselves, we have been able to talk to the explorers who have been there, some of whom have traversed common pathways and some of whom have taken exotic journeys and are bringing back their travel journals to share what they found. We explore the mystery of consciousness with a Christian monk, a Lakota elder, a rabbi, and a Zen Buddhist roshi. We identify the common elements of transformation in the experiences of a Himalayan yoga swami, a transpersonal psychologist, a seasoned oncologist, and a Methodist minister. We found, amazingly, that an evangelical Christian, a successful businessman, a devout Sufi, a skilled athlete, a dedicated physician, a reluctant soldier, a Jewish mother, and an agnostic musician are all walking surprisingly similar paths. We share some of these overlapping cartographies with you in hopes that you will recognize some of the terrain yourself and begin to more consciously create your own path to transformation. *Living Deeply* will provide you with resources to help you maintain your balance while recruiting you to actively collaborate with the forces—both internal and external—that conspire to move you toward wholeness.

THE ART AND SCIENCE OF TRANSFORMATION

In this book, we share what we've learned about transformation through a decadelong program of research, and we explore how our research findings can help you live more fully and deeply. No matter who you are, where you come from, or what your current path is—whether you seek to transform your life completely or to simply make adjustments that will add a layer of richness and depth to your life—we hope that you'll find something valuable here.

The Institute of Noetic Sciences

This focused inquiry builds on thirty-five years of consciousness research at the Institute of Noetic Sciences (IONS). *Noetic* refers to knowledge that comes to us directly through our subjective experiences or inner authority. This type of knowledge might take the form of an intuition that helps guide your decisions, or an epiphany that leads you to a creative breakthrough. Moreover, noetic experiences often carry an unusual level of authority that can help guide you to new understandings and new ways of being. Noetic experiences thus differ from the kind of knowledge that comes through reason or the objective study of the external world. However, we argue that it is both possible and necessary to bring to this realm of intuitive knowledge a scientific perspective and method. Bringing a scientific approach to noetic phenomena has allowed IONS to delve deeply into the nature of human consciousness and its vast potentials.

Edgar Mitchell, an Apollo 14 astronaut, founded IONS in 1973. Having had the remarkable opportunity to walk on the moon, Mitchell then had the window seat on the way home. During the flight back, a moment of epiphany occurred in which his entire sense of meaning and purpose shifted. In that moment he understood that the major crises of our times are due not to aspects inherent to the external world, but to flawed and inadequate worldviews. The mission of IONS is to explore consciousness through both science and human experience in order to advance individual and collective transformation.

In the fall of 1997, our team of researchers initiated a study focused on the process of transformation. We collected narrative descriptions of transformations experienced by people representing many walks of life. From mundane to life-threatening, these experiences led our respondents to fundamental shifts in their sense of self and their way of being in the world. For one man it came during his time as a conscientious objector in Vietnam. Through a specific prayer, in an extraordinary moment, he found inner peace even as he saw his colleagues being shot down. For a mother and daughter, it came when the mother used energy healing to help her distraught daughter find balance during a life transition, leading to profound transformative shifts for both.

We were intrigued by the fact that while the experiences people shared with us differed widely, a golden thread of commonality shone through them all. Some experiences occurred in extraordinary situations; others in ordinary, everyday situations. Some were initiated by experiences of great suffering; others by experiences of awe and wonder. But in each, a radical broadening of worldview and redefinition of identity, meaning, and purpose took place.

Despite differences in content and context, the process of transformation was described very similarly—often even with the very same words. Whether told by a seasoned meditator or a mother of three who had never meditated at all, these stories hinted at a jewel-like tapestry of human experience that transcends cultural differences. As we analyzed the stories for patterns that would shed light on the inner workings of transformation, we found ourselves filled with more questions: What constitutes a transformation of consciousness? What triggers transformation? How can we sustain the moments that move us beyond ourselves? And what impact do transformational experiences have on how we live our lives?

Seeking answers, we took advantage of the wide range of teachers and leaders in the human potential movement living and working in the San Francisco Bay Area and convened three focus groups between September 1998 and May 1999. To our surprise and delight, teachers from different transformational programs came eagerly. They, too, were seeking answers to questions about the mystery of transformation. The discussions were poignant, honest, and often profoundly moving. Together we began to map deep inventories of life experience that led the participants to express gratitude, feelings of connectedness, and a strong sense of community. Often the transformational journey is lonely, even for the masters themselves.

Inspired—and still filled with more questions than answers—we decided to probe the topic of transformation more deeply, and with greater scientific rigor. Beginning in 2002, the three of us invited fifty world-renowned scholars, teachers, and practitioners to participate in detailed research interviews. These teachers were selected specifically to represent a diverse range of transformative practices and philosophies (see figure 1). They represent traditional religions, spiritual philosophies, and modern transformative movements with roots in Eastern, Western, and indigenous traditions, as well as forms that integrate many paths—sometimes referred to as *integral*.

Our overarching goals were to explore the phenomenon of consciousness transformation and learn more about the various transformative paths that lead to beneficial outcomes for self and community. In addition, we launched an online survey, both to begin to answer some of the questions that remained and to test some of our hypotheses (Vieten, Cohen, and Schlitz 2008). Do contemplative practices really foster the transformative process? Is a teacher or a community of like-minded practitioners useful? What kinds of practices are most helpful to what kinds of people? We heard from a schoolteacher in Illinois, a nurse in New York, a businessman in Los Angeles, and many others. Answering dozens of specific and open-ended questions, nearly nine hundred respondents helped us learn more about similarities and differences in the transformative process across people and practices.

While this sample is self-selected, and as such isn't representative of the general public in the way a random selection of all American households would be, it has offered a valuable opportunity for studying transformation in a large number of people who have lived through the process. Over 80 percent of those sampled reported having had at least one profoundly transformative experience, and 90 percent engage regularly in some form of transformative practice. The lives of these nine hundred people have become natural laboratories for studying the transformative process.

Over the years, we have engaged in thousands of hours of rigorous analysis of content and data from our fifty teacher interviews. Out of this work comes *Living Deeply*. We have organized the chapters in our book around the themes that emerged from our research. In each chapter we have carefully selected quotes (italicized text) from these surveys and interviews that illuminate our findings. In each phase of our research program, what has touched us most—what was emphasized again and again, and what we want to share with you—is the fact that transformation is an ongoing, natural process that's available to you right now. It's something that you can cooperate with in ways large and small, every day of your life.

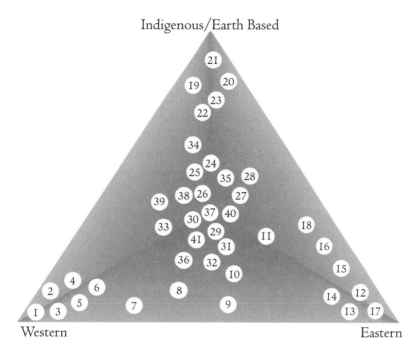

Indigenous/Earth Based

Western

Eastern

Figure 1

1. Roman Catholicism
2. Benedictine Catholicism
3. Lutheran Christianity
4. Episcopal Christianity
5. First Church of Christ
6. Church of Religious Science
7. Judaism
8. Kabbalah
9. Islam
10. Sufism
11. Nondualism
12. Vipassana (Buddhism)
13. Zen Buddhism
14. Shavism/Yoga
15. Kundalini Yoga
16. Transcendental Meditation
17. Bhakti Yoga
18. Himalayan Yoga
19. Yoruba
20. Goddess Religion/
    Earth-Based Spirituality
21. Native American Spirituality

22. Cross-Cultural Shamanism
23. Mongolian Shamanism
24. Psychedelic Psychotherapy
25. Somatics
26. Movement/Expressive Arts
27. Aikido
28. Johrei Healing
29. Transpersonal/
    Humanistic Psychology
30. Consciousness Studies
31. Integral Transformative Practice
32. Attitudinal Healing
33. Avatar
34. Holotropic Breathwork
35. Nine Gates Mystery School
36. Unitarian Universalism
37. Archetypal Perspectives/
    Dream Work
38. Relationship-Centered Medicine
39. Mindfulness/Mind-Body Medicine
40. Religious Scholarship
41. Noetic Sciences

The Perennial Philosophy and Pluralism: Two Guiding Lights

This project has been influenced by a search for common truths across cultures, philosophies, and people. We sought to shed light on a *perennial philosophy* of transformation, a term first used by sixteenth-century Italian philosopher Agostino Steuco in his book *De perenni philosophia libri X* of 1540. In the eighteenth century, German mathematician and philosopher Gottfried Leibniz used this term to designate a universal or shared set of truths that underlie all philosophies and religions, and Aldous Huxley later popularized it in his classic book *The Perennial Philosophy* (1945). Similarly, in our research we sought to find commonalities in the transformative process, across individuals, cultures, religions, and philosophies—a common map of the transformative terrain that would apply to people from all walks of life. As much as there are things that distinguish each of the perspectives, practices, or approaches we studied, our goal has been to find points of intersection.

Indeed, this book is organized as an exploration of the shared ground of transformation that exists across worldviews. However, even though descriptions of transformation overlap among traditions and individuals to an astounding degree, pointing to some important patterns in the transformative process, we realize that there is no simple formula. As we have engaged in this research program, we have confronted some of the challenges that naturally face any attempt to find patterns across different traditions, as well as challenges that typically occur with any scientific effort to objectify the ineffable. Indeed, in research such as this, there is the potential to overgeneralize, thereby trivializing fundamental and important distinctions between the various paths. While we cull out those aspects that are similar, we may be ignoring deep and important differences. These are important concerns, and we take them seriously.

As we engaged in our comparative analysis, we were informed by the work of cultural pluralism. Diana Eck of the Pluralism Project at Harvard University makes the distinction between *diversity*, which is a demographic fact, and *pluralism*, which is the celebration of difference (2006). Pluralism is an active engagement with diversity. It requires participation with "the other." Pluralism recognizes that while there is common and enduring wisdom that can be found in edicts such as the Golden Rule—wisdom that is likely to be equally applicable to all traditions—it's a serious oversimplification to view disparate religious, spiritual, and transformative frameworks as homogeneous.

Our experience thus far is that while commonalities among traditions point to a robust model of transformation that goes beyond sects and cultures, each individual tradition—and each individual person—provides a unique perspective that the others may not have. Forest-dwelling Buddhist monks who have explored the nature of their own minds for hours and years on end in silent solitude are likely to have something different to tell us about transformation than do nuns who have dedicated their lives to serving in urban-jungle soup kitchens. Moreover, both of these groups are different from the busy parent or overworked nurse who are also part of the transformative story.

In our research, and in this book, we have purposely and specifically focused on studying the kinds of transformations in consciousness that happened for Richard Gunther and countless others—to wit, transformations that sometimes quickly, sometimes gradually, but in all cases dramatically and permanently change the person's worldview to one of being more loving, kind, compassionate, altruistic, connected to others, and dedicated toward creating a more just, sustainable, and peaceful world for all.

All science, and all spirituality, begins with the quest to explore and then describe in detail a phenomenon—what causes it, what factors facilitate it, what factors inhibit it, what its outcomes are, and what mechanisms explain its occurrence—often to discover how the process can be facilitated intentionally. A good example is cancer remission. It is as natural for scientists as it is for mystics to delve as deeply as possible into healing events and positive outcomes in hopes that a deeper understanding of the phenomena will yield clues to facilitating or supporting the positive process in others.

For the mystic, this exploration might lead to a deep inward journey, initiation into the mysteries of traditions that seem to hold some keys to the experience, or many years of painstaking spiritual practices that shed light on the phenomenon. For the scientist, it may involve years of data collection and analysis, whether this takes the form of detailed interviews, reams of EEG printouts, hundred-megabyte databases of brain scans, or step-by-step clinical trials that test and retest potential biological targets or pharmaco-logic agents, also to shed greater light on the phenomenon of interest.

In our case, our single-minded focus was on the phenomenon of experi-ences people have, and practices they engage in, that stimulate and sustain a new worldview that may best be described as positive consciousness trans-formation (a term we will unpack in more detail in chapter 1, "Seeing with New Eyes"). We admit freely that our interest in this topic, much like that of a researcher who focuses on cancer remission, is to find out more about how it happens so that we can facilitate it in others.

Throughout our research, and throughout this book, we were dogged in following the golden thread of positive transformation, and in doing so did not take many other paths that may have been just as deserving of deep inquiry. In this book, we do not address in depth many of these paths. For example, what happens in the case of negative transformations in con-sciousness, such as becoming dedicated to a path of harm toward people who do not hold the same belief? What are the negative consequences of experiences of oneness or dissolution of self? What might be the dangers inherent in blending science and religion? Though these topics are worthy of exploration, we were dedicated to leaving these questions to the side for the moment, to stay focused on our goal. Again, we recognize the dangers of oversimplification where these topics are concerned, and we have attempted whenever possible to offer counterpoints to each premise for which we argue. In the end, however, our goal in this book, based on our research, is to make a case for the idea that positive consciousness transformation is possible, is more common than most might imagine, and is best explored by bringing together the perspectives of the scientist and the mystic.

NAVIGATING THIS BOOK

In this book we have drawn from:

- Findings from our own decadelong study of the trans-formative process—from analysis of hundreds of stories of transformation, teacher focus groups, fifty interviews with teachers and masters of transformative practices, and almost nine hundred surveys with people engaged in their own transformative journeys

■ Direct wisdom from a broad cross-section of religious, spiritual, and transformative practices, as shared with us by some of the leading voices in the transformative movement today

■ Scientific evidence from a diverse array of fields—from cognitive neuroscience to physics to psychoneuroimmunology to social psychology

■ Leading theories of transformation

■ Experiential practices for living deeply

Whether you're a seasoned practitioner of a formal transformative tradition, a practitioner of an eclectic array of practices, or a newcomer to the transformative path, you can use our research to affirm, deepen, and inspire your own inner experiences and insights.

This book isn't a new program of growth and change. There are thousands of programs and techniques available for personal transformation: crash courses in healing our internal splits, in reintroducing us to our inner wisdom, in mobilizing the law of attraction, and so on. These programs have been radically life changing for thousands, perhaps millions, of people. However, though this myriad of methods, programs, and techniques for enriching your life exists at your fingertips, it can sometimes be difficult to figure out what's right for you, let alone how to grow your new insights into long-term ways of being.

This book offers you a different approach to constructing your own transformative path, day by day—an approach based on what we've learned through our research and that of others about how transformation is stimulated and sustained. Your path may well include attending a transformative retreat or signing up for an intensive multiyear transformative training program. It might just as easily include a commitment to cook a grand meal once a week, start a reading group, plant an herb garden on your patio, or simply take ten quiet minutes for yourself each day. Rather than provide you with the next surefire formula for a life overhaul, *Living Deeply* will encourage you to find ways that you can add greater richness, meaning, depth, and joy to every moment of every day.

In chapter 1, "Seeing with New Eyes," we ask, What is it that actually shifts in a transformational experience? Chapter 2, "Doorways to Transformation," explores some of the various triggers and catalysts of transformation. In chapter 3, "Preparing the Soil," we identify three key elements that can help you set the stage for a transformation. In chapter 4, "Paths and Practices," we look at common patterns across diverse transformative practices and identify the activities and commitments that teachers across traditions identify as essential. In chapter 5, "Why Practice?" we explore some of the ways that transformative practice works to effect profound and lasting life change. In the next three chapters, we look at some of the major milestones of consciousness transformation. Chapter 6, "Life as Practice, Practice as Life," considers ways you can integrate transformative experiences into your everyday life, bringing them into your family, organizations, and institutions, grounding your transformation and making it sustainable for yourself and others. In chapter 7, "From 'I' to 'We,'" we discuss how transformative practice involves core shifts in your personal identity that translate into lasting changes in worldview. In chapter 8, "Everything Is Sacred," our research suggests that over time, you begin to see glimmers of the sacred shining through even the most mundane and sorrowful of experiences in everyday life. Finally, chapter 9, "No More Floating Clouds," offers a synthesis of what we've learned through our research on transformation. Here we present a model of consciousness transformation drawn from common elements across a variety of traditions. Recognizing the dynamic and nonlinear nature of the transformative process, we hope that this model will be useful for people at any stage of the process.

A TIME OF CONVERGENCE

We write this book at a unique moment in human history. Never before have so many worldviews, belief systems, and ways of understanding reality come into contact. Buddhist monks are sitting down with Harvard scientists to talk about the neuroscience of mindfulness. Indigenous healers are working side by side with physicians to treat patients in major hospitals.

Quantum physicists and living-systems biologists are confirming traditionally held spiritual views of consciousness.

This engagement of different ways of understanding what's real and true is leading to the discovery of new tools for living in the midst of complexity. As ancient spiritual wisdom converges with the latest scientific understandings of the world and our place in it, we are finding new answers to the age-old questions "Who am I?" and "What am I capable of becoming?"

This book weaves together the rigors of the scientific perspective with the deep wisdom of the world's traditions to create a nondenominational, multicultural map to help guide you on your way through the transformations—whether large or small—that impact your life, your relationships, and your community. We've sought to unearth the commonalities of diverse practices, to decipher pathways to transformation that you can use regardless of whether you are religious or spiritual; involved in business, the military, or the PTA; or get your peace of mind from meditation or the golf course. Ultimately, this book encourages you to become the scientist of your own experience and the cartographer of your own transformative journey. The opportunity is yours. Welcome to the adventure.

CHAPTER ONE:

Seeing with New Eyes

A transformation in consciousness effects a kind of double vision in people.
They see more than one reality at the same time, which gives a depth to both
their experience and to their response to the experience.
—*RACHEL NAOMI REMEN (2003)*

For Richard Gunther, who tells his story in the preface to this book, transformation happened in a moment. He stepped out onto a deck and experienced the beauty and splendor of the Big Sur coastline. He felt the sun on his flesh and the wind in his hair. But he also felt something else. Something much more meaningful: a change in his worldview. In one moment he was suddenly "flooded with contentment and the joy of feeling whole, of being blessed." In an instant, he experienced a paradigm shift that changed the way he saw the world—and his place in it.

While not everyone experiences it in a moment, Richard Gunther's experience can best be described as a *consciousness transformation*. Consciousness transformations are profound internal shifts that result in long-lasting changes in the way you experience and relate to yourself, others, and the world. It's not so much that this successful businessman became a different person. Instead, he experienced a change in his perception of reality—and in the process discovered more fully who he really is, independent of the social expectations and cultural conditioning that had previously shaped his sense of self.

Stop and reflect for a moment. Looking back over your life, can you find pivotal moments that broadened your perspective? Have there been times in your life that you identify as turning points—moments after which you saw the world in a more open and generous light? Have you ever felt connected to something greater than yourself, and in that connection felt self-centeredness slip away? Or have you noticed a more gradual process, where over a period of months or years you changed the way you viewed yourself and the world, little by little?

Consciousness transformations happen more often than you might think. Knowing more about what stimulates them, how they work, and what supports the process can help you jump on board rather than be just pulled along, getting bashed about in the process. By understanding transformation, you'll be better able to navigate the enormous changes that face each of us every day of our lives. As a result, you may be able to shift what is difficult and challenging into opportunity and adventure. Our premise is simple, yet radical: your behavior, attitudes, and ways of being in the world are changed in life-affirming and lasting ways only when your *consciousness transforms* and you commit to living deeply into that transformation. In this chapter we explore first what consciousness itself is, and then what consciousness transformation has proven to be for many people.

WHAT IS CONSCIOUSNESS?

Before we begin to delve more deeply into the terrain of consciousness transformation, let's define what we mean by *consciousness*. Consciousness is the quality of mind that includes your own internal reality. It includes self-awareness, your relationships to your environment and the people in your life, and your worldview or model of reality. Simply put, your consciousness determines how you experience the world. Your consciousness, or your perception of reality, is created by the interactions of your *subjective* and *objective* lives. Your subjective life is what exists in your inner experience; your objective life is what's "out there" in the world. The convergence of your self-identity and your perceptions of the world gives rise to your worldview—and thus how you relate to, mediate, and ascribe meaning to both these inner and outer worlds.

As a tradition, Buddhism may have done more than any other to systematically explore the complexities of consciousness and transformation. For thousands of years, Buddhist practitioners have been building a science of inner life, carefully mapping the terrain of mind and consciousness. B. Alan Wallace is one of the best-regarded scholars, translators, and bridge builders between Tibetan Buddhism and Western science. In 2003, he spoke to us about the nature of human consciousness:

> From the very inception of Buddhism itself, we have these statements by the Buddha of the primacy of the mind. This is uniform throughout Buddhism. If you are to understand the nature of reality as a whole, the understanding of consciousness—that by which we are able to observe and reflect upon anything whatsoever—is going to be crucial. It's a marvelous irony that without the mind, without observation, without consciousness, you would never have any science. And yet, it took four hundred years before consciousness actually became a legitimate topic of scientific inquiry.
>
> From this Tibetan Buddhist perspective, the brain is not really a repository of any mental phenomenon at all. It is much more of a conduit, a conditioner. This theory is just as compatible with all current neuroscientific knowledge as the notion that the brain is the ultimate repository or storehouse of memories and so forth. I have never seen any empirical evidence that compels me to believe that any mental event takes place inside the brain, lodged inside the brain. (2003)

Such a view, grounded in over a thousand years of empirical study by Tibetan Buddhist practitioners, is quite heretical when considered from the dominant scientific perspective, which considers all of consciousness as dependent on neuronal firing. In Western science, our experience of the subjective is considered an *epiphenomenon*, or by-product, of the brain. And yet, the study of Buddhist meditation has become a vital area of contemporary brain science. The worlds are indeed converging.

States of Consciousness and Abiding Consciousness

States of consciousness occur on a continuum from being awake and aware of yourself and your environment, to being in an unaware, not-wakeful state of dreamless sleep or coma. While we're most aware of two particular levels of consciousness—being awake and asleep—there are, in fact, many levels of consciousness, including non-ordinary states of consciousness. In the course of an average day, you may experience a range of these states, such as intense alertness, daydreaming, grogginess, sleeping and dreaming, heightened emotional states, or intoxication from alcohol or drugs. If you've ever experienced general anesthesia, you've traveled through many states of consciousness in a very short period of time.

However, consciousness not only refers to these transient, ever-changing states, it also refers to the way that we perceive things in general and across situations. When used this way, *consciousness* designates the overall way that you perceive the world and your place in it. In other words, your consciousness is every aspect of how you experience and understand reality. If all of your experiences, your various states of consciousness, were weather patterns—clouds, rain, rainbows, tornados, hurricanes, or summer breezes—your consciousness would be the sky in which they take place. Your consciousness is the context in which all of your experiences, perceptions, thoughts, and feelings converge.

It is this abiding aspect of consciousness that we're most interested in when we talk about consciousness transformation. The general consciousness you possess profoundly influences the states of consciousness you experience on a day-to-day basis. For example, if you're a person who tends to be generally optimistic, your general consciousness probably includes the assumptions that, overall, people are good and finding a solution to a problem is almost always possible. Thus, in your daily life, you'll react to situations in a generally trusting and open manner. In contrast, if you're a person who tends to react aggressively to difficult situations, your general consciousness probably includes the assumptions that the world isn't safe and you must defend yourself against even the smallest perceived threat. In other words, our various states of consciousness emerge out of our general pattern—personality traits, attitudes, beliefs, behaviors, and so on—of relating to the world. You can see, therefore, how transforming your general consciousness can have profound implications for the way you think, behave, and feel in your everyday life.

Consciousness and Worldview

We use the term "consciousness" to refer to how you experience the world. This use of consciousness includes all of your perceptions, both conscious and unconscious. A closely related term is "worldview." At times, how you experience the world may feel completely involuntary. "I view the world this way because the world is this way—what other way is there to view it?" It can be very difficult to shift a firmly entrenched model of reality. We can get pretty attached to what we think is true, important, and real—even when presented with evidence to the contrary. To a great extent, our worldview determines what we're capable of seeing, and therefore determines our perception of reality. What our worldview doesn't expand to contain quite literally escapes our perception. We just don't see it. This perception of reality colors our reactions and actions, every moment of every day.

A great example of this comes from David Sloan Wilson, who, in his book *Darwin's Cathedral: Evolution, Religion, and the Nature of Society*, speaks of "obviousness in retrospect" (2003, 125). In other words, once we have a theory for something and understand it is possible, we can see things that have been in front of us all along. Wilson recounts how Darwin as a young man studied under Adam Sedgwick, one of the founders of the science of geology. Before it was understood that glaciers had carved out the stunning valleys and gorges that pepper the Earth's landscape, it was thought that oceans (in particular the great flood described in the Bible) created these geological features. In his autobiography, Darwin explains how, along with Sedgwick, he hunted for fossils without noticing the obvious signs of glacial movement:

We spent many hours in Cwm Idwal, examining all the rocks with extreme care, as Sedgwick was anxious to find fossils in them; but neither of us saw a trace of the wonderful glacial phenomena all around us; we did not notice the plainly scored rocks, the perched boulders, the lateral and terminal moraines. Yet these phenomena are so conspicuous that, as I declared in a paper published many years afterwards in the *Philosophical Magazine*, a house burnt down by fire did not tell its story more plainly than did this valley. If it had still been filled by a glacier, the phenomena would have been less distinct than they now are.
(1887, 49)

This story shows how the a priori (prior) worldview of Sedgwick and Darwin actually *determined* what they saw and did not see. When our worldview shifts, new possibilities emerge from the very same landscape we already inhabit. This is one of the fundamental premises of this book—that who you are now, and what you have now, contains all you need for a richer, fuller, and more joy-filled life. The possibilities inherent in each day will become clear when your worldview allows you to see them.

WHAT IS CONSCIOUSNESS TRANSFORMATION?

This worldview shift is the kind of consciousness transformation that lies at the core of *Living Deeply*. We interviewed Frances Vaughan, one of the founders of humanistic and transpersonal psychology, who described it to us thus:

> … *transformation really means a change in the way you see the world—and a shift in how you see yourself. It's not simply a change in your point of view, but rather a whole different perception of what's possible. It's the capacity to expand your worldview so that you can appreciate different perspectives, so that you can hold multiple perspectives simultaneously. You're not just moving around from one point of view to another, you're really expanding your awareness to encompass more possibilities.*

Transformation implies a change in the sense of self. There's both an inner and an outer dimension to it. It requires inner work and an appreciation for how that connects to being in the world, and the outer work of action and service. Transformation involves multiple dimensions of a person: our self-concept, the way in which we relate to other people, how we see the world, and what we feel is worth doing. Transformation really touches every aspect of our lives and has a lot to do with changing values. Transformation is multidimensional. It involves the heart, mind, and spirit, and affects behavior and relationships in the world. (2002)

As Vaughan tells us, consciousness transformations often carry with them profound changes in our core values and priorities. We heard a similar point of view from physician, teacher, and author of *Kitchen Table Wisdom* (1996), Rachel Naomi Remen, who explained to us:

What seems real to me is the shift in experience, the permanent shift that happens for people—sometimes spontaneously, sometimes after years of practice, sometimes in times of crisis. I believe it was Proust who said the voyage of discovery lies not in seeking new vistas, but in having new eyes. The familiar is seen in a completely new way. Nothing changes, yet everything changes. The person is different. This kind of experience shifts a person's values, shuffles them like a deck of cards. And a value that's been on the bottom of the deck for many years may now turn out to be the top card and become the guiding principle of a person's life from this moment on. (2003)

Ultimately, we define consciousness transformation as a profound shift in your experience of consciousness, resulting in long-lasting changes in the way you understand and relate to yourself, others, and the world. We use the term "transformative experience" to refer to an experience that results in a lasting change in worldview, as opposed to an extreme, extraordinary, peak, or spiritual experience that doesn't necessarily translate into long-term changes in your way of being.

Although transformation results in changes in thoughts, feelings, and behaviors, the actual process doesn't require changing these things directly.

In fact, most experts we interviewed told us that consciousness itself doesn't change. Instead it is your *perception* of consciousness that changes. Said in another way, who you are "authentically" doesn't change—rather, as false selves are shed and buried elements of yourself are retrieved and integrated, your expression of your self aligns with who you truly are. Thought patterns, attitudes, behaviors, and ways of being in the world that are incongruent with your core self may drop away.

Mahamandaleshwar Swami Nityananda Paramahamsa, originally from Mumbai, India, spoke directly to this point. Nityananda is a guru in the lineage of Swami Muktananda and Bhagavan Nityananda from Ganeshpuri, India; as a disciple of Muktananda, he was chosen in July 1981, along with his sister Swami Chidvilasananda, to succeed Muktananda and carry on the work of inspiring people to practice meditation and the yoga of self-knowledge. We spoke with him at a devotee's ranch home in Petaluma. On consciousness transformation, Nityananda said:

> *Consciousness is constant—the transformation is in the individual.* [Hindu] *scriptures talk about consciousness as an expanded state of awareness at all times. We talk about the limited self and the whole self or consciousness. The limited self is the mind, the ego, the intellect, the subconscious, the senses, and the organs of action. And it is from this that we actually view the world. But when we say that somebody is enlightened or realized, he or she has understood, "I am consciousness. I am not the mind, I am not all of these other things from which most humans perceive and experience the world."*
>
> *So the transformation is going from being limited and small to being whole. And when you come to the experience of a whole consciousness, a full consciousness, there's nothing else. So the mantra that our families use is, "What is full and what comes from full remains full, and then merges back into the full."*
>
> *Therefore, the wholeness never actually goes away. We are born of the whole, and so even now, in our state of limited experience, we are still whole, still complete, but we are just not aware of that. When we become aware, we simply lose limitedness and become whole again.* (2006)

We heard more about this shift in perspective during our interview with Sharon Salzberg, a master teacher of Buddhist vipassana meditation. For Salzberg, like many of the teachers and writers we spoke with, transformation is a fundamental shift in perspective:

> A transformation in consciousness is something that opens a door for us. It's almost as though we are in a small, enclosed, dark room. We feel constrained, we feel limited in some way, and then the door swings open— and suddenly there's a sense of possibility where there might have been none before. There's a sense of having options where we didn't perceive any before. And there's a change in perception, especially in terms of scope.
>
> I think maybe the best example I've heard was a story of the late Tibetan lama Trungpa Rinpoche, who once took a white sheet of paper and drew in the center of it a floppy V-shaped object. Then he held it up in front of his class and said, "What is this? What's this a picture of?" And apparently everybody responded, "That's a picture of a bird." And he said, "No it's not. It's a picture of the sky with a bird flying through it."
>
> You know that sense of fixation, when we narrow our focus and feel locked in? A transformation of consciousness is the awareness, "Oh! There's a sky there." There's more context. There's more openness than we have perceived before. There's a sense of boundlessness. This is not something that we maintain. This is something that if we're fortunate, we experience, we can renew, and we can reenter—and that changes us. (2002)

From this perspective, you can see that transformation is about opening to new possibilities. It's about recognizing that your current view of yourself and the world is only partial. Seeing with new eyes allows for a new understanding of yourself and your own unfoldment.

The Science of Shifts in Perspective

Is this shift in perspective purely subjective, something that we can only experience firsthand, or can science offer us a more objective understanding of how people come to see the world in a completely new way? Daniel Simons, an associate professor at the University of Illinois at Urbana-Champaign, conducts research on visual cognition, perception, attention, and memory. Particularly fascinating is his research on *inattentional blindness*, which he defines as people's "failure to notice unusual and salient events in their visual world when attention is otherwise engaged and the events are unexpected" (Simons and Chabris 1999, 1062).

Simons's studies build on the work of psychologists Arien Mack of the New School for Social Research and Irvin Rock, formerly at the University of California, Berkeley (Mack and Rock 1998). All of these scientists explore the nature of perception when attention is directed away from a target object. In a series of fascinating studies, these researchers have shown that we can literally miss the proverbial elephant (or in this case, gorilla) in the room if we are not expecting to see it or our attention is fixated on other things.

In one classic experiment, participants are asked to pay attention to a video in which three people in black shirts and three people in white shirts pass a basketball to one another. Participants are asked to count the number of times the team with the white shirts passes the ball to one another. In most instances, participants are quite close to one another in their final figures, some saying sixteen times, a few reporting fifteen times, others saying seventeen times (Simons and Chabris 1999). This discrepancy alone speaks to how people can perceive the exact same situation slightly differently. (If you'd like to try this experiment for yourself before the spoiler in the next paragraph, stop reading right now and visit the Visual Cognition Laboratories' website at http://viscog.beckman.uiuc.edu/djs_lab/demos. html. You won't be disappointed!)

Vastly more interesting is what happens next, when researchers instruct the participants to watch the exact same video, this time without focusing on anything in particular. Almost all participants now see a life-size person in a gorilla suit walk directly into the center of the basketball game, stop, pound on his chest several times, and saunter out. People who participate in this exercise frequently don't believe that this is the same video. It is.

Studies like this one suggest that our brains are wired so that we don't consciously perceive even major aspects of our experience when our focus is fixed on something else. Other types of perceptual blindness, such as *change blindness*, occur when we fail to perceive significant changes in what we're seeing because the change happens very gradually—very much like the frog in the pot who doesn't notice that the water is boiling if it happens slowly enough. In Mack and Rock's book, *Inattentional Blindness* (1998), the researchers emphasize that perception doesn't just depend on having open, functional eyes. Rather, perception depends on attention, and attention depends on underlying cognitive processes. They've concluded from their research that without attention, nothing is consciously perceived. People inhibit their attention from unexpected stimuli, thus preventing conscious perception. This, in turn, leads to significant increases in inattentional blindness.

How does this relate to the role that perspective shifts play in transformations? These findings tell us that when we're focused on something and encounter an experience that isn't expected, we may not consciously perceive its existence. It's possible, particularly in relation to sudden transformations, that when your attention broadens from what has been preoccupying it and is brought into a more open field of awareness, your inattentional blindness is "cured"—what you couldn't consciously perceive previously is now revealed. This fits very well with what many teachers from various traditions told us. There may be much more to your life than you're allowing yourself to be aware of. As we shall see in the chapters to follow, transformation involves not only a shift in perception, but a shift in attention.

Types of Consciousness Transformation

Consciousness transformations of the kind we've discussed appear in every religious and spiritual tradition, and in the lives of many who do not identify themselves as spiritual or religious at all. In some ways, the practices recommended by many wisdom traditions to improve your life seem expressly designed to promote consciousness transformation. Amazingly, even the words used to describe these transformations are very similar across widely varying experiences, practices, and traditions. From neo-paganism to Roman Catholicism, from UFO encounters to giving birth, from a truck driver in Texas to a Buddhist nun in New York, the experience of transformation as a shift in worldview followed by a dramatic restructuring of core values appears to be universal.

However, there are many, many types of consciousness transformation. Some are sudden, seeming to occur in an instant, and some are gradual—like water wearing away stone over many years. Some occur in very ordinary circumstances, while others are sparked by extraordinary moments. Some occur in ordinary states, some in non-ordinary states of consciousness. Like variations on a theme in music, each type holds its own particular beauty and presents its own unique invitation.

SUDDEN OR GRADUAL?

The word "transformation" calls to mind a sudden and dramatic change, but transformation more often happens gradually. Often, even when there is a sudden and dramatic transformative moment, integrating that realization into everyday life can be a gradual process.

For Richard Gunther, transformation happened in an instant. For Joan, one of our survey respondents, a forty-one-year-old professional woman living in Kansas, it was a progression that took place over years, one small step leading to another:

> *The process was not as a lightning bolt, but rather a gradual revealing, or removing of layers, revealing more of what it seemed I already knew, but could only now name. I remember, at the age of twenty-one, driving down the same highway I'd been driving on for months, going to my university classes, when I experienced a sudden sense of synthesis—of everything I was learning locking together to create a seamless whole.*
>
> *I became an observer of my experience, and for a number of years I enjoyed intellectual exploration without considering that there might be spiritual exploration as well. It was not until I was in my late thirties that I ... began to notice that [these experiences] had intensified. In my late thirties, I began noticing an increase in synchronous events, and at the age of forty, realized I could see auras around some people.*

I can say that transformation is constant, though recently some tragic events knocked me off my feet for a while and I experienced nothing but dullness and dread. But the experiences have returned, and … I can again access whatever it is that I access that enables me to think freely and creatively. (Vieten, Cohen, and Schlitz 2008)

For Joan, one experience led to a decades-long journey of change, not instant change. Another of our respondents, Lela, a fifty-seven-year-old business owner, explained the journey to her turning point thus:

My transformation was a gradual process. [I felt] a general dissatisfaction with my life. I had achieved all of my material goals, but still felt that there was something missing. It all seemed so superficial. I wanted to do something different, so I attended a psychic development weekend workshop. This totally opened up and changed my life. I discovered a new world. I now had answers and access to information previously denied. I had confirmation of past talents that were shared by others, along with the discovery of abilities that I was not aware of possessing. I was not alone, weird, or crazy. I laughed and I cried. It was amazing. (Vieten, Cohen, and Schlitz 2008)

Perhaps the best known scholarship on these kinds of transformations of consciousness is that of William James, frequently cited as the founder of American psychology. In his classic work *The Varieties of Religious Experience* (1902), James identified two different forms of change. The first is gradual and continuous, like the opening of a flower. The second is sudden or abrupt. In this latter case, change is often associated with what James calls "mystical states of consciousness."

As we sought more insight into the differences between sudden and gradual life-changing transformations, we had the privilege to consult with Lewis Ray Rambo, minister, author, counselor, and professor at the Graduate Theological Union, San Francisco, since 1978. Rambo is an expert on the conversion experience and spiritual and religious transformation. While our work isn't about religious conversion, the conversion process holds close parallels that make it relevant to our study. According to

Rambo, gradual transformations are relatively common and sudden transformations are more unusual:

> *It's rare that anyone has a conversion or transformation clear out of the*
> *blue. We read books, we see people, we have experiences, we interact with*
> *communities, and so forth. I don't want to say it never happens out of the*
> *blue, but it rarely comes with no preparation, at least in my research…*
> *Most of us have cumulative and gradual experiences. Maybe one parallel*
> *would be when someone falls in love and gets married. You can date the*
> *wedding as being at a particular time and place, but I would argue that the*
> *wedding is the consummation of something that has led up to it. Who knows*
> *when falling in love happened or when the decision was made.* (2006)

Lauren Artress, an Episcopal priest and psychotherapist who serves
as the canon at San Francisco's Grace Cathedral, also shared her insights
on sudden transformation with us, speaking about her favorite topic: the
labyrinth. A *labyrinth* is a pattern laid out on the ground, usually forty feet
in diameter, with a single, circuitous path that winds from the outer edge
to the center; it's used as a Christian walking meditation tool. Based on
her many years of walking—and guiding people along this circular path of
reflection—Artress believes that two levels of sudden transformation can
be experienced by walking the labyrinth:

> *The first is really on the insight level. Something opens and there's a new way*
> *of seeing things. This often happens in the labyrinth itself, but it can happen*
> *afterwards as well. Walking the labyrinth can make it easier for the mind to*
> *be malleable because the body's moving. And so insights can happen, clicks*
> *and ahas! But I think a deeper level of transformation that happens in the*
> *labyrinth—and it happens very frequently—is an insight that comes in so*
> *clearly and so sharply that it is yours automatically.*
>
> *It's a kind of insight that happens on the body level as well. It feels*
> *like an answer to a problem that's been bugging you. It feels like a real clear*
> *flash of light. There's a connection, a sense of joy, a sense of "Wow, there it is;*

there's the answer." And it just comes through so clearly that it's yours. That's what I would call a true transformation with the labyrinth. People find their soul's code. They find their passion in their life. And it's quite dramatic how people's lives change as a result. (2003)

The kind of sudden transformation described by Gunther and Artress is considered in detail by psychologists William Miller and Janet C'de Baca in their book *Quantum Change* (2001). These researchers study sudden, dramatic, and apparently permanent changes that take place in people's lives. Noting that behavioral science had yet to develop even a name for these commonly reported experiences, Miller and C'de Baca use the metaphor of quantum physics to discuss these kinds of sudden transformations. One of the hallmarks of a *quantum change*, the researchers found, is the recognition that something unusual is occurring, something that means your life will never be the same again. Such changes are rarely remembered as willful or voluntary events; rather, the majority of people that the authors interviewed reported that the experience took them completely by surprise; it was both unannounced and uninvited. Another hallmark of quantum change is the sense that what has happened to you is profoundly beneficial and positive. Finally, the authors argue that the sudden change they have studied is permanent. In Miller and C'de Baca's own words, "quantum changes convey the sense of having passed through a one-way door. There is no going back" (17).

MYSTICAL OR MUNDANE?

We use consciousness transformation as an umbrella term for transformations that take place in all kinds of contexts. However, some of the most profound and life-altering transformations typically either have a spiritual component or occur in the context of religious experience or practice. A U.S. General Social Survey in 1998 found that 39 percent of people have had a spiritual or religious experience that changed their lives (Idler et al. 2003). A survey of more than 2,000 adults by the Barna Group found that over half of those sampled described their life as having been "greatly transformed" by their religious faith (Barna 2006). While there are many transformations that have little or nothing to do with religious experience, we will see in chapter 8 that, across traditions and practices, a sense of the sacred or the absolute is often intimately connected with transformative experiences.

However, transformative experiences may also be distinctly mundane. Psychologist Stanley Krippner, cross-cultural psychologist and pioneering researcher of dreams, anomalous experiences, healing traditions, and the impact of war on civilians, explained it thus:

> Sometimes transformations are not mystical or ephemeral at all. Sometimes they are really very simple and very down-to-earth. Like Candide said at the end of the brilliant novel by Voltaire: "We must cultivate our gardens." I have seen people who are very self-realized getting great enjoyment out of growing vegetables, growing fruits, growing flowers. And there's nothing mysterious about that on the surface of it. Yet, you go a little bit below the surface, yes, whenever a flower blooms, whenever a seed sprouts—that certainly is mysterious. (2002)

Krippner speaks to a core theme of this book: transformation is as much part of our ordinary earthly lives as it is about connecting with the deeper mysteries of existence.

IT'S NOT ALL A WALK IN THE PARK

As our research team sought to understand consciousness transformations such as those described by Richard Gunther, Frances Vaughan, and others, we found that transformation is complex. While the focus of our research—and this book—is on positive, growth-inducing transformations, even life-affirming transformations aren't necessarily a walk in the park. Let's not forget, a caterpillar *liquefies* before it becomes a butterfly. Transformation isn't always something we can easily place in positive or negative categories. Some experiences defy such oversimplifications. Transformation entails the whole enchilada, or what Zorba the Greek called "the full catastrophe."

Luisah Teish expressed the complexities of the process when she shared her powerful story of consciousness transformation during one of our initial focus groups. Teish is an initiated practitioner and *iyanifa,* or elder, of the Orisha tradition of southwest Nigeria. A gifted storyteller and spiritual teacher, Teish dropped into her heart to speak to us about the soul of her transformation:

> *For me it was conceiving a child. Participating in something primal and ancient and common to everything. Nurturing something I couldn't see but was dedicated to, and not knowing what it would be. Embracing and nursing a mystery. Having the experience of laboring for twenty-three hours, working for something to be born … and then in twelve hours watching that baby die. I often think: one hour short of a day to birth it, half a day of life, and then it dies.*

We sat quietly as she continued, tears running down our cheeks.

> *"No, he is gone, Mama, he is gone." That statement threw me into being nuts! I couldn't keep my cells together. I slept all day and cried all night, for two years. And then came the words in my mind: "Don't you realize, in a village when this happens to a woman, she then becomes the wise woman who can tell everybody else how to face different things?" A change comes, and it happens in your cells and everything is new. I saw that the conscious part of me had gone crazy: the caterpillar; but underneath, somebody else was putting all of this in order: the butterfly.* (1998)

Teish's story reminds us that transformation is a process that can be stimulated by even the most shattering of circumstances. In fact, some transformations seem to *require* the kind of vulnerability that accompanies extreme loss or grief. This is what separates transformation from more linear processes of psychological development as typically understood. Transformation often asks for something to die so that something new can be born.

SUMMARY

In this chapter we defined consciousness transformation as a profound shift in your perspective resulting in long-lasting, life-enhancing changes in the way you experience and relate to yourself, others, and the world. Consciousness transformations may occur in ordinary or non-ordinary states of consciousness. We found, too, that transformative experiences can either be gradual, taking form in your consciousness over time, or they can be sudden, with triggers ranging from life crises to mystical experiences. While there are no magic formulas for how consciousness transformations come about, our research across different traditions and practices reveals informative patterns. In the next chapter we'll move deeper into the elements that set the stage for consciousness transformation. For now, consider the following exercise as a way of engaging your own transformation.

Experiencing Transformation: Mapping Your Transformative Life Path

The following is an in-depth journaling exercise. You'll need a quiet place, some uninterrupted time, a notebook and pen, and colored pencils or something to sketch with.

On each page (you may use several pages), draw a line vertically down the center of the page. Separate the line into seven equal sections; write the number 0 on the bottom and the number 7 on the top. This represents the first seven years of your life. On each of the following pages, draw the same vertical line for each seven-year interval of your life, numbering them 7 to 14, 14 to 21, and so on.

On each of these lined pages, list on the left side any experiences that you might now see as having opened your eyes to new ways of seeing the world and your place in it. Maybe these were simply glimpses, or perhaps they were transformative experiences that affected your overall patterns of thinking and behaving. These glimpses or transformative experiences could be pleasurable or painful. They could be meeting a person, losing a loved one, reading a life-changing book, traveling, having an extraordinary teacher … the possibilities are endless! The key factor here is your own felt sense that the experience was some sort of turning point or shift in your life.

On the right-hand side of each lined page, note what—if any—transformative *practices or activities* you engaged in during that time period, including both formal practices like going to church or practicing meditation, and informal practices like being in nature, playing sports or an instrument, reading, writing, or exploring a new realm of study. Focus on practices you engaged in specifically to learn more about yourself, to expand your consciousness, or to heal. But don't forget to also chronicle any informal practices or activities that led to your transformative experiences. For example, maybe as a six-year-old you were playing in the garden when you suddenly noticed the light shining through the trees and were filled with a deep sense of peace and knowing.

As you review your transformative experiences and practices, also note down any other factors that might have set the stage for your personal transformation, such as the beginning or ending of a relationship, an illness or healing crisis, a birth, a death, a trip, or a newfound passion. For each of these seven-year periods, map out what helped pave the way for any shifts in your perception of yourself, your relationships, and your sense of the broader environmental and transpersonal world. Make notes, pictures, or symbols in the time slots you have created.

After you have completed each block of time all the way through to the present moment, spend time quietly reflecting on what you have learned about the seeds of transformation in your own life. Name and describe the insights and themes that have emerged and been woven throughout your life. Can you decipher any patterns and relationships between your transformative practices and experiences?

We recommend that you spend some time over the next several days contemplating and completing this exercise in order to let the transformative story of your life unfold so you may document it in as much detail as you would like.

CHAPTER TWO:

Doorways to Transformation

There are many doorways into the inner world…
—FRANCES VAUGHAN (2002)

How do consciousness transformations—the kind that make a long-term difference in your life—begin? You can probably identify in retrospect some turning points in your life, times about which you can honestly say, "After that I was never the same." For example, you may have experienced a shift in perspective after a serious illness, or the loss of a loved one, or a particularly awe-inspiring moment like giving birth to a child or visiting the great pyramids. But these moments are unpredictable. They can seem so random, and so particular to each unique situation, that you may wonder, "Do I just have to wait until I get blown away by some big moment to make a real change?"

In this chapter, we share what we've learned about the many doorways into transformative experiences, both painful and awe-filled, as well as what makes an experience transformative rather than traumatic. We explore the ways that a single extraordinary experience can force you to stretch your worldview and in the process gain valuable perspective on yourself and your life. Finally, we delve into the seduction of the peak experience—and how seeking repeated transformative experiences can become a kind of addiction. The key to transformation is to see how the extraordinary can be found in the ordinary, in each day of our lives.

PORTALS TO TRANSFORMATION

As we explored in chapter 1, transformations can be either sudden or gradual, mystical or mundane. Regardless, most begin with an experience that shakes the foundations of our current way of thinking. As a result, assumptions we've held dear are often proven to be limited or simply untrue.

The Portal of Pain

Perhaps the most robust finding of our research is common knowledge: profound transformations are frequently triggered by intense suffering or crisis. Difficult or painful life events often create new levels of openness or vulnerability, thus setting the stage for a shift in worldview. A brush with death, the loss of a loved one, a mental or emotional breakdown, an injury, loss of a job—such painful challenges can shatter defenses that have taken us a lifetime to build. Whether it's the difficulty of realizing that something isn't working in your life or the suffering you experience when painful challenges cross your path, our research participants identified pain as far and away the most common catalyst for change.

To learn more, we met with Gangaji, also known as Toni Varner. Gangaji teaches in the tradition of her teacher Papaji and his teacher, nineteenth-century saint Sri Ramana Maharshi. Gangaji told us that her unhappiness is what led her to a spiritual path:

My own transformative path was inspired by the unhappiness I felt as a young child. Of course at that age I didn't know it was a spiritual search; I only knew that I was unhappy, and I wanted to be happy. I spent many years trying to get happy in all the usual ways, searching for the right mate or the right "thing" that would do it for me.

In the seventies, I consciously turned toward spirituality. I began many years of spiritual practices, each of which ultimately led me to the same wall. I assumed that this was once again my fault, due to my lack of sufficient practice or because I hadn't found the right teacher. These assumptions were suspiciously similar to previous ones of not finding the right mate or the right "thing"…

When I met my teacher, he said something I had never heard before. He said, "Stop. Find out who you are." When I actually did stop the search and began to investigate, I found that who I think I am doesn't exist; that any idea of who I am is just a thought. Who I am, in truth, is consciousness itself.

Personal suffering, and the searching it often leads to, can be precious gifts. Naturally, I would not wish suffering on anyone. Yet suffering has quite a different quality than pain and hardship, both of which are natural occurrences in a human life. Suffering is how one relates psychologically to pain and hardship. Suffering is something that gnaws at you over time, which you assign to the realms of cause and effect: "If only this would change or that would change, then I wouldn't be in pain." Many people feel great pain, yet they don't necessarily suffer with it. Others may feel very little pain and suffer enormously. Regarding my own early unhappiness and suffering, I bow down to it. I'm happy that it wouldn't let me go, no matter how much I fed it with what seemed to be the best medicine at the time. Ultimately, my unhappiness brought me to the meeting with my teacher and to the discovery of direct self-inquiry. (2002)

As the saying goes, change is what happens when the pain of remaining the same becomes greater than the pain of changing. Perhaps you, like many people, only change when you're backed up against a wall, when you're absolutely forced to modify your life. When transformation requires some kind of sacrifice—whether of a cherished belief, a comfortable habit, or something you think you can't survive without—you may avoid it until there is no other option.

Noah Levine, vipassana meditation teacher and author of *Dharma Punx* (2003) and *Against the Stream* (2007), explained to us how, for him, transformation arose from despair and hopelessness:

> *Mostly I came to my current path and practices—and my interest in and willingness to practice meditation and service and prayer—out of my own personal despair, suffering, and confusion. I came to a place of hopelessness, to a place of really feeling like everything that I'd thought would work in the material world—drugs, violence, pleasure, crime, my own confused attempts to find satisfaction—actually led to great personal despair and suffering. And from that place, there was sort of a realization that what I'd been doing was creating more suffering, not less. Coming around to some place of willingness and saying, "Okay, that didn't work. Maybe this spiritual stuff"—which I had great resistance to and had characterized as being for brain-dead followers; as escapism, a cop-out; as an unrealistic peace-and-love ethic; as hippie shit—"maybe these spiritual folks knew something that I don't know." (2005)*

One of the gifts of intense suffering can be a newfound willingness to make significant changes. For Gangaji, unhappiness fueled a fervent search that led her to her teacher. For Levine, the gift of suffering instilled within him the willingness to try meditation.

Painful experiences can also uncover a longing that we didn't even know was there—or catalyze a search for something we didn't even know we wanted. As Nancy, a sixty-five-year-old retired widow, reported:

> *I had a near-death experience while giving blood for myself before a hip replacement surgery. I was in a tunnel that was dark, but I could see the details of the tunnel clearly. I could hear folks telling me to stay with them, but I could feel the flow of life going out of my body through the tunnel. I did*

not reach the end of the tunnel … I experienced many traumas in my life for
about two years after that (e.g., death of mother, sudden death of husband)
and somehow began a fast-track spiritual path that I was unaware I was
interested in. It was as though I were being led in a new direction. (Vieten,
Cohen, and Schlitz 2008)

External experiences of pain, like illness or injury to yourself or a loved
one, can have great transformative potential. Physician Rachel Naomi
Remen described to us a kind of unstructured, transformative rite of passage
that she has observed over her years of working with people with cancer:

Crisis, suffering, loss, the unexpected encounter with the unknown—all
of this has the potential to initiate a shift in perspective. A way of seeing
the familiar with new eyes, a way of seeing the self in a completely new
way. The experience that I have in watching people with cancer is that the
more overwhelmed someone is at the beginning, the more profound the
transformation that they undergo. There's a moment when the individual
steps away from the former life and the former identity and is completely
out of control and completely surrenders—and then is reborn with a larger,
expanded identity. (2003)

Remen speaks to the capacity of painful and frightening experiences to
loosen our control and dissolve our identities.

But sometimes these painful experiences aren't external—sometimes
they arise from internal identity conflicts. Yoruba chief and storyteller
Luisah Teish draws on her African traditions to describe the kind of transformation that arises when people experience conflict between their choices
and their purpose in life:

The way we talk about it, we would speak of a person realigning their aurie,
their earthly head, with ip'ori, *their heavenly head.* Ip'ori *is that part of a*
person that is connected to spirit, that always has been and always will be.
And ip'ori *knows what your contract with creation was when you chose to*
take a body and come into this world.

In the process of being born and being socialized, we do the best that we can to remember what we can of the original contract, but can get misdirected or redirected through chance and choice. For us there's destiny, chance, and choice. And if, by chance, we make choices that go against our contract, then we experience alienation and various forms of suffering. Or we have the sense of being lost, because we're piling on these things that are not essential to our nature. Then we are struck by lightning. Who we think we ought to be crumbles. And then we are stripped down so that we can transform, or be transformed, into a closer relationship with pure spirit.

So it's kind of like putting on a bunch of attitudes and thoughts and attributes and experiences that have alienated you from your place in nature. And you can do only so much of that before there is some kind of—in this culture we think of it as a breakdown, but I think of it as a breakthrough—where a person has experiences that cause them to rip off all of this and reconnect to their place in nature. And that is what I call the transformation of consciousness. (2003)

As Teish explains, transformation often begins with a deep realization that your life has diverged from your values or purpose. The further you get from your values or purpose, the more painful life tends to become. Psychologists use the term *ego dystonia* to describe those aspects of our thinking and behavior that are inconsistent with—and even repugnant to—our conception of who we are. In fact, many of the participants in our research talked about transformation as an experience that allowed them to recognize that their beliefs, priorities, and behaviors were inconsistent with who they wanted or believed themselves to be. The pain (and sometimes thrilling relief) of this type of realization can open the door to change.

HITTING BOTTOM

This reshuffling of priorities is often reported when people hit some sort of bottom. Sometimes, in order to reconstruct yourself afresh, the complete deconstruction of who you have been is required. While times of extreme personal discomfort can be disorienting, painful, and confusing, they can also open you to new possibilities.

John, a forty-five-year-old married man who is now a minister, educator, and author, described his experience in the following way:

> I tried committing suicide and was found. That same year I started to do a twelve-step program and some seminars. I worked with people who helped me have an awakening, where I heard a voice say to me that I am divine. Now I totally understood that I am a divine being having a human experience. (Vieten, Cohen, and Schlitz 2008)

For John, one event led to another in a process that nearly ended his life but instead helped him discover his own divinity—not a small task for any of us.

Along these lines, many of our respondents used the word "surrender" to describe the moment when suffering becomes so great that a person just gives up. While it can feel like defeat—particularly after fighting a long battle against an illness, addiction, or destructive belief pattern—giving up leads to letting go. Paradoxically, this can open a door to an entirely new way of being.

Marion Rosen, the ninety-two-year-old founder of Rosen Method bodywork, spoke to us from her home in Berkeley about the simple but profound healing power of touch. Rosen's bodywork helps people get in touch with their pain by peeling away layers of resistance and armoring, so people become more open—and eventually surrender to their own healing transformation:

> Some people are not open enough to allow somebody else to touch them, and—without any questions—surrender. When you surrender, to whom and what do you surrender? You allow something to happen and that brings you to a feeling of a higher power, or whatever. I cannot exactly tell you what it is, but this is what happens. (2005)

Father Francis Tiso, a Catholic priest and Buddhist scholar, similarly spoke to us about how personal suffering can lead to transformation through the process of surrender. He described how suffering can become a sacred offering:

> *Your emotional suffering becomes a kind of offering. In Christian terms, it becomes the bread and the wine of the mass that we lift up on the paten at the offertory before they're consecrated. You simply say, "This is what I have. I don't have anything else." And that is good enough right there—you don't have to have more. So the suffering and the pain that you are experiencing, once you've lifted it up in that offertory, suddenly has a glow of sacredness about it.* (2002)

What a beautiful transformative gesture Tiso describes—surrendering your pain and all it represents as a sacred offering.

Noetic Experiences

Of course, not all doorways to or catalysts of transformation are filled with pain. Of our survey respondents, exactly equal numbers became interested in transformation after a difficult life event as due to some other process or event. And although 23 percent said the transformative experience was very unpleasant, 51 percent described it as very pleasant. In fact, the emotions most commonly cited as accompanying transformative experiences included feeling "interested, alert, attentive, and inspired" (Vieten, Cohen, and Schlitz 2008). Moments of profound awe, wonder, or transcendent bliss can provide a glimpse of something that is so compelling, so completely beyond what you've previously realized is possible, that they can instill in you a strong intention to find out more about what happened—no matter what it takes.

What *are* noetic experiences? *Noetic* is a Greek word that refers to knowledge that is subjective—the things you know through your own direct experience. Thus, noetic experiences are those in which there's a deeply subjective and internal experience of knowing. Noetic experiences encompass what James called mystical experiences (1902), what Maslow later referred to in a more secular manner as peak experiences (1970), and what Jung considered encounters with the numinous (1972). We prefer the term "noetic" because it focuses on the common theme shared by all these experiences: an internal form of knowing that is based in direct experience.

In fact, some of these experiences aren't mystical at all in the sense that the word is commonly understood. They don't necessarily have to do with experiences of God, angels, magic, white lights, or astral beings (although these kinds of mystical experiences are all noetic). A noetic experience can also take the form of a deeply rooted, embodied sense of connection to all things, or an awareness of deep love when gazing into the eyes of another. Noetic experiences are often sudden and profound. They include epiphanies, "big dreams" (i.e., those that have a clear significance or emotional impact), and senses of revelation that come in an instant. As you may have noticed, these experiences actually happen quite often; they're neither unusual nor otherworldly.

Noetic experiences can also include some kind of extraordinary human capacity, which can be difficult to interpret. Noetic experiences can take the form of psychic phenomena, including the feeling that you're being stared at, or the knowledge that the phone will ring just before it does, or near-death experiences, or spontaneous healing, or various other abilities and phenomena that arise in non-ordinary states of consciousness (Targ, Schlitz, and Irwin 2000). Transpersonal scholar and archivist Rhea White worked with us in the early stages of our research program. She found that, even though the phenomenology of noetic experiences may differ (e.g., seeing an apparition, sensing mystical oneness with the whole of existence, having precognitive dreams), these experiences can serve as a portal to a new worldview (White 1994).

Noetic experiences—of direct knowing, intuitive insights, sudden revelations, moments of incredible synthesis, and breakthroughs of understanding—can all serve as triggers for transformation. This is true whether the noetic experiences accompany suffering or joy. When you're lucky—or, as many of the teachers we interviewed pointed out, when you're *paying attention*—noetic experiences of awe, beauty, and wonder can create deep shifts in the way you view yourself and your place in the world.

More than a century ago, William James (1902) wrote about the transformative potential of mystical states. He noted that they had several essential qualities: The first quality of the mystical state is its ineffability. Its quality must be directly experienced, as it isn't easily communicated to others. Second is what James called a *noetic quality*—mystical states present themselves as not just a collection of feelings and thoughts, but as actual states of knowledge.

James said of the noetic quality of mystical states:

> Although so similar to states of feeling, mystical states seem to those who experience them to be also states of knowledge. They are states of insight into depths of truth unplumbed by the discursive intellect. They are illuminations, revelations, full of significance and importance, all inarticulate though they remain; and as a rule they carry with them a curious sense of authority. (1902, 380)

Third, James said, mystical states are transient; and fourth, they cannot be controlled. Indeed, in our survey of over 900 people's transformative experiences, more than one hundred years after James's work, 61 percent similarly said that their experience was due to circumstances "out of anyone's control" (Vieten, Cohen, and Schlitz 2008). In his classic chapter on mysticism, James muses about whether these states of mind are essentially windows that look out upon a more extensive and inclusive world. He also suggested that these experiences occur more often as what he called our *field of consciousness*—which includes every idea and perception we are aware of—expands (1902).

Hundreds of our survey respondents recounted these kinds of experiences. For example, Meredith, a seventy-one-year-old homemaker in California, shared the following experience with us:

> *Along with family members, I had been, for five days, spending four hours a day at the deathbed of my friend. He died early in the a.m. while I was staying with the family in their home.*
>
> *The night of my friend's death I was asleep in his office, on the bed where he used to nap and do guided imagery exercises. My face was to the wall and my back to the windows. I was suddenly wide awake, so I raised myself up on one arm and turned toward the window. There I saw a smoky gray square shape; it passed through me. As I looked into it, I recognized*

it as my friend, but in a transcendent state. I thought, "Aha! This is what
transcendence is." It was like looking into the entire universe. There was no
duality. I saw the past, the present, and the future coexisting simultaneously.
Then it was gone. I put my head down and went back to sleep. Some time
later I was awakened again by the sensation that the sheet covering me had
been whipped from the bed. That hadn't happened. (Vieten, Cohen, and
Schlitz 2008)

Another survey respondent, Patrick, a sixty-one-year-old professional who lives in suburban California, shared with us an experience he had that had been brought on by transformative practice:

During a meditation I experienced my body becoming very light, so that
it could almost float. I gently "lifted off" from the Earth and, with vision
focused on the heavens, I moved toward the sun… During most of the
experience, I moved slowly through the darkness slightly illuminated by the
pure white light of stars. At times, though, I moved very rapidly—even the
higher speed was pleasant. I knew, at a cellular level, that I and the universe
and all inhabitants thereof were one. It was a sacred experience. (Vieten,
Cohen, and Schlitz 2008)

This sense of a deep knowing, at what Patrick calls "a cellular level," is the heart of the noetic experience.

Some transformative noetic experiences are *transcendent*, a term that refers to an experience that either lies beyond the ordinary realm of perception or beyond the limits of material existence. These experiences can carry with them an extraordinary quality of numinosity, divinity, or grace, transporting us out of our ordinary worldview. Through our interviews and survey, we learned that such transcendent or non-ordinary experiences are quite common. Meditation teacher Sharon Salzberg told us:

There are experiences of transcendence where quite suddenly you're lifted
out of a sense of limitation and into a whole other vista that some traditions
would call the guru's grace or God's grace. Researchers have asked

*Americans if they've ever had a mystical experience, or an experience of
something completely out of the ordinary. And an enormous percentage of
the population says yes. I think these kinds of experiences are more common
than we might imagine. Sometimes it is very much about love; people feel
an unconditional love permeating the universe. Or a sense of connection to
others. Or sometimes a sense of the divine that's just completely different
from their ordinary concerns of the day.* (2002)

To gain another perspective on the noetic dimensions of transformative
experiences, our team sought the counsel of Gilbert Walking Bull, a Lakota
elder and holy man of distinguished Sioux ancestry. At a young age Walking
Bull was selected to help carry on the spiritual teachings of his people. He
shared with us an important family story of a sudden noetic awakening:

*I had a great-grandmother who was a very kind and wonderful person. She
used to sit outside her teepee and make beautiful beadwork. If you walked
by her, she'd call you over to sit down with her, give you a cup of coffee, and
pretty soon you'd be there all day listening to her stories. One day a little
bitty butterfly fluttered around her while she was working and it landed
on her shoulder. Electricity shot through her body and instantly she was a
holy woman. Spirit came to her in that butterfly. She automatically knew
what medicines to use to heal people. She could tell their futures. That's
how quickly these powers came to her; the spirits didn't waste any time in
choosing her to serve them.* (2006)

Walking Bull further pointed out that noetic experiences—like the one
that transformed the life of his great-grandmother—are given to those who,
according to Lakota tradition, have a lifelong daily practice and way of life
that embodies the principles of becoming sacred human beings.

Some transformative experiences seemingly arrive out of the blue. At
times you may be faced with a potentially worldview-shifting experience,
and you don't have an ongoing transformative practice to help you contain
or interpret it. You may not even have a language for it. Like Darwin's geological experience described in chapter 1, it's hard to see the signs all around

you when you don't have a *cosmology*—a story of how to understand reality and the world—that allows for the possibility of these experiences. And like the research on inattentional blindness suggests, broadening your perspective can result in seeing possibilities and realities that have been right under your nose all along.

Part of the overarching premise of this book, and the main point of this chapter, is that noetic experiences happen all the time. Moreover, they have the potential to stimulate transformation, the very changes you've been seeking to make, in deep and profound ways. But they do require that you pay attention to them and provide them with the fertile soil to grow into true transformations.

IS YOUR WORLDVIEW TOO SMALL?

For Edgar Mitchell, Apollo 14 astronaut and founder of the Institute of Noetic Sciences, it was his journey home from the moon that opened him to the radical and sudden epiphany that changed his life. Mitchell comes from a background of specialized training in engineering; he trusted that paradigm enough to volunteer to join the mission of Apollo 14. (For those of you who have seen the movie *Apollo 13*, you'll appreciate the depth of this trust.) Mitchell's worldview shift was in part due to his noetic understanding, through direct experience, that contemporary materialistic science has only part of the answer to the really big questions about human nature and the meaning of life. He explained during our interview in 2002:

> As an MIT grad and an aeronautics engineer and astronaut, presumably I understood star formation and galactic formation, a little about quantum physics, a lot of classical physics, engineering, orbital mechanics—all of the things that seem to be appropriate to space exploration. And then, on the way home from the moon, looking out at the heavens, this insight—which I could now call a transcendent experience—happened.
>
> I realized that the molecules of my body had been created or prototyped in an ancient generation of stars—along with the molecules of the spacecraft and my partners and everything else we could see, including

the Earth out in front of us. Suddenly, it was all very personal. Those were my molecules.

It was an experience of connectedness. It was an experience of bliss, of ecstasy. The type of experience that brings tears to your eyes, you don't know why. Tears of joy, not sadness. This experience continued for three days. I was working. I mean, I had duties to do, but when I was finished with them I would look out the window again and it would start all over. It was so profound. I realized that the story of ourselves as told by science—our cosmology, our religion—was incomplete and likely flawed. I recognized that the Newtonian idea of separate, independent, discrete things in the universe wasn't a fully accurate description. (2002)

There are times when we struggle to understand the nature of our transformative experiences. For someone like Mitchell, who had been trained as a scientist, such a noetic experience may be very foreign, even disruptive. Mitchell's noetic experience carried with it an unshakable certainty. However, it also propelled him to try to understand what had happened to him. *How* could he know these things so certainly, so directly? Where did this sense of deep, unshakable peace and joy come from? He continued:

I set out to see what the literature had to say about this. There simply wasn't anything in the scientific literature. I wasn't satisfied with religious literature, so I started looking at mystical literature. Some colleagues steered me to the Sanskrit description of samadhi and I realized it fit with what I had experienced: seeing things as separate in the universe but experiencing them as one, accompanied by bliss. I realized my experience had a name—at least, one tradition had a name for it. The more I studied, the more I realized that this type of experience can be found in every culture. And it seems to be roughly the same in every culture.

Over the next few years I had the opportunity to study with people from different cultures—shamans and kahuna, medicine men and mystics. I sought them out to talk about what this experience was… I came to

realize that this tendency to see beyond ourselves or to have this type of
expansive experience was probably the basis of religious experience…

Life didn't seem the same. Suddenly everything seemed different.
Things that were important before were no longer very important. Money
and economics were not very important. Satisfaction, lifestyle, making
things harmonious and loving were important. Understanding what was
going on was important. Nothing else really was. It took a long time to
accommodate all of this experience. (2002)

Mitchell's experience fits with what humanistic psychologist Abraham Maslow called "peak experiences." Maslow used this term to include not just religious noetic experiences but also those that occurred outside of a religious context.

Maslow described the highest peak experiences as "feelings of limitless horizons opening up to the vision, the feeling of being. Simultaneously more powerful and also more helpless than one ever was before, the feeling of great ecstasy and wonder and awe, the loss of placing in time and space" (1970, 164). Like Maslow, we found that these extrapersonal and ecstatic states are often associated with feelings of unity, harmony, and interconnectedness. People often, but not always, describe such experiences—and the revelations imparted during them—as possessing an ineffably mystical if not overtly religious essence.

Non-Ordinary States of Consciousness

For many people, noetic experiences occur in the context of a *non-ordinary state of consciousness*. Charles Tart describes non-ordinary states of consciousness as denoting "alterations in both the content and pattern of the functioning of consciousness" (1975, 16). Stan Grof, one of the founders of transpersonal psychology and pioneer in the study of non-ordinary states of consciousness, argues that transformation comes about when you're forced to reconcile your ordinary worldview with insights gained from extraordinary or non-ordinary experiences.

There is a transformational relationship between the experience of everyday life and the experience of the other dimensions from which we are normally cut off. When you open to these normally hidden dimensions, it transforms you, because you have to take that experience into consideration. Like when people discovered that the world is round, when up to that point they believed it was flat. The experiences that you can have in non-ordinary states are equally radical. You realize that your perception of the world and yourself was not accurate before. You have new experiences that you cannot ignore. You have to integrate them into your everyday experience of the world. This changes both who you think you are and your understanding of the nature of reality. (2003)

Grof and his wife, Christina Grof, have developed Holotropic Breathwork—a non-drug-induced way to achieve non-ordinary states of consciousness through breathing, music, and intention. This tool has served to bring thousands of people internationally into transformative states of consciousness. Holotropic Breathwork and similar methods show that it is indeed possible to intentionally trigger experiences that are often seen as unpredictable or spontaneous.

Non-ordinary states of consciousness can be achieved through meditation, shamanic healing arts, trance, past-life regression, hypnosis, art, dance, music, deep play, sex, being in nature, ritual and ceremony, prayer, the sacred use of plants, use of psychedelics in certain contexts, as well as many other means. These states can also arise spontaneously, as happened for Richard Gunther.

By entering non-ordinary states of consciousness, we're able to gain new perspectives on ourselves and our definitions of self—definitions that have been formed by *consensual reality,* or experiences we share agreed-upon interpretations of with others. Across traditions our respondents propose that the self that we perceive in ordinary reality is but a small part of a much larger self. In fact, in many non-ordinary states of consciousness, the concept of a separate skin-encapsulated ego-self disappears completely.

An even broader view of consciousness takes it out of the realm of the personal "my consciousness" and into the realm of shared, or transpersonal consciousness. Many, including psychologist Carl Jung, view humans as having both a personal consciousness and a collective consciousness. According to Jung (1972), this collective unconscious is shared by all; it's thought to originate in the collective ancestral experience of humankind. Jung's collective unconscious is a kind of universal psychic repository of our human history—a repository we can access—that contains the totality of human reactions to the world. This collective history manifests itself in conscious awareness through images, emotions, and behaviors. It appears, moreover, in the mythology and personal experiences of people across cultures, even before they've had enough contact with one another to exchange cultural symbols. According to this theory, when unconscious archetypal patterns enter your conscious awareness, profound changes in consciousness result.

Indeed, the glimpses that the collective unconscious offers of mystical and transpersonal realms of experience often lead to profound consciousness transformations. As Grof explained to us:

> In non-ordinary states of consciousness we can have various kinds of mystical experiences, for example, a vast mythological realm of the collective unconscious opens up for us, where we can visit various archetypal realms and encounter the beings who dwell there. So, generally, for me psychospiritual transformation is associated with the awareness and experiential knowledge of dimensions of reality that are not available to us in our everyday state of consciousness. (2003)

Paying attention to noetic insights—those that arise from direct experience—becomes important as you seek transformation and greater self-discovery.

Teacher and author Starhawk—one of the most respected voices in modern Goddess religion and Earth-based spirituality—spoke to us about attending to the collective realms of consciousness and the entire world of interrelations and interconnections as a way of reclaiming our natural consciousness:

A range of different types of consciousness is available to human beings. It's a kind of anomaly that postmodern Western culture has narrowed the range of consciousness that we are encouraged to have. Maybe it is not so much a transformation we are speaking of, but an opening. It's a reclaiming.

A natural consciousness is readily available to human beings as a birthright. It is not so much a supernatural awareness as it is an awareness of being present in this world and open to understanding the interrelations and interconnections. It is about being aware and thinking in terms of patterns and relationships rather than separate isolated objects. (2006)

Perspective shifts are natural openings of awareness; they reveal to us a more expanded world of relationships than we've previously perceived. Both Starhawk and Grof remind us of the importance of non-ordinary states of consciousness—often including experiences of the collective unconscious and the realm of interconnectedness—as tools for moving out of habitual ways of seeing life. For many of the teachers we interviewed, transformation involves an open-minded approach to what is possible for each of us.

Psychedelics

About 10 percent of our survey sample found psychoactive compounds an important part of their transformative experience (Vieten, Cohen, and Schlitz 2008). To learn more about non-ordinary states of consciousness experienced through the use of psychedelics, we spoke with Ram Dass, formerly Harvard psychologist Richard Alpert. Over the last forty years Ram Dass has become one of the most beloved of Western spiritual teachers. Ram Dass told us his own story of worldview change, stimulated in large part by his experimentation with psychoactive substances and the altered states of consciousness they induce. Like others we interviewed, Ram Dass found psychedelics to be a doorway into an expanded view of reality:

When I was a psychologist, God was a figment of human imagination. I was into the anthropological ways of understanding different people and

*their myths. And then Timothy Leary took pity on me… He took me
through mushrooms.*

*Mushrooms showed me a part of myself that I had never known
through Western psychology. It was a place inside of me that I call home.
It was extremely familiar, but I could not remember ever having been there
before in this incarnation.*

Then Aldous Huxley gave us The Tibetan Book of the Dead *and
that made me stop… I had had an LSD session on Saturday night; on the
next Tuesday he gave me the book and I sat and read it. There were aspects
of my session that I just couldn't talk about—and here was this book
describing it!* (2003)

James Fadiman, transpersonal psychologist and cofounder of the
Institute for Transpersonal Psychology, shared with us a similar story of
transformation brought about by psychedelics:

*I was totally awakened by the selective use of psychedelics … that is what
opened up everything… Before that I was a kind of unattractive, bright,
neurotic human being who was perfectly pleasant to have around. I
probably would have ended up making a lot of money for a psychotherapist
over the long run! But with the psychedelic opening I began to look at
the serious mystical traditions that talked about what I had personally
experienced with psychedelics. By day I was a graduate student who would
tell my professors what they wanted to hear; at night I would be reading
the* I-Ching *and* The Tibetan Book of the Dead *for my own education.*
(2003)

For many clinicians, healers, and teachers, non-ordinary states of
consciousness have important therapeutic value for themselves and their
clients. For Charles Grob, a psychiatrist at UCLA, psychedelics have
proven to be a useful therapeutic tool for patients. When we spoke to Grob,
he explained that a number of therapeutic benefits have been identified for
psychedelics, including reduced fear of death in terminally ill patients, relief

from psychopathology, and, in healthy volunteers, psychological insight, enhanced creativity, a reorientation of values toward less materialistic goals, and transformative spiritual experiences (2005).

Today Grob is leading an FDA-approved study of psilocybin to see if it can help terminally ill cancer patients sort through emotional and spiritual issues. Patients take a modest dose of synthetic psilocybin and then spend the next six hours in a comfortable setting with a psychiatrist, thinking, talking, and listening to music through headphones. According to Grob, early results have been impressive. Patients report an amelioration of anxiety, improved mood, increased rapport with close family and friends, and even significant and lasting reduction in pain.

Similarly, researchers at Johns Hopkins Medical School (Griffiths et al. 2006) are engaged in studies of psilocybin, the active ingredient in "magic mushrooms." Under rigorous laboratory conditions in double-blind protocols, they have shown that with appropriate preparation and in specific conditions, administration of psilocybin causes experiences that meet the criteria of full-blown mystical experiences. In the study, one-third of subjects rated the experience as the single most spiritually significant experience of their lifetimes, and two-thirds rated it among the top five. Nearly 80 percent of subjects reported moderately or greatly increased well-being or life satisfaction two months after the experience.

Please bear in mind that all of those who mentioned using psychedelics to induce consciousness transformations also said this was best done under the careful direction of a trusted other. This is because your intention and surroundings are powerful determinative factors for the nature of the experience. This is known in the consciousness literature as *set and setting*. Indeed, none of our interviewees recommend that mind-altering substances be taken in a casual or recreational manner.

Meeting a Teacher

Meeting an individual who embodies or expresses some truth we've been seeking is a common inspiration for beginning the transformative journey. Whether it's the sparkle in this person's eyes, a sense of being known deeply (though you may never have actually met the person), or a simple admiration for how the person navigates life, finding a teacher with whom you connect deeply is one of the most tried-and-true ways of opening yourself up to deep shifts in perception. In fact, although some traditions make the practitioner's relationship with a teacher central (such as Hindu-based guru-devotion traditions), and others are more focused on an individual's development of inner authority, almost all traditions include some form of guidance and support from another person who has "been there." Mahamandaleshwar Swami Nityananda explained to us why this might be:

> When we meet our master, our guru, what he does is plant a seed within us. He awakens us to our potential, and tells us, "Do this." It's like the instructions on the seed packet: if we follow those instructions, we may grow into a beautiful plant. (2006)

For Ram Dass, an initial mystical opening was expanded through a trip to India, where he both encountered deep suffering and met his spiritual teacher. He explained:

> My guru was the map that I was looking for. He knew every plane in my consciousness, and could meet me in any one. He provided the miracle of having read my mind to keep me busy while he operated on my heart. At least that's the way I experienced it. (2003)

Ram Dass described, too, the unconditional acceptance he felt from his spiritual teacher, telling us that the guru seemed to know his every thought and reflected back love with no hint of judgment.

Robert Frager, transpersonal psychologist and cofounder of the Institute of Transpersonal Psychology in Menlo Park, California, has been a shaykh in the Halveti-Jerrahi Order for twenty years now. He told us how, for him, unexpectedly finding the extraordinary bond of love between master and disciple led to his transformation—and to he himself becoming one of the most respected American Sufi teachers. Within Sufism, loving God and your fellow human beings is the key to ascension:

My colleagues had invited a Sufi master from Istanbul to come visit the
school, be a guest teacher, and do a ceremony for the public. I was sitting
in my office when a man walked by my door, turned, glanced at me, and
walked on without stopping.

Time stopped when he glanced at me. I had the very powerful sense
that in this timeless moment, all the data of my life had been fed into a
high-speed computer, through some incredible modem, and it had all been
integrated. Somehow that man knew how it was, how it is, and how it was
all going to come out.

There was this amazing sense of being seen in a metaphysical and
existential sense of what I was and where I was going. And then the thought
came to me, "Gee, I hope that's the spiritual teacher, I hope that's the head
of the order—because if this is that guy's student, I don't want to meet the
teacher of someone who just did this to me. This is enough!"

Sure enough, it was the head of one of the great Sufi orders. I found
out years later that in the Sufi literature this powerful glance of the master is
considered an initiation.

I fell in love with my teacher in a very deep sense. It was very powerful.
It was not intellectual, it was more than emotional—it was very deep. I
never would have chosen it. It was not a choice. It happened to me. (2002)

In each of these three stories, we find a kind of surrender to a larger
calling, catalyzed by meeting a teacher. Nityananda, Dass, and Frager—
individuals from three different traditions—each unexpectedly met a spiritual teacher who offered a way into transformation.

Angeles Arrien, a cultural anthropologist and the founder of the Four-
Fold Way Program, pointed out that transformation often involves unexpected synchronicity, and that external catalysts of transformation—like
teachers or mentors—can lead us to internal insights:

The transformation process involves synchronicity, the numinous, and
some coincidence or the unexplainable. It most often is signaled by an
experience of expansion and upliftment and a deep peace and grounding.

It's a fire that mobilizes you to do something outside of yourself. It's something that wants to alleviate suffering or create more happiness in the world in some way. I think most of the transformational process, 80 percent of it, involves the unseen.

There are a few catalytic figures in our lives that serve to honor the sacred covenant of mutual growth that helps deliver us into another phase; [these may be] *mentors or teachers or loved ones or losses. There are many different catalysts. If I'm not paying attention internally, there will always be an outer catalyst, whether it is a circumstance or person...* (2002)

Finding the Extraordinary in the Ordinary

You don't have to be in an extraordinary place—in an ashram in India, flying across the galaxy in a space capsule, under the influence of mind-altering substances, or in the presence of a guru—to have a transformative experience. Transformations also happen in the everyday places we inhabit in the course of everyday experiences. Many of the people we interviewed and collected stories from experienced shifts in consciousness through ordinary actions. For some, transformation was found in fatherhood; for others, in tending a garden. Some even reported transformative experiences triggered by simply reading a book or being introduced to a new idea. In the end, we learned that while extraordinary experiences can offer glimpses of what's possible—and that even a single such glimpse can have a profound and lasting effect on your worldview—transformation isn't just about having a classically mystical experience. The sun shining through autumnal leaves, mist hanging in a lush valley, a baby grabbing your finger, eye contact with a kindred spirit on the bus, a disagreement with a loved one—these are all choice points that allow you to change the way you attend to a situation and choose to open to its meaning rather than push it away or rush past it.

For example, sports, martial arts, and other forms of physical activity can serve as triggers for transformation. Michael Murphy, founder of the Esalen Institute—a center for transformational learning in Big Sur,

California—and author of *Golf in the Kingdom* (1972), told us about the transformative potential in the sport of golf:

> *For thirty-five years, since I published that book, people have been telling*
> *me about their extraordinary experiences on golf courses, and some of them*
> *resemble mystical or occult experiences. By now, countless people have told*
> *me about their telepathic experiences, psychokinesis, sudden visual acuity,*
> *or other events that they cannot account for. So that's led me now to look*
> *at this in all walks of life. This transformative process goes unnamed and*
> *unrecognized, because nobody thought to do this with golfers.* (2002)

Later in our interview, Murphy referred to these unrecognized processes as "covert" transformational practices. Clearly, you don't have to have what we think of as a classical or mystical experience to find a door that opens to consciousness transformation. Transformation can and does occur naturally in the course of everyday experiences. These transformative experiences are more akin to the peak experiences that Maslow believed people encounter throughout their lives—precisely because the doorways to transformation are everywhere.

TIME IN NATURE

For many of the people we interviewed, just being outdoors held great potential for a shift in consciousness. In a house nestled in the northern California redwoods, Anna Halprin—expressive arts originator, choreographer, dancer, teacher, and pioneer in the use of dance as a healing and transformative art in the contemporary Western world—shared with us her great love for nature:

> *Especially now that I am eighty-two, when I dance with tree, or ocean, or*
> *wind, I feel transposed. It takes me to a place beyond life, beyond death.*
> *And it helps me to accept death, and that's a big one for me—to find a way*
> *to look at death as a cycle of life. I find that transformative quality when I*

relate to the natural environment. I can't explain why, but it's a partnership
that changes my consciousness. (2002)

Drawing on a cross-cultural perspective and her Basque ancestry, Angeles Arrien's program, the Four-Fold Way, integrates ancient but universal practices into the modern world. Incorporated into the program is an archetypal wilderness experience (a period of solitude in nature) of three days and three nights to help people experience the way that nature can mirror our inner state to us if we look carefully and quietly. Arrien explained:

> *Each individual is touched by nature and in silence in their own unique*
> *way. There's no magic formula—it's arrogant to assume that there is a*
> *formula. One factor is the willingness of each individual to spend some time*
> *contemplating where they are in their life. What has meaning and what*
> *doesn't? On our three days–three nights wilderness experience—often*
> *known as a vision quest among traditional societies of this continent—the*
> *transformational crucible is the outer world. In many ways the outer is really*
> *a mirror of what the person is doing internally.* (2002)

Being a sacred and mysterious force unto itself, nature often reveals new self-knowledge to us, and thus serves as a catalyst for transformation. Physician Gerald Jampolsky described to us a simple but transformative moment of inner reflection he had while contemplating a leaf floating down a river:

> *Maybe twelve years ago, I spent a month in Australia, just in nature—not*
> *reading, not talking, just looking at the outside world. One of the peak*
> *experiences I had was being on a big rock in the middle of a stream and*
> *watching water go by. I saw a leaf fall from a tree; I watched it go this way*
> *and that way. To my surprise, it came to right beside me and it stayed there*
> *for about five minutes. Then the wind picked it up, put it in the water, and*
> *it went down the river. Seeing that leaf was an important lesson for me. I*
> *identified with the leaf as me letting go, not being afraid of what was going*

to happen, trusting in the flow of the energy. And that was a big moment for
me; it was about letting go of the body and fear of the future. (2002)

James, a respondent in our survey study, similarly reported:

I was in the woods, sitting next to the river, reading, and I looked up.
Everything looked immensely beautiful, like I'd entered another world.
Leaves sparkled with golden light, the sun was brilliant, and sounds such
as bird calls and the flowing of water were magnified. I was in awe at the
feelings I experienced. It left quite an impression on me for the rest of my life,
and made me a seeker. (Vieten, Cohen, and Schlitz 2008)

Nature can provide a quiet, reflective place to listen to your inner voice
and your way of being. Looking deeply into simple natural events—a leaf
floating in a river, sunlight sparkling through trees—can tell you about
your own life journey.

Nature can also teach us about the interconnectedness of the universe.
Lakota elder Gilbert Walking Bull explained to us that it's when you see
the sacred energy that infuses all of creation that you come to know true
religious or spiritual power. According to Walking Bull, this awareness of
interconnectedness is what gave birth to the Lakota tradition of becoming
a sacred human being:

True spiritual power exists in the world. In our Lakota world, we call it
taku skan skan—*something that moves. What this refers to is how the*
energy of the Great Spirit, Wakan Tanka Tunkasila, is connected. The
atom world is connected to everything Grandfather created. We call it the
Fire Within All Things Moving Alive—the atom world is this. True spirit
is the atom. It is in everything. When you know how everything is connected
to everything—I grew up knowing this—out of this comes the seven sacred
principles connected to our tradition. (2006)

For Walking Bull, nature isn't only an entry point to the sacred, it's
sacred in itself.

PERILS AND PITFALLS

Sometimes transformative experiences can be so unsettling, and so out of the ordinary that they're difficult to distinguish from psychosis. Psychiatrist Stan Grof, psychotherapist Christina Grof, psychologist David Lukoff, and others have distinguished between *spiritual emergence,* or "a gradual unfoldment of spiritual potential with minimal disruption in psychological/social/occupational functioning" (Lukoff 1998, 22) and *spiritual emergency,* which can cause significant disruptions in those areas. Lukoff further points out that making a differential diagnosis between psychopathology and spiritual emergence is challenging because the unusual experiences that are sometimes associated with transformation can look like symptoms of mental illness. The desire for silence may be seen as depressive withdrawal, the inability to articulate a noetic experience may be seen as loose associations, and near-death experiences may be diagnosed as hallucinations.

We mention this because transformative experiences aren't always welcome and can sometimes be confused with pathology. While not all transformative experiences are pathological, some are. Part of the challenge we face in transformative experiences is staying grounded amidst openings to new views of reality—views that often don't fit with the dominant cultural model of what's true or acceptable.

Cultural Inhibitions

Potentially transformative experiences can fade when they aren't honored. Benedictine monk Brother David Steindl-Rast told us that, because of cultural inhibitions, people can be quite reluctant to integrate mystical experiences into their lives and worldview. The author of more than thirty books, Steindl-Rast is renowned for teaching gratefulness—a practice of living with a fundamental appreciation for life. This practice, according to the sprightly octogenarian, can lead to restored courage; joyful recognition of truth, goodness, and beauty; and the understanding that we're united on a heart level. Steindl-Rast believes we can heal relationships and the Earth itself by practicing gratefulness. Drawing on the work of Abraham Maslow, he explained to us what separates great mystics from others:

59

Maslow called the peak experience first "mystical experience" and wrote about it under this term. He discovered very soon that it didn't come across too well in psychological literature and then changed it to "peak experience." Throughout his life he insisted that what he called peak experiences could not be distinguished from the so-called mystical experience we find in spiritual literature in many of the great traditions.

He discovered that the peak experience, or this little mystical experience, is accessible to everybody. And, to the extent to which we can generalize, we find it everywhere. Everybody has this experience… One of the most prominent features of peak experiences that was underscored by Maslow is an overflowing gratefulness.

So, if everybody has these mystic experiences, then the great question that arises is "Why aren't we all mystics? Why aren't we all spiritually evolved?" Maslow's answer was that, while many people have these experiences, they repress them, forget them, or are ashamed of them because they don't fit into our cultural frame of reference.

After people spoke to him about an experience—often with some prodding—they frequently said, "I've never spoken to anyone about it. I thought it was a momentary insanity." He would suggest to them that maybe this was actually the one sane moment in their lives!

So, the answer to the question of what makes the great mystics great mystics and us, with all our little mystical experiences, not really great mystics, is that the great mystics differ from the rest of us in allowing this experience and the memory of this experience—and therefore the energy of this experience—to flow into everyday living.

What you have experienced wants to be translated into everyday life. It's not a compartment in your life, it's the matrix for your whole life. It wants to be the energy that enlivens your life on every level. And that means spiritual living, and that means what the great mystics do. (2006)

Living your life based on a model of reality that goes against the grain can be challenging. Sometimes all you need is permission from a trusted other to feel that your noetic experiences are real in order to begin to integrate their insights into your life.

The Seduction of the Peak Experience

Most practitioners we spoke with viewed transformation as an ongoing process. As writer and integral philosopher Michael Murphy described during our interview with him, transformation can be "incremental and practically invisible, or completely invisible" (2002). Anthropologist Angeles Arrien also made this point clearly, warning that transformation can often be a subtle process:

> It's a disservice to think that transformation is a Fourth-of-July fireworks experience. I think most Westerners have the illusion—or delusion—that it happens all at once. There is nothing in nature that happens all at once. There's always a gestation or an incubation period. There are graduated stages of unfoldment. The changes within the individual are subtle yet distinct and witnessable, just as the seasons in a year. (2002)

When we experience a sudden shift in worldview—after which it often seems nothing will ever be the same—this change can take a lifetime to grow into. Shedding old habits, recalibrating deeply worn grooves, even reconditioning your neurochemistry, may be required to catch up with your new expanded worldviews and reshuffled priorities. Like water wearing away stone, or the slow laying down of layers of sediment to form mountains, integrating transformative experiences into your core way of being often requires time, patience, and inner work.

Arrien also noted that within the growth process "there are peak experiences or breakthroughs, but those are not the transformative points. The transformative points are always gradual, subtle, refined" (2002). Most of the teachers we spoke with warned about the dangers of getting too attached to these peak experiences. Trying to re-create peak moments over and over again, rather than settling into the more subtle, less glamorous work of integrating the realizations from these experiences into your daily life, can be a problem. Lutheran reverend and therapist Dennis Kenny shared his view about the role peak experiences play in transformation:

> I think those events are a part of the transformative process, but they're not transformations in and of themselves. I believe that many of these experiences are actually catalysts in the process of transformation, but they are not the end… They are part of the process that can lead us to understand ourselves and the world around us differently. And that's the end. The end is transformation—conversion—so that we live more fully as we walk.
>
> When Jesus was transfigured and gathered his disciples and zipped up into heaven in this wondrous miraculous event, they wanted to stay there, build shrines, build a temple. And the word was, "No. Go and do the work." And I think we all have that in us, the "This is so wonderful, it feels so good, I want to stay." But although these events are for a purpose, and are a part of the process, they are not the end. (2006)

Kenny's remarks suggest, too, that transformation is something that must be lived into—true transformation isn't just a set of remarkable experiences that are an end in and of themselves. Others in our focus groups, interviews, and surveys held similar positions. Even many of the people who'd had mystical or extraordinary experiences pointed out that these experiences themselves didn't dramatically change everything. For example, Peter Russell, author of *From Science to God* (2004), told us during our interview:

> I've had dramatic sudden shifts of awareness, or been in other states which have been quite remarkable. The memory of them has certainly stayed with me, but they haven't changed me. Afterwards, I drop back to the old baseline. It's that baseline which is gradually, gradually changing—the baseline of how I am, with all its wobbles and variations. While those peaks are certainly inspiration to continue with the work, on their own they don't make major shifts in my baseline. (2002)

So then, what does it take to transform? As both Kenny and Russell tell us, simply having an exceptional experience isn't enough. A transformation in consciousness is a fundamental shift in perception; it entails an entirely new way of being in the world. Living deeply involves an engagement with life, in all its various complexities. It is a moment-by-moment process. As Catholic priest Father Frances Tiso told us:

> All the great traditions talk about this idea that somehow the ideal thing would be for every moment to be a revelation, every moment to be a mystical experience—but not because you're having visions, but because of the beauty of the moment. The beauty of this moment is very, very great. This is a very great opening. Every microsecond of the conversation has the temptation for us to almost get lost in it. So these are good things ... hugging the dog, walking outside, or seeing that the real mysticism is here. (2002)

Of course, being present for all that life offers isn't always easy. It may require that you learn how to attend to life in new and different ways. And it may require that you adopt practices that actively reinforce these new ways of being. We will discuss some of these practices further in chapters 4 and 5.

SUMMARY

As we've seen, there are many different catalysts for transformation. People have found doorways into the transformative process through pain, loss, and illness, as well as through ecstatic and mystical experiences and communion with the natural world. And we've seen, too, that although extraordinary transformative experiences can be profound, transformation can also occur in the course of mundane, everyday experiences. We've explored differences between exceptional and transformative experiences—not all exceptional experiences lead to lasting worldview changes, but many act as catalysts along the way.

In chapter 3, we'll discuss more ways to move yourself toward the openings that can lead you to a life more full of wonder, awe, and surprise. We'll explore how to cultivate a soil that will help you grow in vital, sustaining ways. For now, you may wish to consider your own insights about transformation through the following exercise.

Experiencing Transformation: Integration

The following is another in-depth journaling exercise. You'll need a quiet place, some uninterrupted time, a notebook, a pen, and something to sketch with. The questions were drawn from a study done by psychologists Dacher Keltner and Adam Cohen in their lab at UC Berkeley as part of their research on experiences of awe and wonder (2003). Inquiring deeply into your own transformative experience can allow you not only to honor these experiences, but also to see patterns, retrieve elements that have been lost in translation, and integrate realizations from these experiences more fully. Like dreams, these experiences often have layers that are only revealed when revisited.

Think about a transformative experience in your life, one that has had a profound impact on you. It may be of the spiritual or religious variety. It may have been in response to something in nature. Or it may have resulted from relationships with other people, art, music, or many other things. The very first experience that comes to your mind is probably one that is asking to be explored in greater depth. Answer the following questions:

How old were you when the experience occurred?

Describe in detail what you were feeling at the time.

Describe in detail what happened to cause you to feel this way.

What were you thinking at the time?

What did you say, if anything, and how did you say it?

What were the physical signs of the experience?

How did you act, if at all?

How did the experience change you?

Were there pleasant aspects? Unpleasant?

Did you resist the experience, or did you surrender to it? Why or why not?

Sometimes, trying to express an experience with words is limiting. Perhaps you can write a poem about your experience or draw a picture, either of it or of something that symbolizes it. Maybe expressive movement would best capture this transformative experience—put on some music you love and let your body speak to you of the experience. Have you learned anything new?

CHAPTER THREE:

Preparing the Soil

The moment of realization or aha! is the outcome of dedicated effort.
Constant and daily effort is important and necessary in any individual's life.
—SWAMI NITYANANDA (2006)

What exactly is it that makes an extraordinary experience transformative, translating into true and lasting change? Clearly, not all extraordinary experiences end up being transformative. And some experiences that seem quite ordinary can be utterly transformative. Rabbi Jonathan Omer-Man, pioneering teacher of Jewish meditation and mysticism, told us that the transformative experience itself is less important than what comes next:

> *The question is, what do you do with the epiphany? The teaching that I have received is that all great moments of insight, all great epiphanies are ephemeral, and fade very, very quickly. It's like a wonderful moment of intense love. You are filled completely with affection for another human*

being and then get irritated by the way they burp after dinner. It's still the same person, the relationship is there, so what has happened?

The technique of the spiritual life is to cultivate what we call the reshimu—the subtle imprint that is left after the great opening. There is an opening in which we see all, the doors of perception are cleansed; then it's over. How does one retain the imprint of a moment of overwhelming love for another human being? What is there the next morning? Something is there. That is the essence of the work. The experiences themselves are almost meaningless. Or even dangerous—as when they become commodities, and the spiritual life becomes a quest for the next experience. (2006)

How can you nourish and grow the seeds of change that already exist within you? How do you cultivate the "imprint left after the great opening"? Indeed, how do you translate moments ripe with possibility into opening and growth, instead of just closing back down around them and waiting for the next invitation to come?

The garden is a powerful metaphor for transformation. In the garden, seeds are planted and—with adequate light, water, and soil nutrients—they grow. As a gardener, you don't *make* plants grow. Rather, you provide the ideal conditions for plants' natural growth to take place. Similarly, most of the teachers in our studies talked about transformation as something that happens naturally. Even though you may have an internal resistance to change, you also have a natural inclination toward growth. Like the gardener, rather than *making* transformation happen, we create the ideal conditions for natural transformation to flourish.

Through our research, we've identified several elements that can help you prepare the soil of your life. Some of these soil fertilizers—or *soul* fertilizers—are qualities you can cultivate within yourself. They involve the decisions you make about who you want to be and how you want to live. Others are choices you make about the external support system you provide yourself with and the support you offer to others for your mutual flowering. Whereas the last chapter focused on what the transformative experience brings to you, this chapter focuses on what *you* can bring to the transformative experience.

THE TRANSFORMATIVE EXPERIENCE: A CHOICE POINT

Why is it that some powerful experiences—sometimes even just one—can change your consciousness in deep and lasting ways, while other deeply powerful experiences don't seem to have any effect at all? A well-established theory from developmental psychology offers some suggestions as to what differentiates exceptional experiences from truly transformative ones.

Jean Piaget, the Swiss-born biologist and pioneering developmental psychologist, together with his colleagues, observed that when a child is presented with a new experience, that new experience is most often *assimilated* or incorporated into their current beliefs and attitudes (Inhelder and Piaget 1958). Or, if a child's beliefs and attitudes cannot assimilate a new experience because it's too challenging or different, their cognitive structures must alter to *accommodate*, or make room for, the new experience. For example, when children see a zebra for the first time, they often call it a horse. Having no concept for zebras, children *assimilate* the experience of the zebra into their current mental structures and decide that it's just an unusual horse. Eventually, a child will learn that there exists an animal similar to a horse in shape but actually a different animal altogether called a zebra. This process is the child *accommodating* her worldview to include the possibility of zebras.

Thus, as we learn, we're naturally forced to stretch and revise our worldviews. This cognitive process may partially account for the profound shifts in consciousness that we've heard about over and over again in our research. But what makes it more likely that we'll accommodate rather than assimilate new information? Psychologists Dacher Keltner from the University of California at Berkeley and Jonathan Haidt from the University of Virginia study experiences of awe and wonder, an area previously ignored by scientists. These two pioneers propose that awe has two essential components: perceived vastness and a need for accommodation (2003). In other words, it may be that some experiences are so vast, so profound, so far beyond what we've previously perceived, that they in effect *demand* that we transform our worldview in order to accommodate them. Rather than simply trying to assimilate these experiences into our constricted framework, we are forced to broaden that framework. This may explain why some of the experiences described in chapter 2 have the potential to be life-changing.

But still, why do some experiences that challenge your belief systems result in positive transformations while others result in trauma or greater rigidity and fear in your worldview? Psychologists Keltner and Haidt suggest that it's your ability to accommodate new experiences—to shift your current structures—that may determine whether these awe-inducing experiences are terrifying or enlightening. Taking this even a step further, Louise Sundararajan, psychologist and religious historian, proposes a model in which only assimilation failure leads to attempts at accommodation (2002). In other words, if you can somehow squeeze this new experience into your current worldview, you won't stretch or revise your current structures at all. Conversely then, when the process of assimilation is challenged by a new experience but accommodation *fails* (we don't stretch successfully), the original belief structure can end up getting rigidly reinforced to defend itself against future threats to a cherished worldview or sense of identity.

Following that, when the sheer power of experiences makes accommodation the only possibility—but we are, for whatever reason, unable to acknowledge or embrace a big shift in our internal structures—the result can be trauma rather than transformation. Sundararajan proposes that it is *self-reflexivity* that allows for successful accommodation. Self-reflexivity is your capacity for metacognition—your ability to take a step back and reflect upon yourself and your thought processes. This ability may be linked to successful accommodation, Sundararajan says, because it can bring you back to square one for a radical revision of your model of the world. Isn't it interesting that one of the essential components of transformative practice, across traditions, is the cultivation of this capacity to step back and look at ourselves? From the confessional in the Catholic tradition, to insight meditation in the Buddhist tradition, to taking inventory of your behavior in steps four and ten of twelve-step programs, transformative traditions often include a practice to cultivate your capacity for self-reflexivity. Being able to step back and examine your thought processes makes you able to notice the outdated beliefs and attitudes you're holding on to despite a wealth of new information calling for you to transform.

Traumatic vs. Transformative Pain

As we've noted, not all painful experiences lead to transformation. So what's the difference between pain that's traumatic and pain that's transformative? Now that we're aware of our tendency both to disregard new information and, when we do notice it, to try to fit it into our expectations (as described in the inattentional blindness section in chapter 1, and the description of assimilation and accommodation in the previous section), what qualities can you cultivate to help you attend to and get the most out of potentially transformative experiences?

Buddhist teacher and author Noah Levine spoke about the need for wisdom when encountering pain and suffering along the transformative path:

> In my experience, there's been a balance between feeling much more connected to others and feeling isolated and disconnected. To be awake in a world that is so asleep can feel very isolating and very lonely on some levels because, ultimately, everything is connected and everyone is doing the best they can, but also … the best that people can do isn't very good. In general if you look at the world … the suffering and the oppression and the vast ignorance that rules this realm of existence, it can be quite painful. The more awareness and the more sensitivity, the more need for balance with equanimity and understanding—even saying to yourself "Oh, this is just the way it is" may help.
>
> It's my work to wake up and to help others wake up. At times I take it personally. It can be quite difficult and painful to handle doubts like, "Is my work really making any difference? What about the 15 million children that starve to death every year?" Being aware of that and caring about it, even if it's a feeling of compassion, is painful.
>
> The Buddha says compassion is a quivering of the heart which, when it's not balanced with equanimity, is quite painful. When compassion is not balanced with wisdom it is very painful—and for me, I get out of balance. That can be quite difficult and as a result I feel very alone sometimes.
> (2005)

For many of us, this sensation of being overwhelmed by the challenges and suffering of the world can be hard to take—it can lead us to feelings of isolation and even impotence. As Levine points out, the more open and sensitive you become, the more you will feel—both more joy and more pain, of your own and of others. Compassion is the willingness to open to the suffering of others. To balance this increased sensitivity, Levine recommends cultivating wisdom and equanimity through meditation practice.

Equanimity refers to an evenness of mind or a state of inner unshakability in the face of all the highs and lows of our various experiences. A fundamental element of not only Buddhist practice but of psychological health in general, maintaining a strong equanimity can make our deepest pain and grief bearable—and leave us in a better position to act rather than collapse or simply avoid issues because they're too distressing. Of course, this is easier said than done.

It's no wonder, then, that so many of the world's transformative traditions include some version of a practice to foster equanimity and wisdom along with practices to enhance compassion. To "endure the quivering of the heart," you need to cultivate equanimity, wisdom, and insight. Like the Christian Serenity Prayer in which one asks God to "Give me the willingness to accept the things I cannot change, the courage to change the things I can, and the wisdom to know the difference," a balance is called for in our response to pain and suffering. Having this balance can make a painful experience more transformative and less traumatic.

Curiosity and Inquiry

In addition to cultivating a capacity for equanimity in the face of difficult or out-of-the-ordinary experiences, one of the most important ingredients that you can bring to your transformative path is a strong sense of curiosity and inquisitiveness. Rather than be suspicious of new information that seems out of the ordinary or counter to what you've always believed, you can approach these moments—whether pleasurable or disquieting—with a sense of adventure and exploration.

For many people, states of innocence and wonder are nutrients for the seeds of transformation. Some call this quality of openness the *second naiveté*, in which curiosity reminiscent of a child's takes you beyond your critical mind to the re-enchantment of the world and a desire to directly know things for what they truly are. Similarly, many teachers pointed to *beginner's mind* as one of the fundamental attitudes needed for mindful living. Beginner's mind is a way of approaching situations with openness, curiosity, and interest—a way of approaching situations as though they were happening for the first time, even if you've had numerous similar experiences. An old Zen saying goes, "In the beginner's mind there are many possibilities; in the expert's mind there are few."

Charles Tart, psychologist and author of *Altered States of Consciousness* (1990), spoke to us about the importance of bringing curiosity to the transformative path:

> One of the most essential aspects of this path—and, interestingly, one that is very seldom mentioned in traditional teachings—is curiosity, just wondering what things are really like. Curiosity, coupled with the desire not to be fooled (even though it's very comfortable to be fooled sometimes) but to try to get a better and better understanding of the way things actually are.
>
> I remember when I was a kid, I used to wake up excited each morning. It was an excitement that was both intellectual and emotional. It was sort of, "Wow, another day! I wonder what is going to happen today?" You know, life was very interesting.
>
> And then I gradually became more normal as I was socialized. My path, in a sense, has been to get back to that curiosity—to what's happening now. Curiosity about my own mind has been a major part of that. Why am I thinking the things I am thinking now? Why am I feeling this way when I don't want to feel this way? Curiosity and a desire not to be fooled are fundamental parts of that.
>
> The commitment to keeping curiosity alive takes a fair amount of work. For a lot of people the whole socialization process narrows curiosity down fast. That's a real shame. I think one of the greatest kicks in life is to look at very, very young babies when their eyes are open and they're looking

around like, "Whoa, what is this place?" There is something sacred and inspiring about that. (2003)

What Tart tells us here is more than simply "be playful." Rather, he encourages us to cultivate both curiosity and discernment in our lives. For him, the desire "not to be fooled" by paying attention only to what's on the surface or taking things at face value comes from an appreciation for the multiple ways that we can know reality—for the range of epistemologies (all the ways that we know what we know) that's available to us. For example, if you were raised within a worldview that valued only material accomplishments, your capacity to see beyond materialistic goals may have been unintentionally shut down. However, by exercising your curiosity and striving to understand what lies beneath the surface, you can gain greater insights into your own spiritual being. By cultivating a childlike curiosity, you create a dynamic between your inner and outer worlds.

Similarly, several teachers described the importance of cultivating an *I-don't-know mind.* Being able to tolerate uncertainty rather than immediately rushing to safe, habitual beliefs—and staying with that uncertainty despite the discomfort it can bring—is an ability that can lubricate the transformative process. Certainty, though seductive in making us feel safe, can also close down the potential for considering alternatives. If you already know the answer, what's there to be curious about? Uncertainty is actually ground zero for both curiosity and inquiry. And open-minded curiosity and the courage to inquire deeply are both qualities that, when cultivated, can provide fertile soil for positive change.

Andriette Earl, an assistant minister at the East Bay Church of Religious Science in Oakland, described to us her work helping people "get the hang of spiritual inquiry":

What I find is that a lot of people don't know how to inquire. They know the questions, but they don't know how to use them. It's like thinking that because you have a hammer in your hand you know how to build a house. Just because you have a profound spiritual question, it doesn't mean you know how to use it.

The first thing I do is try to teach people how to use a deep spiritual question—which is meant to get us to the experience of not-knowing almost instantaneously. "What am I?" "I don't know." "What's it like not to know?" One second ago you thought you knew, but now, in a split second, you know that you don't know. Before you try to know, what's it like not to know?

People push so hard to get an answer—they think they're in school and this is a test. If they're sitting in front of me, usually the first thing that happens is their eyes start to roll up in their head. This tells me that they're thinking. They immediately go into the thought process. Why is it that when we ask ourselves, "What am I really, ultimately, essentially?" most people go into thought?

I'm stretching something out that happens in a split second, which is why people miss it. When they look within they don't find anything. This isn't what they expected to find. They expected to find the true self, the enlightened self, the higher self, the better version of me. And they don't find anything, so the mind instantly concludes, "That can't be right. I looked in to find what I really am and there's nothing there."

I find that the first thing you know when you ask the question "What am I really?"… is that you don't know. We don't have to think about things we know. We don't have to roll our eyes in our head and think about it for even a split second.

When you really start to get the hang of it, you understand what inquiry is actually like. You find the questions that naturally fit your experience. They just help you take in the mysteriousness of your own self. But if you don't know how to use a question, you can't go into the mysteriousness of your own self. Instead you go into your mind or what you read in a book or what someone heard that someone else said, and it has no power. (2006)

Indeed, what is it like to not know? Earl's question brings home the point that being mindful of not knowing, maintaining a healthy curiosity, and cultivating the skill of inquiry can lead you to a space of creativity and imagination. And in that space, great breakthroughs can happen.

Creativity

Making time in your life for creative expression can be a challenge. Expressing your creativity can feel like a luxury, like something you should do only after other more pressing or more important things have been taken care of. Creativity often translates in our minds as a hobby or pastime. While it can be—and often is—fun and enjoyable, creativity also serves a very important function: it's a crucial part of preparing the soil for transformation. The creative process is a breeding ground for new ideas and new connections between previously unrelated aspects of your self. Creativity can provide you with a context for seeing the unseen world.

Creative self-expression can transform your body and mind and support the healing of your whole being. Various forms of expressive arts therapies, including drama, dance, painting, making music, sculpting, and writing, have been shown to ease symptoms and improve quality of life in a variety of populations. For example, *expressive writing*—unstructured journaling engaged in thirty minutes per day, four days a week—has been shown to improve health in cancer patients; benefits include increased vigor, improved sleep, reduced number of doctor visits, improved coping, and fewer physical symptoms (Frisina, Borod, and Lepore 2004). Conversely, psychologist James Pennebaker's work shows that *inhibition*—keeping thoughts and feelings hidden—is a stressor that can negatively impact immune and vascular function, as well as the workings of the nervous system (1990). Clearly, finding pathways to self-expression and learning to listen to your creative urges can be both liberating and health promoting.

Anna Halprin, mother of expressive-movement art therapy, told us that she began by using her life to create her art, but then, after engaging in deep internal inquiry, began to use art to create her life. She explained more fully:

I've always been an artist. But I'd never connected art so closely to life experience until I was stricken with cancer in 1972. That was a big shift for me. I began to ask all kinds of questions: What am I doing and who am I doing it for? Why am I dancing? What difference does it make anyway? The shift was that I began to use the art experience to reveal real-life issues and to find ways to transform them.

Modern dance at that time was dancing about things—Martha Graham was dancing about Greek mythologies—or dancing in relationship to music, or other very abstract themes. I was no longer interested in dancing about abstract things. I began to explore ways to dance about themes that had to do with real life—my life—and the life of those whom I related to.

For me, transformation has to do with how the artistic experience can bring about positive change. Positive change enables the individual to release from their wholeness anything which interferes with creativity. It enables them to cope with whatever comes to them in terms of their particular life experience. We need tools to cope creatively and artistically with our lives. And that's what leads to transformation and to a continuous growth.

Life is constantly going to bring up unprepared-for situations that will tap into areas within yourself that, up until that moment, you didn't know existed... You have to commit yourself to looking at whatever comes up—without knowing what the outcome will be—and dealing with the outcome creatively. What comes up may be very difficult; it may be challenging, dark, and uncomfortable. But the ability and the commitment to use the art process to overcome the blockage—that creates. (2002)

The transformative process is filled with opportunities for surprise and wonder—imagination, creativity, and the generative impulse are all waiting to be nourished in your life. If creative expression feels like a dusty relic of the past, it's time to dust off your crayons.

Introspection and Inner Authority

As you seek to foster curiosity and creative expression, the importance of making time for silence and solitude cannot be overstated. Quiet the external noise. Unplug your radio and turn off the television. Take a walk in the woods. Stop and spend five minutes without moving before your next appointment. Slow down and enter a sphere of quiet to allow yourself the chance to cultivate inner knowing, to listen and understand your life in a new way.

For Jeremy Taylor—Unitarian Universalist minister and author of several books integrating dream symbolism, mythology, and archetypal energy—deep listening has taken the form of paying attention to the complex messages of dreams:

> My dreams have been the most important ongoing influence on my life and work. I always pay regular attention to the specific content of the dreams I am able to remember from sleep. One reason I do this is that it gives me a vivid sense of living in the midst of an unending flow of creative energy. The dreams have also given me specific inspiration for virtually all my creative efforts—writing, teaching, extemporaneous public speaking, drawing, painting, and all the other projects and constructions I get involved with.
>
> Dreams also play a crucial role in my relational life—particularly my long-term, evolving relationship with my wife Kathryn. It's fairly easy to imagine that if we had not been sharing our dream memories regularly with one another over the whole forty-plus years we have been together, we might not even be together now… Dreams bring these potential insights to us all in a marvelously impersonal way, a way that allows us to see our lives with fresh eyes and to talk about problems and make the necessary adjustments in behavior and attitude so that we stop dealing pain to one another unintentionally.
>
> Paying attention to my dreams on a regular basis has also continued to give me heart for the nonviolent social change work I have engaged

in all my life—even in the face of the relentlessly depressing news of this country and the world. It's really quite difficult to stay filled with hope and enthusiasm and creative energy while things keep spiraling into worse and worse configurations. Many of my old social activist friends are burnt-out, exhausted, embittered, and cynical. And I can understand why—they have every rational reason to feel that way. I believe that the primary reason why I have been able to avoid that state of moral exhaustion is that my dreams constantly give me this tangible sense of being in the midst of a flow of creative energy and possibility. Aboriginal people would probably call it a sense of being supported by spirit allies—which is a perfectly reasonable way to talk about it. There are forces at work in the collective psyche that are more subtle than the screaming headlines. These energies are often difficult to catch sight of in the waking world, but they are much more visible and accessible in the dream world. These energies have proven themselves to be much more powerful than the billiard-ball economics and violent stupidities that, dare I say it, keep knocking the towers down.

Dreamwork also provides me with an intellectual tool of analysis that offers hope because it offers names for the evolutionary forces that are at work in the psyche, forces that are clearly the equal of the forces that brought us articulate speech and the ability to imagine our own mortality. My personal conviction ... is that we are on an evolutionary cusp right now, where something as important and transformative as the development of articulate speech is at work in us. But we don't know what it is yet; we have not yet evolved to the point where we can recognize it consciously, but everything I know points to it and says that it is there, growing and evolving in our dreams... (2006)

Deep listening can take many forms. Swami Veda Bharati, a teacher and spiritual leader in the tradition of the Vedas and the Himalayan yogis, told us that by enduring silence we can enter the space of our hearts and by doing so access what is imperceptible to our outer senses:

*Why do you want to see outside what you can already see inside? Silence …
endure silence. Now you can measure brain waves. But by that, you cannot
convey the silence. In that silence, something else happens. We talk of the
entire universe as being an entity in space. Something in the space of your
heart grows and expands. It encloses the whole universe. All the living beings
are embraced in silent space, which you have entered in this cavity of the
heart.* (2002)

Entering the realm of silence requires that you pay attention to your
daily rhythms and natural cycles. Spiritual teacher Gangaji shared with us
the story of how her teacher taught her to find her natural rhythm and state
of being by slowing down to a complete stop:

*I met Papaji at a time when I was earnestly asking for a teacher. For me, it
was essential that I meet him. I had tried many different paths, and I had
had many beautiful experiences. Still, the transformation I was searching
for had not yet been established. When he said to me, "Stop all your paths,
stop all your searching, don't do anything," a huge and deep fear arose.
If I stopped, what would that mean about all that I had attained and all
the time I'd spent attaining it? Yet I recognized Papaji as my teacher, so I
decided to stop and see what he really meant.*

*Stopping doesn't happen instantaneously, but the willingness to stop
happens instantaneously. There is an "okay, I'm willing." Not as in giving
up or resigning, but "okay" as in surrender. In that moment of surrender,
I discovered how much mental, physical, and emotional attention had
been about getting something for me—my happiness, my fulfillment, my
enlightenment—or keeping away my unhappiness, my lack of fulfillment,
my ignorance. Papaji had spoken with the force and the authority of his
own direct knowing, and because I recognized that force, I was willing not to
immediately run out the door, following my own agenda.*

*It is very simple: Whatever is going on, good or bad, underneath that
circumstance is usually a thread of suffering. If you will only stop to directly*

investigate what is deeper under that, it is possible to discover an infinite field
of happiness, truth, silence, and bliss that is your essential nature. (2002)

If there was one thing the majority of teachers we interviewed agreed upon, it was this central thread of looking inward. Intentionally stopping and being in silence is a simple practice that may at first feel uncomfortable, but over time can become a refuge. In a way it's like being in nature and seeing the flash of a buck. In order to get a closer look, to truly encounter this wild and majestic being, the ideal strategy is to stop and be utterly still. In the same way, to truly encounter the wild and majestic aspects of your own inner self requires being still and silent.

For Zorigtbaatar Banzar, a Mongolian shaman and leader of the Center of Shaman and Eternal Heavenly Sophistication in Mongolia, transformation comes from what he describes as "eternal power." To find this power, one must slow down and listen to the messages of the Earth:

In the place where I live in Mongolia there is much eternal power and
information on our land. To find this eternal power I lived with my master,
a very powerful Mongolian shaman, in a cave in the mountains for thirteen
years, studying shamanism. If people can find the power of this eternal
power and the power of their own body, they can live happily. They can find
the real meaning of their life and what they need. Patience overcomes all
difficulties, all pain, all sufferings in our life. If you have great patience, then
very positive results are waiting for you.

The most important thing for you is to know yourself. You are a very
precious and sacred person. You are a god for yourself and you are a heaven
for yourself. So you need to open yourself. We need to communicate with our
sacred treasure. After we know ourselves and each other very completely, this
eternal love blossoms and becomes stronger. (2006)

To achieve inner stillness, silence, or eternal power, you don't have to find a spiritual teacher, embark on a different spiritual path, or live in a cave for thirteen years. Instead, you can simply cultivate deep listening.

In doing so, you may find yourself guided to that teacher, new practice, or cave after all!

Most of us are primarily familiar with the *discursive intellect*—the "computer brain" part of us that knows things through thinking, figuring, planning, strategizing, comparing, and evaluating. But you may also be familiar with the kind of knowing that comes from intuition, hunches, or gut feelings. By cultivating silence and deep listening, you can open yourself up to these inner realms of knowing and broaden your previous understanding and experience.

DIRECT KNOWING

Our research suggests that when the facilitators of transformation we've described in this chapter are present—awareness of the natural tendency to assimilate rather than accommodate; the cultivation of curiosity and inquiry, creativity, and space for introspection—a very natural and authentic source of knowledge, what could be called *direct knowing*, will arise from your own awareness.

Of course, we aren't recommending an exclusive reliance on gut feelings to navigate you through your life. The rational mind, when used properly, is a powerful tool, particularly in relation to the material world. As the old adage goes, be open-minded, but not so open-minded that your brain falls out! The transformative process is about establishing a more equal balance between head and heart, intellect and intuition. If you're someone who tends to overrely on your judging rational mind, the various forms of transformative practice can move you toward melding your rational discursive intellect with noetic/subjective understanding. Likewise, if you're someone who is highly reactive and driven by emotion, transformative practice can help you find greater discernment and self-regulation. Weaving knowledge gained through objective observation and logic together with direct noetic knowing allows you full access to both what can be physically observed and what's actually being directly experienced in your life.

A Scientific Perspective on Direct Knowing

For more than a century psychologists have been curious about what happens in people's brains during *aha! moments*—those moments of clarity when the solution to a vexing problem falls into place through sudden insight. A series of experiments (Kounios et al. 2006) has begun to identify what leads to aha! moments. First, the research suggests that aha! solutions to vexing problems are often actually preceded by brain patterns that begin much prior to the act of solving the problem—sometimes even before a problem is presented. This suggests that how a person is thinking *before* problem solving begins may be just as important as the kind of thinking involved in reaching the solution—it's almost as though you put your mind into a receptive state that primes it for insights and integrations.

Second, as people approach an aha! solution, brain activity suggests that attention focuses inwardly. It appears that, to switch to new trains of thought, irrelevant thoughts must first be actively silenced. To facilitate this, the brain momentarily reduces visual input. This produces an effect similar to closing your eyes or looking away—physical tricks we often unconsciously employ to help solutions emerge into conscious awareness.

Furthermore, Kounios and his colleagues also found the mental preparation that leads to aha! solutions to be characterized by increased brain activity. Increased activity was seen in the temporal lobe areas (associated with conceptual processing) and the frontal lobe areas (associated with cognitive control or "top-down" processing). Learning to focus attention inwardly, to reduce visual and auditory inputs, and to silence irrelevant thoughts temporarily can all set the stage for moving into a different kind of cognitive processing—one that includes increasing insight-based knowledge along with the traditional "figuring it out" knowledge. It's amazing that so many transformative practices, like the vision quest, already foster qualities like introspection and internal silence that scientists are only now discovering as key factors in growth, learning, and transformation.

SUMMARY

Just as soil can be prepped in anticipation of a beautiful garden, consciousness transformation can be nurtured and cultivated. By fostering curiosity, creativity, and introspection in your life, you can open yourself to expanded dimensions of your being. These are ways of being, within the everyday circumstances of your environment, that can help you increase the transformative potential of your experiences—and allow any transformative experiences that come to take hold more easily and firmly, with less resistance or trauma.

Once you've prepared the ground and a seed of transformation has been planted, you begin the growth cycle. Before you can harvest your bumper crop, more work remains ahead. What sustains you on the transformative path? What keeps you moving forward when the terrain seems impassable, or when you're tempted to settle for a familiar and comfortable stopping point that's less than your full potential? Many of our research participants emphasized the importance of practice. In the next two chapters, we'll consider the different paths of practice available to each of us and some elements common across them. For now, consider the following exercise as a way of clarifying your own intentions for transformation.

Experiencing Transformation: Preparing the Soil

Growth and transformation happen all the time—they're aspects inherent to both nature and human nature. The degree to which growth and transformation proceed on a slow, agonizing, bumpy course or flow easily through your life is partly up to you.

Over a half century ago, Abraham Maslow (1954) proposed that when human beings' basic needs for food, shelter, and safety are met, they seek to satisfy higher needs for things like friendships, intellectual stimulation, and beauty. In this exercise, we explore the possibility that so-called higher needs may need to be met in order to fully meet what had previously been considered "lower" needs. Examining to what extent your needs are being met can shed light on the conditions for transformation present in your life.

Take out your journal and find a quiet place to reflect. What is the condition of your soil right now? How conducive is your life to the transformative process?

You may or may not have your basic physiological needs for food, shelter, and safety secured. Explore whether your basic physiological needs are really being attended to by answering the following questions:

Are you eating enough nutritious foods on a fairly regular schedule?

Are you giving your body enough exercise, sunshine, and nutrients?

Do you have aches, pains, or discomforts you could be attending to more consciously?

Are you getting enough rest and sleep?

Are your environments at work and at home safe, and are you taking whatever precautions you need to in order to feel safe?

Do you have an appropriate balance of work and time for rest and renewal?

Does your housing really suit your needs?

If you're feeling frustrated in reaching your highest potential, perhaps these more basic needs aren't being adequately attended to. While they may seem mundane, they're just as important to your mental, emotional, and spiritual well-being as are more lofty spiritual and philosophical pursuits.

Next, flip it the other way: are you having trouble reaching your goals in relationship to the basic needs of balancing your life, eating healthily, treating your body well, and so on? It's possible that you've delayed your higher needs too much, maybe thinking, "When I get everything in my life settled, then I can move on to things like learning to be more loving; enhancing my capacity for trust, generosity, and forgiveness; and actively cultivating joyful and creative experiences." Our so-called "higher" needs are as fundamental to our quality of life as our basic needs. Explore whether your "higher" needs are really being met by answering the following questions:

Do you have friends and family members who are supportive and worthy of your trust and respect? If not, where can you seek at least one connection like that?

Do you regularly engage in at least one activity that brings you uncomplicated joy?

Is there a regular time for creativity in your life?

Do you spend daily time in quiet contemplative reflection? How about time in nature?

Right now, make—and commit to—a plan to fulfill at least one of the basic needs and one of the "higher" needs you've identified in this exercise.

CHAPTER FOUR:

Paths and Practices

Realization isn't something we can do, it's only something we can be ready
for. Practice isn't the cause of realization, but it helps you to be more open
and ready to receive what the universe has to offer.
—*ZENKEI BLANCHE HARTMAN (2003)*

So far, we've considered common doorways to transformation and how you can prepare the soil of your life so that seeds of transformation are more likely to take root. But this is only the beginning of the journey. How can you grow a plant from that seed—a plant that's a perennial, not just a single-season bloomer? How do you translate extraordinary—or even ordinary—life experiences into transformations that result in significant, long-lasting changes in your consciousness?

Most of our interviewees and survey respondents emphasized the importance of practice. Of our self-selected survey sample, 68 percent reported engaging in a formal practice, with the most common practices being meditation and devotional practices such as prayer. A full 73 percent reported engaging in informal practices, including writing, reading, visualization, studying spiritual or consciousness-oriented topics, walking in nature, personal prayer, music, art, and affirmations (Vieten, Cohen, and Schlitz 2008).

Even when a transformative experience is deeply profound, new realizations can be fragile. To take hold, transformations must be reinforced. As Reverend Lauren Artress told us, "Transformation disappears if you don't honor it" (2003). Changes in your worldview can happen in an instant, but mastery of new kinds of thought or behavior often requires the cultivation of new ways of being. George Leonard, author of *Mastery* (1992), put it this way: "If you want to catch the grace of the wind, you must put up your sails. Practice!" (2002).

WHAT MAKES A PRACTICE?

There are literally thousands of different ways to engage in transformative practice. Moreover, transformative practices themselves can take many different forms, ranging from contemplative prayer to mindfulness meditation, from the twelve steps of Alcoholics Anonymous to Holotropic Breathwork, from walking a labyrinth to growing a garden—and many more. With all this diversity, it's fair to ask, what exactly makes something a transformative practice? While we don't want to gloss over this rich diversity of forms, our research suggests that there are some essential elements of transformative practice that appear across widely varying traditions.

Traditional and Emerging Practices

In traditional forms of transformative practice—such as those found in organized religions—practitioners follow formal, prescribed traditions with ancient lineages. Some traditional forms have remained relatively unaltered as they've been handed down through the ages and adapted to new cultures. And some have evolved, at times spinning off new traditions. For our research, we sought out active participants of the world's leading religious and spiritual traditions, including Buddhism, Judaism, Islam,

Christianity, and Hinduism. We also spoke with representatives of long-standing cultural traditions in which spirituality is deeply rooted, such as Native American and European shamanism. In considering these various practices, we sought to identify the common elements that could be useful to each of us in developing our own transformative path.

In traditional forms of transformative practice, maintaining continuity with the past is strongly emphasized. By replicating well-calibrated practices—ones that have been developed and refined over millennia—it's thought that you'll benefit from the wisdom of the ages. These methods are essentially technologies of transformation that have been refined through trial and error—finely tuned over centuries to achieve specific results. The rituals, symbols, and sacred texts of formal traditions are often regarded as themselves imbued with the power to transform the individual. For example, in the ritual of the Eucharist (in some Christian traditions), the consumption of consecrated bread and wine is believed to transmit the spirit of Christ into its participants. In some Hindu traditions, the word "om" is believed to contain the essence of the universe; it's thought that by chanting "om" you connect with the primordial essence of life. There is great beauty, comfort, and authority in these formal rites.

However, following a traditional path isn't the only way for people in the twenty-first century to engage in transformative practice. The last century—and in particular the last half of the twentieth century—saw an explosion in nontraditional religions, spiritualities, and transformative practices (Kripal 2006). Many of these new practices have been created to correspond more directly with the values of contemporary culture. These forms tend to be eclectic and are often amalgams of various ancient practices and more modern views. In our research we intentionally sought out and interviewed respondents from various modern forms of transformative practice, including Holotropic Breathwork, the Four-Fold Way, Nine Gates Mystery School, A Course in Miracles, Integral Transformative Practices, neoshamanism, neo-paganism, and many more.

To help us better understand the distinctions between traditional forms of practice and emergent forms, we turned to comparative religions scholar Huston Smith. From his home in Berkeley, he described to us the tension between more established religious practices and the emerging new forms of spiritual expression, which he identifies as "cut-flower" traditions:

In the past, each religion was in a kind of cocoon; there wasn't much contact with others. But now, with globalization, they're all rubbing shoulders with one another. This poses a constructive problem for those who are seriously interested in religion. How can we combine depth with breadth? Depth means solid grounding in one's own religion. Knowing its history, its creed, and its magisterial minds. You can spend your whole life and still not get to the bottom of one religion. How can you have depth, through grounding in one's own religion, and breadth—which implies an openness to learning and respecting other religions? We can draw a distinction between religion and spirituality. Religion is organized spirituality. Spirituality is free-floating, it doesn't get together, have worship services, or whatever…

In my work I like the Irish tailor's definition of trousers: they are singular at the top and plural at the bottom. All religions have a central core of great, enduring truths that are mirror images of each other. Simple ideas are stated in different idioms. However, the great religions are certainly not carbon copies of each other. You get the central truths that are shared in common, but each tradition ferrets out a different cavity in the human spirit and speaks insightfully to those truths. (2006)

This comparative approach has been an anchor of our own research. We've considered transformation much as Smith's Irish tailor does trousers: celebrating differences while seeking areas of core connection. More specifically, we've sought to identify common elements that shed light on the mystery of transformation and how you can apply transformative experiences to your everyday life.

FINDING *YOUR* PRACTICE

You may celebrate the fact that you live in an era and culture that allows you to choose your own unique transformative path! You might choose a transformative practice connected to deeply rooted, long-lasting, tried-and-true spiritual or religious traditions. There are many benefits to this choice. For one thing, there will most likely be opportunities to engage in this practice in your own community—you won't have to trek off to the heights of the Himalayas or the depths of the Amazon to connect with a teacher or practice community. Indeed, you may be able to find members of your group almost anywhere you travel. And there is definitely something special about the idea that thousands—if not millions—of people around the world, past and present, are engaging in the very same practice. It can feel very safe to be part of something so steeped in tradition that it undergoes change only very slowly and thus remains predictable.

On the other hand, you may identify with people who have become disillusioned with organized religion and seek alternative forms of spiritual practice to provide meaning and purpose. Our survey sample reflects this movement: although 60 percent were raised in a religious household and 40 percent were not, only 30 percent identified themselves as religious without another spiritual practice, while 70 percent identified themselves as spiritual, not religious. Moreover, a full 95 percent reported that they were very or moderately spiritual, whereas only 22 percent considered themselves very or moderately religious (Vieten, Cohen, and Schlitz 2008).

Many groups and programs have emerged as alternatives to traditional forms of practice. Spiritual teacher and author Andrew Cohen refers to his spiritual perspective as "evolutionary enlightenment." In his words, Cohen teaches a "spiritual path for the twenty-first century" (2003). He spoke to us about the cultural context in which new spiritualities are born and old traditions are translated in new ways:

> *Many people from my generation who've become interested in the possibility of enlightenment, or the experience of higher states of consciousness, have grown up in a secular context. The world we are living in is very, very different from the world in which the great spiritual traditions emerged thousands of years ago, and naturally we have outgrown many of the moral, ethical, and philosophical precepts of those traditions. But the problem is, we have found little to replace them. And therefore, when we discovered the higher states we were looking for, a lot of these experiences occurred in an inner context of profound narcissism. This narcissism is unmediated by any strong moral, ethical, or philosophical context that would help put our*

spiritual experiences in a much bigger perspective, a perspective that would give them real evolutionary power, drive, and force. Unfortunately we have all kind of gotten stuck in this way, because we have lost the big context. (2003)

Swami Nityananda has spent the last twenty-five years traveling and teaching people in India and the West. Like Cohen and Smith, he notes that there can be grave dangers to not planting your roots in deep soil. He suggested another way to consider—and utilize—the smorgasbord of transformative practices available in America today:

I think America is a country that was founded to be different. A little bit of what I see in the generation of today is possibly those same principles of "I'm not going to be bound to one thing. I'm not going to be limited to one thing. I'm going to keep trying different things."

I agree that until you find a path, a teaching, a way that works for you, you can look at different things. But I think at some point, you should decide which one you're going to follow. The example I give is: There's a freeway, there's a highway, there's an open road, and maybe a dirt road. And all of them will bring you from point A to point B. But somewhere you have to decide whether you're going to take the freeway, the highway, the local road, or the dirt road. You cannot say, "You know what, I would like to travel on all of them at the same time," or even at different times. Because you'll only waste time getting off the freeway, going onto the highway, going onto the local road—you might end up going around and around. You'll never get to your destination that way.

On the path of spirituality you try out different things, realize different things, but then decide which one you are going to follow. And then stay with that. Because our mind is such that, if it doesn't have a dedicated, committed practice, it is not steady, it wavers. (2006)

Of course, not everyone agrees that committing to a single, laid-out transformative path is necessary. Psychologist James Fadiman has a very different perspective, perhaps exemplifying his own eclectic spirit. He explained:

> *Maybe taking different paths is a little like taking a multivitamin—the reason they say "take a multivitamin" is that one individual supplement isn't appropriate for a complicated physiological being. It seems to me, given the opportunities that we have, a single spiritual path isn't appropriate for the contemporary American experience. We have these incredible riches. You also find spiritual teachers who say, "Well, I may be a Tibetan but there is this wonderful book by Yogananda that you may appreciate and there's a Pilates teacher that will really help you because I can see the way that you are holding yourself isn't going to be useful for you as you age … and maybe it would be good for you to go to Esalen because there is someone there who is teaching journaling!" Now that is a prescription, like a bunch of vitamin supplements. And every person benefits from a different prescription.*
> (2003)

Indeed, almost exactly equal numbers of our survey participants said that a formal practice was important in their transformation as said a formal practice wasn't important. Similarly, equal numbers found a teacher or guide important as did not (Vieten, Cohen, and Schlitz 2008).

So now, after all that's been said, what constitutes an effective practice? If practice can be traditional or alternative, formal or informal, guided or teacherless, then what are the essential elements that make an activity a practice?

THE ESSENTIAL ELEMENTS OF TRANSFORMATIVE PRACTICE

The word "practice" is both a verb and a noun. You can practice something in order to learn it—"I am practicing being open and honest with others"—and something can become your practice—"It is my practice to be forthcoming." Thus, practice is both the act of performing a set of exercises and the form, philosophy, or worldview underlying these exercises. Most commonly, practice is thought of as the act of repeating something over and over for the purpose of learning and gaining experience. In the course of our work, we have come to define *transformative practice* as any set of internal or external activities you engage in with the intention of fostering long-lasting shifts in the way you experience and relate to yourself and others.

What are the essential elements of transformative practice across traditions? We asked teachers and survey respondents to describe in detail *their* practices—what their practice entails, the essential elements of their practice, and how often they engage in it. We learned that transformative practices aren't defined by specific rites, rituals, texts, or belief systems. While these elements are very important for each practitioner and differentiate practices from one another, none of our respondents told us that "having a cross on the wall" is absolutely essential, or that "chanting Hare Krishna for one hour each day" was a fundamental requirement. What we learned is that transformative practices include four essential elements: intention, attention, repetition, and guidance.

The First Essential: Intention

One of the first steps to any conscious transformative path is personal choice—the will to change, emotional volition and desire, motivation, or, put more simply: intention. *Intention* is the determination to act in a certain way.

While it is true that transformative experiences, such as the ones we described in chapter 2, often seem to arise spontaneously, one of the elements that determine whether or not they take root is the intention you hold toward personal growth and transformation. It's an interesting paradox: even though transformation is a natural process—one that you primarily need to recognize and surrender to—it also requires making the choice, each moment of each day, to be in greater alignment with who you are at your core.

Holding the intention to be open to transformation at all times can help you recognize the opportunities for transformation that present themselves in your daily life. Despite promises made by popular books and movies, your own positive intention may not make transformation a walk in the park or be the answer to all of your concerns; however it *can* go a long way toward easing—and perhaps even accelerating—the transformative process. With intention, it's almost as though you become a coconspirator in your own evolution, as opposed to being dragged through it kicking and screaming.

Religious Science reverend Andriette Earl has a strong and powerful presence, filled with radiance and vitality, but under her dynamism is a person who has struggled to find her way. Learning she had choices was an important lesson for her, as it is for many of us; she describes the intention to grow and transform as essential to her being:

> I think, most of all, my practice is born out of an absolute intention to live life fully. I do whatever it takes in order for me to show up as best as I can in that energy. It's often difficult. It's often very, very difficult.
>
> My own life story is one of having made two suicide attempts as a young person, having been raped, and then going through deaths of intimate family and friends, and divorce—you know, the manner of life experiences that we all have.
>
> In all of this, I choose as best I can to stay present and conscious to what my options truly are. That's new. I hadn't always known that there were options. It used to feel as if I had to live life in reaction to how it showed up for me. And now I'm finding that I've always called it into being the way it is. Now I have an opportunity to shift what I'm calling in.
>
> It's seldom as immediate as I would like. But there's something that calls me to just stay there. To keep chipping away at the parts that I don't want to continue to experience. And so I think my practice is this chipping away. It's being still enough to recognize when it's out of alignment, and courageous enough to know that I can pull it into alignment using the right tools and resources. (2006)

Perhaps the moral of this story is that transformation rests in part upon your commitment to listening for that something that calls you to stay with the process, that something that calls you to keep chipping away to reveal the beautiful form that is you. Sufi Shaykh Yassir Chadly, coming from a different tradition than Earl, told us a similar thing:

The bottom line is intention. What's the intention? If the intention is for God, then God makes sure that person will be shown the right way. God looks for us the way we look for God. God said, "I am a treasure, I wanted to be found, so I created you." God created you, you are His treasure. As soon as your intention is for God, God will guide you to His prophets or His saints that represent the prophets. Once your intention is like that, then the teacher appears, because God will send someone to you. God listens and hears your heart and your desire for finding God. "You want to find me? Then I will send you the people that will bring you to me." If there is no one around, God will show you Himself through anything—through an ant, a rock, a mountain. He has a variety of ways to show you paradise. (2006)

For each of these teachers, intention is a choice you make about where to place your awareness. For Earl it is deciding to stay present in the choices she makes; for Chadly it is the intention to continuously look for God. Focused commitment is essential to translating potentially transformative experiences into new ways of living and being.

Spiritual teacher Andrew Cohen goes even further, arguing that once you've had an experience of awakening, it's your *responsibility* to join the evolution of consciousness itself through intention:

To me, the experience itself, especially if it's a very deep experience, is not a free ride. We taste or experience our own potential, and in that, we awaken to an evolutionary imperative to evolve. And when one awakens to the evolutionary imperative, one's spiritual conscience or higher conscience is awakened. So the higher conscience is what I would interpret now and understand to be an evolutionary impulse. It's a call from one's own authentic self to begin to participate in the evolutionary process for the sake of the evolution of consciousness itself.

> *One recognizes in this kind of experience that for consciousness to be able to evolve and develop from our stage of development to the next one, we have to begin to consciously engage with this process. You have to consciously participate in this process. In other words, it's not going to happen by itself. For evolutionary development to continue to a higher level, our conscious, intentional, committed engagement is the only way it's going to happen.*
> (2003)

This big-picture view of individual growth as part of a larger collective evolution was a common theme in our interviews with teachers. Similarly, identifying oneself as part of a larger movement toward greater awakening was a common theme among our survey respondents (Vieten, Cohen, and Schlitz 2008).

As we've seen, transformative practice isn't always easy or enjoyable. In fact, it's often tough for people to stick to. Like any other repeated practice (and like life itself), moments of the sublime or the deeply profound are interspersed with boredom, discomfort, and the unfamiliar. Often our commitment wavers. It is deep, strong, pure intention that rekindles it. Sylvia Boorstein, teacher of vipassana meditation and author of several books, including *Happiness Is an Inside Job: Practicing for a Joyful Life* (2007), explained to us why it's important to have clarity of intention:

> *I like to think about practice as a way of becoming aware of the habits of the mind—either through wisdom or through intention and dedication—and changing these habits through the understanding that this will lead to a happier life… I tell people it's so important to have clarity of intention. And I really need to tell them that thirty years ago, when I started, I didn't have clarity of intention. Thirty years ago meditation was more or less the interesting thing to do on a weekend with your friends. It took me a while to catch up with my intentions.* (2005)

Intention not only fuels the transformative process through commitment, it also imbues actions with transformative potential. In other words, bringing strong intention to any constructive action can make that action transformative. For aikido master George Leonard, transformative practice is based in an integral philosophy where mind, body, and spirit are called into harmony. His practice borrows from traditional aikido training (*aikido is an ancient Japanese form of martial art*), but blends ancient forms with emerging ones. For Leonard, the definitive element of practice is the intention brought to an action, rather than the action itself. As he explained:

> *A practice is any nontrivial activity that you engage in in a long-term, patient, diligent way primarily for its own sake. If you, for example, grow roses, that could be your practice—if you love the roses, love the feel of the soil; if you love the beauty that you're creating, and even if no one sees the roses, you still love it. But if you're growing roses just to impress your neighbors or to win medals, then that's not a practice.*
>
> *For me, a practice is something that you do primarily for its own sake. Now, there's a wonderful paradox there, for if you do it primarily for its own sake, you are more likely to win prizes and more likely to impress your neighbors. But we want people to love the activity, to be in it, to be in the present moment, to be centered, to be moment-centered. Not way out there—just here.* (2002)

As Leonard points out, a practice is something you do primarily for its own sake. This idea was echoed by many of our respondents. What does this "for its own sake" mean though? Aren't you practicing in order to get somewhere, to change something, to get healthier and happier?

Paradox is inherent to both the role of intention in practice and the role of practice in transformation. While you may begin a transformative practice with the goal of reducing your own suffering or reaching your full potential, in a seemingly contradictory way, many of our teachers explained that you must let go of this striving and just practice to practice. Within the Buddhist tradition, for example, this concept, called "nonstriving," is considered so important that it is recognized as one of the fundamental foundations of mindfulness or awareness. Zen Buddhist teacher Zenkei Blanche Hartman told us of her meditation practice:

We sit, just to sit… A good deal of our practice is seeing just that this is it. This is my life, just like this. Once we actually realize that, then we begin to take care of this life more carefully. We begin to appreciate this life as it is and not look outside for something else, but actually give some attention to this life as it is. (2003)

So, while it can seem a bit confusing, the key here is to bring a strong, pure intention toward authenticity, growth, and transformation into every activity, at the same time letting go of the striving and goal orientation sometimes associated with the word "practice." Through this process, we can begin to bring our whole self into each of the activities of our life. Maybe it's best summed up by Australian psychiatrist W. Beran Wolfe, who lived only to the age of thirty-five, and in 1932 wrote the book *How to Be Happy Though Human*, which went on to become a best seller. He says:

If you observe a really happy man you will find him building a boat, writing a symphony, educating his son, growing double Dahlias in his garden. He will not be searching for happiness as if it were a collar gold button that has rolled under the cupboard in his bedroom. He will have become aware that he is happy in the course of living 24 crowded hours of the day. (32)

The Second Essential: Attention

As Wolfe suggests, and as we have shown in previous chapters, a key component of the transformative experience is a shift in perspective—you begin to look at the world with fresh eyes. In the process, you begin to notice things in a new way. You may find that you're no longer as preoccupied by self-centered concerns—your race to work, remembering to get the groceries, wondering if there is enough money to pay the bills, etc. With new eyes, you're no longer locked into seeing the world through the filter of old beliefs about what is and isn't possible. And in the process, you may naturally develop a deeper way of attending to the world in which you live.

A transformative practice you can start today is paying greater attention to your everyday habits. For psychologist Charles Tart, developing awareness is critical to consciousness transformation. He told us:

> The path that interests me the most, personally and professionally, is what
> you might call a path of awareness. It's based on the assumption that
> in ordinary consciousness a great deal of what happens is automatized.
> Ordinary consciousness is only sort of semiconscious, and there is a
> mechanical nature to it. Whereas, if you begin to apply to it various kinds of
> mindfulness practices that give you insights into the way the mind functions
> as well as certain concentrative abilities—this can speed insights and enable
> you to focus your attention in a particular direction. (2003)

Most transformative practices involve bringing your attention to activities in a particular way. Although different transformative practices may require different kinds of attention—devotional practices require attention to a deity while martial arts practices require attention to balance, and so on—attentional training is an aspect shared by most of them.

As Tart indicates, attention is closely related to awareness. Psychologist Frances Vaughan described to us how shifting our attention can lead to fundamental reorganizations of how we view ourselves and approach our lives:

> I think we have to start with self-awareness. Most of our education is
> outer-directed. There is a lot to learn about the world—it's endless. Often
> in therapy we turn attention inward for the first time. When you begin
> to explore awareness through meditation, psychotherapy, or some other
> discipline such as yoga, it is the turning of attention inward that is an
> important first step. In this way we discover that there is an inner world and
> we can begin to see how the mind works. We begin to recognize the power
> of the mind and how the inner is often the cause of the outer, instead of the
> other way around. (2002)

Similarly, our research suggests that by bringing attention to your mind and body you can make any activity transformative, and thus live more deeply. Ron Valle, transpersonal psychologist and author, spoke to us about the value of meditation practice for cultivating the awareness of *witness consciousness*—the ability to observe yourself and others in a nonjudgmental manner. As Valle explained:

> *If you wish to change the nature of your mind in this very basic, direct way, I recommend meditation as a practice. It's a matter of just doing it. I often describe it as like brushing your teeth: you do it because you do it. You don't struggle with, "Well, should I brush my teeth tonight or not?" or "Should I spend one minute tonight brushing my teeth or five?" You just do it. Try it and see how you feel. And then observe and trust your experience. Experience is the bottom line. Don't believe anything anyone says unless you experience it yourself.*
>
> *The second thing, the being-in-the-world part, is to hold the intention to be aware of that witness or observer as you go through life, no matter what it is you're doing—talking or doing the dishes, the particular isn't what's important, it could be anything. It's the remembering or awareness to observe your mind. By making meditation a living practice, life becomes meditation. There's the formal sitting, working with a mantra—or whatever your practice might be that you use to quiet your mind—and then there's taking that into life. After twenty to thirty years, the mantra that I primarily practice is there all the time. While I'm speaking with you, I can feel it. (2002)*

At its core, transformation requires becoming more conscious, or as Valle indicates, becoming more aware of your own mind. Through this greater self-awareness, you develop the capacity to see more clearly into the minds, feelings, and intentions of others, a skill psychologists call *mindsight* (Siegel 2001).

Likewise, Gay Luce, founder of the Nine Gates Mystery School—a newer form of practice grounded in the ancient mystery schools of Greece—explained that practice helps you shift your attention to the witnessing of yourself:

> There is an activity which is essential throughout all different paths I've followed: to keep on inspecting, witnessing. Keep alert, present; watch what is going on internally as well as externally, but mostly internally... It's not just daily practice. A daily practice is helpful, a meditation practice is helpful, but more important is the commitment to witness one's self, to introspect, to look at what one is doing, to think about how those thoughts are beginning to shape a life and affect others—to be aware. (2002)

If you're like most people, transformation may require that you break free from some pretty deeply ingrained patterns of thinking and behavior—many which may have become habitual. Habits, unconscious thought patterns, and assumptions can drive your behavior and cause suffering; they can also prime you for what you will and will not pay attention to in the course of your daily life. As Shakti Parwha Kaur Khalsa, an American-born woman who has become a Sikh and kundalini yoga teacher, noted during our interview, "We have embedded patterns of thought and behavior that we're not even aware of—and yet, they manifest in our daily lives, actions, and relationships" (2002).

There are a variety of behaviors that we're classically in denial about, including addictions, jealousies that drive aggressive interactions with others, and unconscious narcissisms that lead us to function solely in our own self-interest despite consequences to others. Before changing any of these behaviors, we must become aware of them—we must bring them into consciousness. Many transformative practices are designed to help you—and in some cases, to *force* you—to become more aware of the self-limiting habits of your mind and behavior. Meditation allows you to observe the workings of your mind and body. Dreamwork encourages you to intentionally work with messages being delivered from your unconscious to your conscious. Prayer helps you find the connections between your individual self and your collective self. Body-oriented practices reveal to you truths that have been stored in the wisdom of your cells, muscles, and movement.

As you expand your awareness and learn to direct your attention, you can begin to choose what you focus on, rather than simply have your attention pulled to the most compelling sensation of the moment. Needless to say, this isn't always easy. Vipassana meditation teacher and author Sylvia Boorstein spoke with us about how challenging it can be to sustain focused attention on what is important in the face of the many distractions that compete for your attention:

> *It's very easy these days to get caught up in the stuff of life and forget that the intention is to keep clear about it. We get caught up in something that arouses ire, arouses anger, arouses desire, and do not see we've lost it, because it's what everyone else is doing. Life is so compelling!*
>
> *Life is jam-packed with possibilities to get overwhelmed or anguished or angry or lustful with everything that is pulling at us. I think the greatest difficulty or stumbling block towards integration is that we're swimming upstream. This practice of waking up and living out of clarity and kindness and compassion is actually a very countercultural kind of behavior. That is to say, in spite of whatever happens, maintain a mind of wisdom and a heart of love. This is a very countercultural thing to do. It's not what everybody around us is doing. (2005)*

Cultivating mindful attention and awareness is an act of liberation; it's a self-determined assertion that you can be free to be who you choose to be, even in a world filled with clinging and cruelty, a world that doesn't always support creative unfolding. As vipassana meditation teacher Noah Levine (2003) tells young people in juvenile detention centers and prisons: being awake and aware is one of the most radical, rebellious things you can do!

As we have seen, the most common way to shift your attention is to quiet your mind. Turning the TV off, listening to the birds in your neighborhood, or taking a walk in nature can all be ways to shift your attention. In doing so, you may find a place of stillness and contentment that will serve as an inner refuge. You may see, too, ways to replenish yourself and nurture your sense of wholeness and balance. Contemplation, whether through a formal sitting meditation or informally, through sitting quietly in nature, was identified by the respondents in our studies as by far the most common tool used to cultivate awareness and attention.

You can use many means to train your attention, from monitoring your breath to observing various bodily sensations; from concentrating intently on one image to attempting to maintain a broad and open "bare aware-ness" of your whole experience, without evaluation or judgment. A range of techniques for learning to discipline your mind is available, and there are many ways to bring mindfulness into your practice. For example, when Reverend Lauren Artress found that she couldn't fruitfully focus her atten-tion in a sitting modality, she adopted a walking meditation. She explained her method to us:

> For me, the key is walking. The Buddhists have a walking meditation. The Shiite Muslims have a walking meditation. Part of my work is to give people in Christianity a tool that they need. People often think going to church on Sunday morning and sitting in a pew, praying for a few minutes, and listening to a sermon is what transforms consciousness. Sometimes it does; but rarely—rarely as compared to the frequency of when people walk the labyrinth. So, I walk the labyrinth.
>
> Once a woman came up to me and said, "I don't get the labyrinth at all. I think it's the wrong metaphor. There's not one path to center, or one path to God or the divine or holy, or to transformation." And, of course, I agree with that. It's as unique as each person walking it. And I didn't know what to say to her. So I asked her, "Have you walked the labyrinth yet?" and she said, "No," and I said, "Well, walk it today and then come on back and in our process session we'll talk about it again." So at the end of the day she came back in and I said, "Okay, let's talk about it now." And she said, "Never mind, never mind, I got it. I got it." So that sense of the one path is the many paths. The many is one and the one is many. (2003)

THE SCIENCE OF ATTENTION

Increasingly, research supports the value of silence and the cultivation of mindfulness, not only for inner peace, but for the health of our bodies. A wealth of data in the area of mind/body medicine supports the value of attention-based practices.

For example, meditation has shown promise in relieving headaches, insomnia, psoriasis, chronic pain, heart problems, symptoms associated with cancer, and psychiatric conditions such as depression and anxiety (Astin et al. 2003; NCCAM 2006). African-Americans with atherosclerosis (hardening of the arteries) who engaged in regular meditation for six to nine months showed a decrease in thickness of artery walls, reducing their risk for heart attack and stroke by up to 15 percent (Castillo-Richmond et al. 2000). Meditation also appears to reduce risks of heart disease and stroke in the overall population (Larkin 2000). In cancer patients, meditation was found to improve quality of life, decrease stress, and improve immune function (Carlson et al. 2003). In another study of cancer patients, practicing meditation for only seven weeks improved energy and reduced depression, anxiety, and heart and gastrointestinal problems (Speca et al. 2000). While mindfulness—or the awareness of inner experience—and meditation hold great promise, more research is needed to find out what exactly works and for whom. It appears, though, that taking the time to quiet your mind not only stimulates transformation, it also has benefits for your physical and psychological well-being.

The work of Richard Davidson and colleagues (2003) at the University of Wisconsin–Madison offers an intriguing example of the ways in which the mind and body are connected. Davidson's team has shown that the brains of monks who have meditated for thousands of hours function differently than those of individuals who haven't engaged in this level of practice (Lutz et al. 2004). While engaged in a compassion meditation, the monks showed dramatically increased activity in the left prefrontal cortex (associated with positive emotions and an optimistic outlook) in comparison to the right prefrontal cortex. Of course, it's possible that even before they engaged in meditation training, these monks were different from the control group of nonmeditators, as noted by Davidson and his colleagues.

But other work in Davidson's lab shows that individuals trained in mindfulness meditation for only eight weeks showed a similar pattern of greater left to right brain activation—even six months after receiving the training (Davidson et al. 2003). It appears that a relatively short period of intensive meditation training can alter brain function in a lasting way. It seems that your brain, like your muscles, can be trained to perform in ways that will promote life-affirming transformations.

What's fascinating about this is that a practice that focuses on changing your consciousness in a disciplined way can not only change the function of your brain and body, but also the physiological structure. Similar research, focused on Western-style meditators, by Sarah Lazar and colleagues at Harvard suggests that meditation is associated with an increase in cortical thickness in the brain (Lazar et al. 2005). These findings are important as they suggest that meditation may protect against the cortical thinning associated with aging. All this is by way of saying that transformative practices have been shown to have positive and life-enhancing effects on our bodies as well as our spirits. (To learn more about the science of meditation, check out www.noetic.org.)

The Third Essential: Repetition

Just as physical exercise helps form your musculoskeletal system and improve your cardiovascular health, transformative practice helps you live into a new way of being. And in the same way that learning to play the violin requires repetition, so too does learning to live more deeply. Part of practice is the building of new habits—it makes sense that you'll need to engage in the process on a regular basis to reinforce them. As transformation teacher Angeles Arrien told us:

> In the transformation process, the tools need to be used daily, not just whether it's crisis, or things are working well or not. If I'm going to really maximize the change or the transformation process, I need to be working with my tools daily … or my practices daily. I don't believe there's really a change without practice. (2002)

As we have seen, the transformative practice of meditation has been shown to cause changes in the brains of those studied. Our brains are far more adaptable than was previously thought. *Neuroplasticity*, or the capacity of the connections between neurons in the brain to change in response to experience and our environment, extends well into old age (Markham and Greenough 2004).

Neurons and neural connections adjust in response to new activities—especially activities that are repeated. Repetitive behaviors—whether functional or dysfunctional—actually change the way our brains work. In their review of the literature (2004), Julie Markham and William Greenough note a number of important findings that may have relevance to transformative practice: For example, after injury, a process called synaptic reorganization can help people regain important functions. Synaptic pathways that are used frequently are strengthened while those that are rarely used can become weaker. Entirely new pathways can be formed; moreover, recent research shows that in some parts of the brain (including the all-important hippocampus), *neurogenesis*, or the formation of new nerve cells, continues throughout life. Functions can be transferred from one part of the brain to another, and the brain's baseline functioning can itself be altered. Since the brain continuously reorganizes itself, repeated transformative practices may allow us to consciously shape our brains and our behaviors.

The Fourth Essential: Guidance

Of course, just as not all habits are worth cultivating, not all practices are transformative. Many teachers and survey respondents said that guidance from experienced teachers is helpful to learning a practice correctly and staying on course over time. Studying a particular form of meditation, developing correct posture in a somatic practice, reading the appropriate books, and so on, can substantially increase the transformative potential of a practice.

For transformative teacher George Leonard, instruction is essential to creating a transformative practice. We're practicing all of the time, he explained, so what happens if we're actually practicing doing things the wrong way? Building bad habits in golf or tennis may allow you to play, but it *doesn't* allow you to play your best game. The same is true in transformative practice. In Leonard's words, this means that "You're not achieving your potential. So you need instruction. Learning to practice good things— being a more loving person, for example—that's worth practicing. We're practicing the bad things and the good things all the time" (2002).

Rabbi Omer-Man shared with us the essential aspects of his own transformative practice of Judaism, speaking to the many different types of practice that can be helpful:

> I've always been a spiritual anarchist. The struggle for discipline has been an issue throughout my life… I've always maintained a practice, but lack the kind of formality and consistency that even some of my students have! I would say one of the central aspects of my practice and one of the central components of my work is to maintain, strengthen, and refine my integrity. The integrity of being-in-the-world. I'm talking about a perpetual transformation of consciousness. I'm talking about the ongoing refinement of being. A locus of this work is meditation.
>
> Other practices that I've been involved in are finding good teachers, a certain amount of ritual, a certain amount of sacred study (as opposed to intellectual study), and a certain amount of prayer. I try to limit the areas of self-deception, of self-aggrandizement.
>
> Sacred study is that which nurtures the soul and works through the holy imagination, as opposed to the unholy imagination. It refines the soul, opens the heart in a nonindividualistic way. Sacred study is learning from sacred tradition. It isn't personally intuitive. It is receiving from beyond one's self.
>
> Also important is to be part of a dedicated community. Through challenging community and challenging friendships, we open up a place for joy in the life of spirit. A central teaching in the Torah is a commandment of reproof, the commandment to call on one's brother or one's sister when you think they are off the path. But it has to be a reproof out of love… Let me give an example: if someone says, "Jonathan, you're becoming a heretic" (this has happened a few times in my life), it could be a way of excluding me, but

it could also be shining a light, offering me a mirror of my soul. This latter
kind of reproof can't take place in a " feel-good" community of convenience.
It demands love and seriousness. (2006)

Like Omer-Man, many of the teachers we interviewed spoke of the
importance of ritual, prayer, sacred texts, and reliable guidance, such as that
found through like-minded communities and good teachers. Rina Sircar,
Burmese Buddhist scholar, teacher, and nun, spoke to us of the importance
of both repetition and having a good teacher:

If you just do a practice for one retreat, one Saturday, and then you don't do
it for three years, where are you going to end up? Nowhere! There must be the
right effort, commitment, and continuity. If you do not strive for anything
that is worthwhile, how can you get it?

Another important factor is that once you take up a practice, to begin
with you'll need to practice with a teacher you feel good about… You need
a good teacher, a teacher who will help you—this is something to do with
the dharma [life path]. And dharma should be given from the heart. Your
teacher must create interest in you. If this practice is a very new thing to your
life, you'll need the teacher to give you some kind of incentive. Otherwise,
how can you have interest?

Then, once you get into this practice, you have to keep up the
continuity—it doesn't matter what or where the place, or how many hours
you do it. Today people are very busy and they often give the excuse that
they don't have much time, but at least they can do five minutes! If you don't
have five minutes, that means you have two minutes. Do it! Sit! Don't give
up the practice. (2003)

It's important to remember that not all guidance is external. External
guidance must be balanced by your own internal wisdom. Some of this
guidance is simply trial and error. Is the practice having the intended
results? Is the way you are engaging in the practice helping you learn about
yourself? Is it resulting in new insights? Is it helping you be the best person
you can be? While your own point of view can be biased and an external

guide can see into your blind spots, there is also value in your own assessment of whether or not a practice is working for you.

For many, the most profound guidance is not of the intellectual or rational variety. Inner guidance seems to speak the language of symbol and metaphor. Frequently, guidance can be found in dreams, altered states, or synchronous events. Stories abound of finding solutions to dilemmas, or charting an unanticipated but fruitful course, based on the contents of a dream.

Guidance for many people and across many cultures comes from entities perceived as deities, spirit guides, animal helpers, visions, or voices within. In some indigenous traditions, for example, sighting an eagle might indicate a need to broaden your sense of self or to gain a more expansive perspective on an issue. The appearance of an otter might signal the need for greater playfulness or nurturance. In Hindu traditions, students often perceive their guru to be communicating with them directly, even when the student is not in the guru's presence. A current Christian practice that has become popular enough to earn an acronym is to ask oneself "What would Jesus do?" And still more people are simply guided by hearing a quiet voice from deep within that speaks only in the context of silence and solitude. By bringing intention, attention, and repetition, grounded in guidance from both skilled teachers and your own inner knowing, you can discover many ways of being that can become valued practices in your life.

KEEPING PRACTICE IN PERSPECTIVE

Thus far, we've seen how practice can help sustain the transformative process. While spontaneous and potentially transformative experiences are a part of everyday life, practice increases the likelihood that such experiences will be integrated into your daily experience.

However, another paradox we unearthed in our research is that an overly strong emphasis on practice can be counterproductive: we can become too attached to a spiritual or transformative practice, making the practice the end rather than the means. Benedictine monk Brother David Steindl-Rast is a man who understands practice. Although he believes that life ultimately becomes a form of practice, he reminded us that practice is about preparation—it's not the end in itself:

> When I say practice, I am always careful to stress the fact that it's practice. It's like practicing the violin so that you will be able to play it in concerts. The practice prepares you for doing it. If you sit on a cushion and you practice letting go of your thoughts and being in the present moment, you can't spend the rest of your life sitting on a cushion. You have to get up, prepare your food, eat, walk, or other things. There is quite a distance between sitting on a cushion and using your computer or keeping your relationship going.
>
> I'm looking for a practice where the practice is closely associated with the doing. When your mother teaches you to make a tossed salad, you are actually making the tossed salad in the process of learning how to… That's a practice that's very close to the actual doing.
>
> In the same sense, being grateful, or cultivating gratefulness, is as close as I have found to being in the present moment. By practicing gratefulness, you are, at the very moment, doing what you hope to do after your practice…
>
> You can still distinguish between the practice of grateful living and the actual grateful living. The little difference here would be that you remind yourself to be grateful. We need reminders.
>
> When I came back from Africa, where I had no drinkable water or electric lights, I was overwhelmed by having water. You turn on the tap and out comes drinkable water.
>
> I wanted to remind myself of that gratefulness for water because it was starting to wear off after a while. So I put these little stickers that come with postage stamps on the water faucet and on the light switch. Every time I want to switch on the lights, there's a little sticker on it. What's that? Well, it's a reminder to be grateful that I have electric lights. This was one little private mnemonic device that I devised for myself. The best suggestion is to find your own reminders because different things work for each of us. To remind yourself is a very important aspect of practice. (2006)

Steindl-Rast's words remind us that preparation and doing are connected but not identical. For him, an important aspect of practice is to remind us of what we intend as the practice's outcome. Wink Franklin, past president of IONS, went even further, to encourage a de-emphasis on formal practice (a viewpoint shared by a minority of our participants):

> A lot of transformational change comes from our life experiences. I think we probably draw too sharp a distinction between "practice" and "life experience." Rather than viewing them as separate deals, we can view them as deeply interconnected. Either practices or life experiences can lead to shifts. It can be 80 percent one and 20 percent the other, or 90/10 or 50/50 or 20/80 the other way; but usually both are interacting and both are functioning.
>
> I have to say that I think that some of the emphasis on practice is overdone. It's a part of our Western mind that wants to be in control and wants to work and accomplish something (and I'm one of the worst at that). If we could relax some, I think it might happen just as fast. On the other side, I think that discipline and practice are useful to crack the cultural malaise that we're in. It's useful as a counterforce. If you could wipe out cultural influence and family influences … the natural way would probably be pretty easy—and it doesn't require practice per se. (2003)

As a counterpoint, Noah Levine argues that it can be dangerous to eschew formal practice:

> It seems that people have a lot of difficulty integrating big spontaneous experiences or insights. We hear a lot in the Buddhist community about people who are on retreat and they have these big insights—and then don't know how to walk in the world, don't know how to relate. It seems like it is a challenging thing for a lot of people. A danger that I've seen with teachers and students is having those kinds of experiences and mistaking them for enlightenment and then going off and making all kinds of claims and stuff and then seeing, "Oh, no, that was actually an impermanent experience,

too. It wore off." You know, it was this aha! and everything seemed to be transformed, and then… It's gone, I'm still suffering, I'm still attached, I'm still lustful, greedy…

Some people have these big spontaneous awakenings without much practice and then go out and say, "Practice is not necessary. Just be awake right now. I am. If I can be, then everybody should be able to just be awake in the moment. It doesn't take training." I have a lot of personal concern about this approach, and the damage that may be caused to those who hear these teachings and want them to be true because we are so lazy. We don't really want to do the practice anyway. But it doesn't actually work… I feel like there is a real danger sometimes when teachers don't give people the tools to gradually train and transform—especially when it seems that 99 percent of people need to do a gradual transformational practice. (2005)

Ultimately, you need to find your own balance between convention and innovation, between the tried-and-true and the emerging forms of transformative practice.

SUMMARY

In this chapter, we've considered the role of practice in the cultivation of transformation. By harnessing the inner resources that shape your interpretations of life events, you can begin to build new ways of reacting to your daily circumstances. In addition, transformation can actually change the circumstances you find yourself engaged in. As your inner experience calls on you to grow and change, you may find yourself altering your outer realities, building new social networks and moving away from situations that generate stress. Moving beyond old habits naturally implies building new ones. Through a discipline or practice, you can train your mind and body in new ways. As you seek to develop more adaptive traits, you can condition yourself in ways that will reduce negative emotions and promote your capacity to flourish, even under difficult circumstances.

There isn't just a single way to engage in transformative practice. Indeed, different approaches work for different people at different times in different settings. Through our research, we've identified four essential characteristics of transformative practices: intention, attention, repetition, and a generous dose of guidance to round out the practice equation.

We've also seen that practice on its own isn't enough: if practice becomes an end rather than a means, it can become an obstacle to the transformative process. In the next chapter we'll explore the ways that practice brings transformation more fully into your life. For now, you may find the following exercise helpful in exploring your own practice, whether formal or informal.

Experiencing Transformation: A Path to Practice

We asked the teachers, masters, and scholars in our studies, "What are the essential commitments of your path or your practice, both internal and external?" Take a moment to discover your own answer to this question.

First of all, what is your practice? Write down exactly what your transformative practice includes. Be broad—include both your formal and informal practices. Does your practice include meeting with a group of like-minded individuals at a sacred space, or is it solitary? Does it involve time for silent reflection? Perhaps it includes some daily method of expressing devotion, or moving your body in a particular way. List all the elements of your practice and how often you engage in them.

Next, look at your personal practice with respect to the three qualities we've identified in this chapter. How do you bring intention to your practice? Do you have ways of reminding yourself of your intention? Which activities in your life do you bring attention to, and which do you complete essentially on autopilot? Are you engaging in enough repetition? Or are you hoping—perhaps unrealistically—for your insights to create changes in your life without any repetition? Are there activities essential to your practice that it's hard to make the time for? Can you find even just a few minutes of each day to make these a priority? Are you asking for guidance around your practice, checking in with trusted elders from time to time? Are you paying attention to guidance that may come your way in the form of symbols, metaphors, dreams, or synchronicities? Is there enough time for silence and solitude in your life to allow for that quiet wisdom from within to be heard?

On the other hand, have you made your practice itself more important than integrating transformative insights into your everyday life? Are you practicing activities that don't support your growth, or that are no longer essential? If so, can you replace these with more life-affirming activities? Spend ten to twenty minutes journaling on these questions. And if you decide to explore different practices, the companion DVD to this book, *Living Deeply: Transformative Practices from the World's Wisdom Traditions*, offers guided experiential exercises from nine different teachers of transformation.

CHAPTER FIVE:

Why Practice?

Of course, ancient swamis and yogis, rabbis and priests,
nuns and monks didn't develop mind-body techniques to get
cholesterol down … or perform better at board meetings. Their
techniques are tools for transformation and transcendence.
—*DEAN ORNISH (2005, 305)*

In the last chapter we explored the four essential elements of transformative practices: intention, attention, repetition, and guidance. These elements can help you integrate transformative realizations into long-term shifts in your worldview, thought patterns, behaviors, and, indeed, your very way of being. But questions still remain: What does practice do? How exactly does it work? How can sitting in silence for a brief period every day have far-reaching and profound effects on your life? Why would moving your body in particular ways every day affect your mental and emotional health to a large extent? Indeed, how do contemplative practices, such as meditation, prayer, or walking in nature, actually move us through the process of transformation? In this chapter we explore how practice appears to work, across individuals and across traditions.

HOW DOES PRACTICE WORK?

The answer to this question may surprise you. On the surface, a practice like meditation probably seems like a good way to relax. You may start meditating in hopes that by cultivating an internal state of peace, you'll have more peace in both your mind and your life. Similarly, you may commit to a practice of prayer in hopes that the answers to your prayers will come in short order. Practicing A will lead to B, you think, so you jump into your favorite new form of practice gung ho.

As we've said, transformative practice *does* appear to bear some similarity to learning a language or a new musical instrument—for example, as you become more physically flexible and relaxed through yoga practice, these qualities also appear in your thinking and behavior. But transformative practices are more than just learning new habits or skills—and they don't always work in the linear, goal-oriented fashion we're accustomed to in our secular, physical lives. Transformative practices, in many ways, appear to work indirectly—by creating the best conditions for the natural processes of growth and awakening to take place.

For example, if you try insight meditation, you may not achieve a sense of inner peace and relaxation right away. Typically in this kind of meditation, you're instructed to closely observe your experience, whatever that may consist of. By following this instruction, you get an up-close and personal view of your mental habits. It is through seeing these habits of mind clearly (attention) and being willing to change these habits (intention) that you begin to naturally engage in ways of being that cultivate inner peace. As kundalini yoga teacher and author Shakti Parwha Kaur Khalsa told us:

> *Of course you can perfect things and become more adept … but because yoga is a living science, it's not like something you can learn by rote or from a book. In fact, my teacher wouldn't even let us put anything in writing for almost three years. He said, "People really need to be with a teacher."*

He made what he taught us that first year so doable and so easy, that it's what I teach to beginners now—and then they can progress as the practice becomes more complicated. If you are consistent, changes take place without your actually knowing about it… I think that's where transformation comes in. (2002)

As Shakti points out, many of the benefits of practice can happen below the threshold of conscious awareness. It may not be causal in any literal sense.

Insight

So, given that A may not lead to B in exactly the way that we expect, how does practice actually work? Many practices start by cultivating *insight*—the ability to discern or grasp the true nature of a situation. Transformative insights can help you identify the roots of problems within yourself, whether these are faulty assumptions, dysfunctional behaviors, or beliefs that no longer serve you. Seeing a situation clearly is the first step toward determining what changes need to be made; sometimes insights even reveal what steps are required to make those changes.

Rina Sircar, one of the first Buddhist vipassana meditation teachers to come to the United States, spoke to us of how practice can lead to insights, particularly insights about personal identity and purpose:

Once you find the transient nature of things—that there is nothing but impermanence, changing from moment to moment—you will find, "Oh, everything in the world is like this!" And you will then wonder, "Why am I craving, clinging, and grasping for something to keep with me, and where is me after all?"

This is what practice teaches us: who am I, what am I, and where am I going? Practice opens our eyes. Now I'm in darkness, my mind is clouded, dark, full with ignorance. They say that a remote forest is very dark, midnight is very dark, and the cloudy day is very dark, too. But the darkest of all … is the ignorance of the mind. Therefore, to get rid of this

ignorance—to get rid of the cravings and the clinging and the grasping of
our life—we practice. (2003)

Practice then, is a sort of flashlight that you can intentionally shine on your inner world—as Sircar says, on who you are, what you are, and where you are going. With the illumination of practice, blocks to transformation—and often ways to remove them—can become clear.

Riding Your Ego

Most of us have an *ego* that runs the show. The ego, or the sense of a self as separate from other selves and the world, is the thinking part of your mind—the one that evaluates, judges, plans, strategizes, compares, and categorizes. It's the part that navigates the material world and keeps you functioning—paying your bills, being at carpool on time, getting food on the table.

However, despite being useful and necessary in many ways, the ego can also become a real tyrant. An overactive ego can keep us out of our bodies and in our minds, out of our hearts and in our heads, out of the present moment and stuck in the past and the future, out of our intuition and deep wisdom and concerned only with the next task—in short, it can keep us living shallowly. An overactive ego can lead to narcissism and self-centeredness, both blocks to transformation. In fact, as spiritual teacher and editor of *What Is Enlightenment?* magazine Andrew Cohen told us:

> *We can measure how much an individual has transformed by the degree*
> *to which they are able to free themselves from the attachment to—and the*
> *belief in—the fears and desires of the narcissistic self-sense which has been so*
> *deeply conditioned by the particular culture that we've come from.* (2003)

One criticism of the human potential movement—which brought many of these transformative practices to the West in the 1960s—is that it encourages self-indulgence (think "the Me Generation"). Setting aside work, family, and other obligations for a yoga retreat, self-improvement workshop, or women's circle can seem selfish. Indeed, your friends and family—even your own mind—can imply that these pursuits are luxuries and should only be engaged in after all other obligations have been satisfied, if at all.

Paradoxically, many of these practices are actually designed to deconstruct your self-centeredness. One of the primary functions of many transformative practices is to reestablish the internal balance between ego and soul, mind and body, self and other, doing and being. These practices take the ego out of the driver's seat for a while and allow the many other parts of your being—your feeling self, your creative self, your intuitive self—to have a turn at the wheel.

Using the metaphor of the ego as a donkey, Sufi imam Yassir Chadly explained how the daily practices of his tradition work to put the ego in its proper place:

> The whole art form of Islamic rituals—washing your hands three times, your mouth and nose, your face, your arm, right foot, left foot, and then praying, five prayers a day—all of that is to create tension inside of you. Inside what? Inside the ego, because the ego doesn't like to do this. "Why should I wash and do this and that? I can just sit down and read a spiritual book on my couch and I can get spiritual …" because the ego likes to be lazy. So they put the ego through this training and give it a frame—so you can have the bit on the ego, so you are the one riding. Riding your ego is the first step toward spirituality and to understanding that what makes all these human beings hate and harm each other is their donkey riding them.
>
> If their donkey is wild, kicking, you can see that they have no mastery. This is very close to Buddhism, where they tell you to control this donkey. Except we don't make the donkey our target. We say that the donkey should take you somewhere. The donkey is our ride to Allah. He gives you this donkey to ride. Islam is for love and peace and respect and dignity and honor, for majesty and grace…
>
> The donkey is very clever—sometimes it kicks you and does what it likes. When this happens, then you have to put it back. The five prayers help limit you, help stop you from doing anything bad or harmful to anyone. That's the caging of the ego. We give you five prayers to cage this wild

animal. Once you cage it, then you can start the next step, which is Sufism.

So we work … first to help reveal the divine part of yourself—the soul that is beyond ego. In Sufism, the bottom line is Allah. If everything you do is for Allah, this is good. If you do everything for your ego, then the ego is Allah. The teachings show you how to ride your ego, like riding a donkey. Your ego can take you there—they don't say kill your ego, they say ride your ego. (2006)

Across traditions, mind/body practices include ways to help you learn to ride the donkey, rather than be ridden by it. Rituals, contemplative practices, dreamwork, devotional practices, dance—these practices serve to connect you with parts of your being other than your ego. Your creative self, your intuitive self, your spiritual self, your body—all of these are sources of deep intelligence. And when these parts of our being are expressed, our lives are enriched and deepened.

As Chadly and many of our other respondents told us, this process isn't about *eliminating* the ego. In fact, many have pointed out that before you can transcend your ego, you first need to have a healthy ego. In psychology—one of the great wisdom traditions of the West—there is an emphasis on strengthening the ego. Similarly, the transformative process involves cultivating greater self-awareness and a stronger sense of who you are. However, there comes a time in the transformative process when the sense of self is redefined, and the limits of ego-centered consciousness are recognized and transcended. (We'll explore this more fully in chapter 7.)

Teachers from many different traditions noted that through practice, your very deepest assumptions about who and what you are can be called into question. As you begin to explore the nature of your authentic self, you see what elements of yourself aren't in alignment with that self. Outdated beliefs, thinking patterns that are no longer useful, and dusty old baggage that you no longer need: all of these are revealed by repetitive, intentional, attentional practice. And, wouldn't you know it, many practices have built-in ways to cleanse these blocks to living deeply.

Purification

Purification practices exist in many different traditions. What looks like a simple practice of washing, as Chadly described in his Islamic tradition, can be deeply transformative when done with intention, attention, repetition, and guidance. Whether through baptism, touching holy water upon entering a church, being *smudged* with the smoke of sage (having smoke whisked around your body), engaging in *pranayama* (rapid deep breathing), cleansing with salt and water, or simply clearing the mind of all external stimuli, purification is about removing whatever blocks you from being true to your authentic self. As the windows of your soul are cleansed, the Christ light, Buddha nature, divinity, universal energy, or simply love begins to peek through more and more. In many traditions, it is thought that this element need not be cultivated, only revealed, because it's actually your true nature.

For Charlie Red Hawk Thom and Tela Star Hawk Lake, the healing that comes from purification practices isn't just for your individual self. Charlie is a full-blooded Karuk Native American elder, medicine man, and hereditary spiritual and ceremonial leader from northern California. Tela is a traditional Native American healer and teacher, and one of the last female shaman-doctors of the Yurok tribe. Tela described to us the purification practice of the sweat lodge (a practice used by many North American First Nation peoples, in which several hours are spent sweating, singing, and praying in a hut heated by coals from a wood fire); she spoke, too, of the profound transformations that can transpire through the sweat of the body and the prayers of the medicine man:

> When we gather the people for the lodge with a medicine man, we say that that lodge is our mother. We are going to be reborn. We tell people, "When you go in today, the way you see physically, spiritually, and emotionally will be different from when you come out. When you come out you're not going to be that same person; something's going to change. When you come out, your friends and family are going to see something different." It's like you lose

something. It's like you're shedding a shell. Because maybe you're getting rid of something you were holding on to. Maybe it's a grieving process. Maybe you're having a hard time making a transition and you're struggling.

When you go into the lodge and you pray, and the medicine man prays for you, he's praying for you physically, spiritually, and emotionally. We're looking at you as a oneness. When the medicine man goes into the lodge, he says, "I'm going to purify you."

You have to purify your body first. This means getting rid of all the poison, all the toxins, all the chemicals; anything that we've done to our bodies that's bad. You're sweating because you're pulling that poison out and you're giving it to Mother Earth. When you come out, you wash yourself, cleansing yourself with water.

When we sweat, we change our lives, because the medicine man works on our left and our right brain—your thinking, your spirit, your heart. He makes us look at mirrors, because we're a reflection. He makes us look into ourselves, because … we forget to stop and look in here, within. In here are the questions—in here is what we're looking for. (2006)

Catholic priest Father Francis Tiso told us that washing before prayer times in the Islamic traditions, the sweat lodge in the Native American tradition, washing rituals at Buddhist shrines, and the use of holy water (in baptism, upon entry into a church building, and in the sprinkling rite at the start of Mass) in the Catholic tradition all share some common elements. For one, these purification practices often require patience. Sometimes it can take repetition after repetition before the practitioner becomes aware of benefits. People may wonder, "What am I doing this for?" And yet, as Tiso points out, an important purpose lies behind the various rites of cleansing and purification:

These traditions may use varied languages of sign and word to describe it, but what is going on is very clear. Purification is partly about washing your body. However, purification in the greatest sense is about cleansing the consciousness itself; keeping in mind that consciousness is not understood in depth unless it is linked to embodiment. The greater purification is most certainly about cleansing sinful actions that we have committed in thought, word, deed, and omission (of doing something good that we should have done). On the basis of moral purification, practice can then proceed on the level of subjective awareness to unblock our understanding of who God is and what the true self is, including necessarily the embodied self. We are, in short, describing the transformation of the whole person. (2002)

Not all purification is ritualistic. Bodywork pioneer Marion Rosen told us how transformative touch in Rosen Method bodywork can have profound effects on clearing out blocks and old baggage:

Many people who get in touch with their feelings lose their physical pain or difficulties by getting in touch with what had happened before the pain. There was a lady who was seventy-nine years old when she came for treatment. She was supposed to have a hip replacement, and I gave her just one treatment. I asked her about her life. She said everything was fine: she had a nice husband, they lived well, she was a psychiatrist, she had good work—and then, all of a sudden, something happened: her eyes got red and she started to cry. I told her, "Are you aware that you are crying?" and she said sharply, "I am not crying," and I said, "There is something very wet there, so I don't know." She said, "Yes, there was something I was thinking about…" She explained she had a pupil, a pupil she had liked very much, who had done something very unethical, and how much it had hurt her, and how disappointed she was. All that came out and then she got dressed—and as she was leaving, I said, "What about your cane?" and she said, "What about my cane?" and the pain was gone from her hip. Now she is ninety-three, and she has never had the hip replacement. The moment she has a twinge, she comes for treatment, and then it's alright again. When people get in touch with their real hurt, then they can also let go of that hurt. I don't know how it works, but it works. (2005)

Of course, not all physical pain has a psychological basis. Still, many teachers report that removing blocks through various forms of touch, movement, and ritual can clear the way for healing, sometimes to a profound extent. Indeed, consciousness can be an important part of healing (Schlitz, Amorok, and Micozzi 2005).

Living in the Moment

If you're like most people, you're not beginning a transformative practice because you want to be more present. In fact, you may want to escape from—or at least improve upon—your present circumstances. You may want to feel happier, to find deeper meaning, to enjoy greater success. Often, these goals can seem like they're achievable only at some point in the distant future. But, as author Peter Russell told us, transformation is about "waking up" to the present moment:

> The experiences that I've had of waking up are not suddenly entering into a different consciousness. They're having exactly the same experience, but with a complete letting go—and this is where it's inevitable we start losing words—it's a different context for holding that experience. One experiences the complete inner freedom, joy, love, and the bliss that the mystics speak of. And it's realizing that that's there all the time, but we keep ourselves constrained and held back from it. That's why I think there's some truth in what's often said: "You are already enlightened, you just don't know it." Except it's a long hard journey to go from the not-knowing to the realization of it. So that's why I don't like the term "transformation of consciousness"—because it implies we're going somewhere different, as opposed to waking up to the present moment and not being lost in a whole train of thoughts. (2002)

How can we find that deeper sense of joy and love that Russell and so many others have alluded to? The vast majority of our respondents told us that part of transformation is recognizing that what we're looking for isn't to be found elsewhere, in the future or in some far-off land. It's available to us right now, in the present moment. And indeed, many transformative practices are engineered specifically to bring you more fully into the present. In fact, if you really think about it, connection, meaning, purpose, freedom, and happiness can *only* be experienced now, in the present. Over and over again, we heard that learning to live in the moment is an essential aspect of living deeply.

For David Steindl-Rast—Benedictine monk, author of *Gratefulness, the Heart of Prayer* (1984), and contributor to Gratefulness.org—surprise, gratefulness, and chanting offer powerful methods for being in the present:

> *The goal of any practice, to me, is to be in the present moment. Whatever helps you with this: Zen, Sufi whirling, devotion. The thing that gets me into the present quickly and easily is grateful living. If somebody says that you can't start with gratefulness, you can start with surprise. Have you ever been surprised at anything? It's nice to be surprised. Allow yourself to be surprised by everything—your eyes when you open them in the morning, the idea that there is anything rather than nothing. Finding meaning starts with surprise. When you start being surprised, you begin to be grateful for the things you have taken for granted. So surprise is the first baby step.*
>
> *The next step organically evolves from this one—that's gratefulness. Gratefulness puts you in the present moment; this takes you out of the rat race, the maze, the merry-go-round. Before you know it, you are evolved—or at least on the road to evolving.*
>
> *As a Benedictine monk, I do a lot of chanting. In the monastery we chant once during the night and seven times during the day—often just for five minutes or so. These chants put you into a trance… Whatever tradition I have had the privilege of chanting in—Buddhist chanting or chanting with Hindus—… if you do it well it puts you into a trance. It's not a mindless trance, it's a trance of mindfulness—a full presence in the present moment. That is what I feel the chants do for me in the Benedictine tradition. Chanting is my favorite devotional activity in the monastery. (2006)*

Ultimately, practicing being present helps us to let go of those things in life that we cannot control or hold on to. As David Parks-Ramage, both a Christian minister and a Zen practitioner, told us:

> What worked yesterday doesn't work today—and what works tomorrow may not work today. Just being present here, just being right here, right now means that you leave the past and you leave the future.
>
> This can be painful. Being present, you let go of the ideas that you have about your children when they're not the way you want them to be. Life itself is one big preparation for the big let-go at the end. As you age and as you grow, you've also got to let go of your parents. And, too, there's your self-image you have to let go of—like your ability to get out of bed … and stand up straight, without that pain in your lower back. Then, finally, we've got to let go of it all into this mystery that we've had these glimpses of. It's pretty clear nobody gets out alive.
>
> So, what do you do in the meantime? You get ready and then you catch these glimpses of where you've already let go of everything—and then death itself isn't as scary anymore. Being present, you act more in accordance with the spontaneity of the universe, God, or self. (2006)

Parks-Ramage reminds us of the power of being present, and how it can lead to transformations in your perspective on, and behavior toward, fundamental existential issues.

Surrendering to Mystery

By repeatedly engaging in a transformative practice you cultivate insight—seeing your situation more clearly, and becoming more aware of your limits and strengths. Your sense of self becomes stronger and more authentic; at the same time it may expand and begin to move beyond self-centeredness. You may find yourself living more in the present moment and worrying less about the past or future.

All of this requires strong intention and discipline. Each day, you must make the choice to act in alignment with your highest truth, to overcome the external and internal pressures to maintain the status quo. As Luisah Teish, Yoruba priestess, told us: "It takes courage and commitment" (2003).

However, our research over the past ten years suggests that in the transformative process, there is another, equally important requirement: the willingness to surrender to the mystery and grace of life itself. As we've said, transformation isn't always—or even typically—a linear process. As much as we may want it to, A doesn't necessarily lead to B. In a way, this is a good thing: if we just got what we'd wanted in the beginning, we'd most likely shortchange ourselves dramatically! As past president of the Institute of Noetic Sciences Willis Harman once said, "If my life had unfolded in the ways I'd planned, it never would have been as interesting" (1994).

Transformation is at least as much about letting go and releasing effort as it is about working hard and making choices. As Zenkei Blanche Hartman told us, "Realization isn't something we can *do*, it's only something we can be ready for" (2003).

Just what is surrender? In part, surrender is a *radical acceptance* of our lives just as they are. Psychologist Marsha Linehan, developer of one of the only successful treatments for chronic suicidal, self-harm, and borderline personality disorders, defines radical acceptance as accepting your direct experience exactly as it is (1995). Radical acceptance is an active turning of the mind from willfulness (resisting or trying to change what is) to willingness (meeting what is or accepting life on life's terms). This doesn't imply becoming passive or condoning an unacceptable situation; instead, radical acceptance is an active engagement with whatever is happening in the moment. Linehan finds that, paradoxically, radical acceptance of even the most painful or difficult feelings and thoughts can reduce their intensity and increase your tolerance of them (1995). This, Linehan says, can allow you the freedom to make decisions from the place of *wise mind*—the middle ground that relies equally on rationality, emotion, and intuition.

Many of the teachers in our study spoke with reverence of *mystery*, or the unknowable aspects of life that resist simple rational explanations. Physician Rachel Naomi Remen spoke eloquently to us of the importance of remaining connected to the questions or mysteries of life, rather than just seeking answers:

I was trained to look for answers—the more answers you had, the more you'd be able to live well. And what I've learned is that it's the questions that give you the power of living well, not the answers. We are always in the presence of mystery. Being aware of that can give you a sense of aliveness, a sense of engagement with life, a sense that something may happen that has never happened before. And not wanting to miss it … not wanting to miss it. (2003)

Transformative teacher Angeles Arrien reminded us that transformation often unfolds differently from how you've expected—and that the practice of letting go can help prepare you to open to "mystery's plan":

There's a lovely Inuit saying that there are really two plans to every day: there's my plan and there's the mystery's plan. In the process of transformation I may have a whole plan about how I will transform and do my inner work. This is an egoic plan.

But there's a deeper plan that is much stronger than any egoic plan. This plan gets revealed in silence, with specific intention and attention. What often happens for people in silence and in nature, in prayer or affirmation, is that once they let go and really listen, something else emerges that wasn't on the agenda. And it often reveals something greater than what was on their egoic agenda. I encourage them to pay attention to that.

I really trust the mystery. I trust what comes in silence, what comes in nature when there's no diversion. The lack of stimulation that takes us out of our addiction to intensity allows us to hear and experience a deeper river—one that's constant and still and vibrant and real. (2002)

While we can intentionally engage in practices to help prepare us for the transformation of our self-identity and worldview, as Wink Franklin—past president of the Institute of Noetic Sciences and a man who lived with an open heart and an everlasting faith in people and the world—told us during our interview, there are some things we just can't know or prepare for. For Franklin, this is why it is important to trust and honor the mystery and our "unknowing":

As we enter the deeper levels of awareness and reality itself, we know less and less about cause and effect. There's a top-down as well as a bottom-up causation. I don't think we can know a lot about top-down causation. That's where the mystery and awe is—and it's also where the trust comes in. It's imperative that we trust that there is a deeper knowing in the universe than our own knowing.

This doesn't mean we don't keep trying to know. We keep trying to know that there's a knowing and rightness about the world that we don't understand; we have to honor and trust in the mystery and the awe. All the spiritual paths talk about the fact that you can't describe the indescribable. The practice then, is not only to trust the unknowing, it's really to honor and appreciate and love that unknown, and to really embrace it as the life force that is the ultimate energy and ultimate source. (2003)

While we live in a culture that values certainty, an important aspect of transformation is finding comfort in not knowing.

Getting Out of the Way

Starting a transformative practice implies that you've formed an intention and are taking action. Many people we interviewed, however, felt that something bigger was happening "to" them; they didn't need to do anything except get out of the way (not as easy as it sounds!). For many, practice was less about training like an athlete to transform through strength and will, and more about cultivating the conditions for the natural process of transformation to occur. Michael Murphy, cofounder of the Esalen Institute and author of *The Future of the Body* (1992), explained it this way:

You can't speak of a practice without [speaking of] the relationship of volition and grace. They all have it. In Buddhism there is the doctrine of nonattainment. In Christianity, the idea that graces are given. Practice is like planting a vineyard. In meditation itself, for example, the primary act of being present, however you do it—vipassana, zazen [a Japanese form of

silent meditation], *prayer, or the prayer of simple regard in the Christian*
contemplative tradition—involves recollection. If you take this act of
recollection as in a vineyard, you are planting a stake on which the vines
will grow. What happens is that these vines start to grow, leaves appear, the
grapes come, and then wine can be made… But you don't make the grapes.
They just happen. All you're doing is planting the stake and making sure
it stands up against the elements. Sometimes it droops over, and you put it
back up, until those vines are well established. The vines blossom through
your process of practice and more practice. (2002)

Many of our respondents said that one of the fundamental purposes of practice is to connect to some form of truth that transcends the physical. Many transformative practices are designed to cultivate the attentional and physiological conditions that are most conducive to connecting with and expressing what is called the numinous, the divine, the sacred, the mystery, or simply "what is."

Developing a regular transformative practice allows space for these numinous moments to come forth more reliably, thus keeping us in frequent contact with the mystery of life. Pagan teacher and writer Starhawk told us:

I think it's long-term work that lays the groundwork for moments of
epiphany. If you do the long-term work, you'll have the epiphanies; they'll
come. If you don't do the long-term work, sometimes they'll still come. The
long-term work makes them almost, you know, reliable epiphanies. If you
do … some sort of personal practice—some sort of training of the mind
so you can move into altered states of consciousness and the deepened sense
of connectedness that you get in ritual—you can learn how to create these
epiphanies. You can't necessarily guarantee every ritual is going to be an
epiphany, because there's mystery and epiphanies have a life of their own.
But you can pretty much expect that a lot of rituals will be epiphanies,
because you have learned how to open that door. Once you've learned how
to open that door, it's like a well-oiled hinge—it opens very easily. (2006)

Wink Franklin similarly argued that transformative practices open us to more profound understanding of the most fundamental human core:

I think practices and spiritual activities actually work by continually opening doors to different levels of understanding that take us to a deeper place. That understanding is simultaneously a deeper understanding within our self and an understanding of the world. (2003)

This deeper understanding is what you are called to in your efforts to live life more fully and deeply.

SUMMARY

In this chapter, we've shared some of the ways that practices—whether prayer, meditation, dreamwork, ritual, or some other kind of practice—can support transformation.

First, many transformative practices work to help you cultivate insight: seeing your situation and the true nature of things clearly. Second, transformative practices can help return the ego back to its appropriate role: a useful tool for navigating the ins and outs of the material world, but only one of many aspects of your internal life. Practice can make room for other aspects of your being—creativity, intuition, surprise, emotion, physicality, etc.—to emerge and take their rightful places as sources of inspiration, information, and motivation. And as you build a more complete self-structure, you can transcend the limited, self-centered, egoic sense of self. You learn to ride the ego; it serves you rather than you serving it. Third, as you become more in touch with your authentic self, you begin to clear away whatever is out of alignment with that self. Many transformative practices include elements of purification that can help you rid yourself of outdated beliefs and habits that no longer serve you. Fourth, as these blocks are cleared away, you become better able to move out of the past and into the present, into a place of power and acceptance. Living in the moment becomes a way of finding the beauty in all your thoughts and deeds. And finally, our research suggests that transformation requires a balance between courage, determination, discipline, and choice on the

131

one hand, and letting go, acceptance, and surrendering to the mystery of transformation on the other. Releasing control and learning to embrace the unknown is as important to transformation as is sustaining a strong intention and motivation to live deeply in each moment, for the transformative journey can take you to places that you would never have dreamed, through circuitous routes that you could never have predicted. In the next chapter, we'll see how life can become your practice—and practice your life. For now, take a few moments to consider more deeply the qualities of practice you seek.

Experiencing Transformation: The Inner Workings of Practice

Review the practices you've engaged in that you've found to be personally transformative. Whether it's a formal spiritual practice of prayer or meditation, a body-oriented practice such as yoga, tai chi, qi gong, or martial arts, or a less formal practice like running, dance, singing, gardening, sailing, or surfing, how does your practice work for you?

Get some paper and a writing utensil. Write the name of your practice on one side of the page, maybe 15 to 20 times. (If you don't have a regular practice, choose something that you enjoy doing that gives you peace.) Then, starting at the top, for each line complete a sentence about what this practice brings into your life.

For example:

Walking the labyrinth makes me feel peaceful.

Walking the labyrinth is sometimes boring.

Walking the labyrinth brings me closer to God.

Walking the labyrinth makes me remember who I am.

Walking the labyrinth brings a sense of sadness.

Walking the labyrinth grounds me.

Don't edit your sentences. Let whatever comes naturally be written down, even if you don't immediately understand it, even if it isn't politically correct, even if it isn't the "right" answer. Next, go back through your answers and add the words "which teaches me" to each sentence.

For example:

Walking the labyrinth makes me feel peaceful, which teaches me that I have peace within me.

Walking the labyrinth is sometimes boring, which teaches me that I can tolerate boredom and it sometimes leads to creative ideas.

Walking the labyrinth brings me closer to God, which teaches me that I am always close to God.

Walking the labyrinth makes me remember who I am, which teaches me that I actually like the person I am.

Walking the labyrinth brings a sense of sadness, which teaches me that I have deep feelings and need some space to grieve.

Walking the labyrinth grounds me, which teaches me that the ground is always beneath me, wherever I am.

Do the same for every important practice in your life. You may be surprised by what you discover. You can even try this with practices you'd *like* to try. What do you think they would bring you? What do you think you might learn? This process can help you clarify both what you're getting from your own transformative practice and what you need or want from practices you're considering.

CHAPTER SIX:

Life as Practice, Practice as Life

If you are really awake, conscious, and aware, then your life is a practice. Then everything you do is a practice. Most of us aren't that aware or awake all of the time.
—*WINK FRANKLIN (2003)*

Changes in the way you view yourself and your world obviously affect all arenas of your daily experience. Transformative practices, however, can sometimes seem separate from the rest of your life. If you're like many people, you may find yourself racing through your days, working hard to get everything done so that you can take a walk in nature or squeeze in a yoga class. You may work sixty-hour weeks so that you can fit in a ten-day meditation retreat. You may have a deep and profound connection to the sacred when you are in your church, temple, ashram, mosque, zendo, or garden, but at work, in your car, and even at home, you may feel that the sacred is far away—that you need to go to a special place to reconnect with it.

Vipassana teacher and author Sharon Salzberg spoke to us about understanding transformation as a form of spirituality integrated into all aspects of life. She recalled the perspective of a teacher visiting from India:

> When we were first starting to teach here we took one of our teachers from India around, to show him all the vipassana meditation groups that were springing up. We were very excited and proud. "Isn't it great what is happening in America?" And he said, "It's wonderful, but in some ways what's happening here reminds me of people sitting in a rowboat: they're rowing with great effort and sincerity, but they refuse to untie the boat from the dock. People want great transcendent experiences, but they don't pay attention to how they speak to one another, or how they earn their living, or the things of day-to-day life."
>
> In the West, there isn't a seamless understanding of what spiritual life is. It's more specialized, like, "I'm going to meditate on a cushion, and something great is going to happen." The classical understanding is that a spiritual life is how we live every day. It's how we relate to our children, how we relate to our parents, how we earn a living, how we speak to one another, how truthful we are. That's something that hasn't translated completely into our culture. (2002)

In fact, many teachers said that transformative practices are often misunderstood as prescriptions for being more spiritual, when, in fact, they're meant to provide a road map for life.

At some point in the transformative process, you recognize that there's no difference between who you are in the pew or on the aikido mat and who you are in the grocery store, on the freeway, or at your office. The same mindful attention brought to the placement of your legs in a difficult yoga pose can be brought to a challenging conversation with your child. The same peace and joy brought to a beloved community of fellow practitioners can be brought to a PTA meeting. The same reverence that arises from spending three days in the wilderness on a vision quest can be brought to the clouds in the sky and the spindly trees in the mall parking lot.

As ecological and spiritual teacher and activist Satish Kumar told us:

> I use meditation as a practice—to focus, to learn how to be mindful, how to be present in the here and now. But for me the distinction between meditation and action must evaporate, must come to an end. Every action—whether I'm gardening or cooking or speaking or writing or talking to a friend or being with my children—everything is to be done mindfully, fully present and attentive and aware. Meditation becomes part of everyday living. (2005)

In this chapter, we'll share with you what we've learned through our research about how, in ways shared across traditions, people integrate their transformative practices and insights into everyday life. Like Kumar, many people reported that living life to the fullest can bring transformation into being. Engaging in a daily mind, body, and spirit practice; finding a like-minded community; sprinkling simple reminders of your core values, purpose, and intentions throughout your environment; taking time out from the hustle and bustle; manifesting your realizations by giving them a form and body in this world; and being of service to others are all ways to create a more seamless fusion of life and practice. We identify little ways in which you can weave what has meaning for you through each and every day.

INTEGRATING LIFE AND PRACTICE

The Venerable Pa Auk Sayadaw, a Burmese Buddhist monk and carrier of a tradition of vipassana, or insight meditation, told us that once you're convinced of the benefits of spiritual practice, you begin to integrate the benefits into your being (2003). Sayadaw identified five positive spiritual factors that are important for the integration of the more common short-term realizations into long-term shifts in worldview or way of being. The first factor is the *desire* to change and the *conviction* that practice will result in your transformation. The second factor is effort, without which Sayadaw argues nothing will happen. The third factor is vigilance. Strong determination can keep you from falling back or losing sight of the path to spiritual well-being. The fourth factor, one that is central to Sayadaw's vipassana practice, is concentration, which he describes as "the consistent integrity of consciousness" (2003). This is not, he says, an innate quality, but rather something that has to be developed by practice, something you can learn. The fifth factor is right understanding—accurately perceiving the nature of reality. Sayadaw explained to us that once you have even just a couple of these qualities, "you are sure to progress on the path. You will be able to shift short-term gains into long-term benefits in life" (2003).

No matter what practice or tradition you engage in, you can make a conscious choice to use the following tools to make your life and your transformative journey one and the same—because, of course, they are!

Going Beyond State-Dependent Learning

Psychologists have found that people are better able to recall information when in the same state or situation as when the information was originally learned (for example, if you learn algebra in a yellow room filled with rows of desks, you're more likely to ace an algebra test when taken in a similar yellow room with rows of desks). This long-studied cognitive phenomenon is known as *state-dependent learning.*

For many people, transformative realizations seem to be subject to state-dependent learning: it's easier to recall your true priorities or get in touch with your capacity for deep compassion in the same setting as your first experiences of these things. For example, most transformative traditions include regular visits to a particular place of worship or practice. However, too great a dependence on these sacred places can lead to a constant search to recapture the *states* of your realizations—which are temporary—rather than the development of these realizations into sustainable *traits.* The key is to begin to integrate these realizations in to all arenas of your life.

Many people spend years chasing transformative states, attending workshop after workshop, group after group. Often people will feel exhilarated at a workshop, only to come home and have difficulty integrating the realization the moment of exhilaration pointed to. As a result, they may simply start searching for another workshop to replicate the intense experience. Indeed, this cycle can be especially challenging when you live in a society that doesn't support the integration of your practice into your daily life. As Catholic priest Father Francis Tiso told us:

> *Remember, the great yogis went into retreat in the mountains from cultures that were traditional, religious, and favorable to at least some of the goals that the yogis were pursuing.*
>
> We *live without retreat, in a society that is inimical to* [the transformative process]. *We are attempting to be part-time yogis... If you're going to get any kind of results out of this, it's probably going to take awhile—and they also might be a little on the thin side: very fragile, easily torn. You may get a glimpse or an insight, and the day afterwards, you'll seem not to have had it. It's evanescent. Don't be discouraged by that.* (2002)

In addition to extending beyond state-dependent learning, there are many ways to utilize it to help bring transformation into your everyday life. For example, one is to make your home and your workplace—even your car—more similar to places in which it is easy to experience your deepest self. Many places that are thought to be sacred incorporate elements of beauty, simplicity, images, light, or music to facilitate deep experiences of the numinous. You can integrate these elements into your own environment—lighting a candle, playing comforting music, etc. can all help you create a space that nurtures transformation. Another way to utilize state-dependent learning is to make your mental and physical state as similar as possible to what you experience in your practice environment. Many retreat settings (though not all) emphasize elements like silence, solitude, creative expression, and a peaceful pace; they also often incorporate healthy food, fresh air, and exercise. Bringing these elements into your everyday life can make it more conducive to recalling what has heart and meaning for you.

Finding a Like-Minded Community

When we asked our teachers how to integrate transformative realizations into everyday life and long-term shifts in ways of being, the most common response we received was to connect with a like-minded community. In fact, many teachers said that finding a like-minded community with whom you can share your transformative process is essential. Having people in your life who support your metamorphosis can help fortify the results that Father Tiso called "fragile" and "easily torn" (2002). Moreover, your community can serve both as a crucible for your transformation and as a sanctuary for exploring new ideas and insights.

Psychologist Frances Vaughan noted that being part of a community is also vital to the part of transformation that involves learning how to behave with other people. She suggests that you ask yourself:

> *Am I more compassionate? Am I more caring? Am I more considerate, or am I less so? You can evaluate these questions subjectively as well as asking others what they observe. It's this latter form where I think it's important to have a community that you work with. You may think you are having a wonderful enlightenment experience—and the people may feel that you are off the wall! You have to balance the inner and the outer, I think. It's not either/or, it's both/and.* (2002)

Similarly, Zenkei Blanche Hartman told us how the practice of Zen, particularly in a monastery, works to enhance a sense of interdependence—and how, in the process, practice helps to polish people's dull and rough edges:

> *The monastic practice helps people to see how connected they are to everyone—how they affect others and how they are affected by others. To develop some compassion—that is, some feeling for others—is part of the way we live together at the monastery. At Tassajara, where we have the monastery, we live together, we eat together, we work together, and we read together. Pretty soon everybody sees who you are. You might as well forget yourself.*

To understand this, we use the metaphor of rocks in a tumbler.
You take some pebbles and put them in a tumbler with some water and
some abrasive. Then you put them on the roller. Have you ever seen a rock
tumbler? It rolls and it rolls. The rocks keep falling and bumping. Then there
is the grit, or abrasive, which I think may be the relentless monastic schedule.

We follow a very strict schedule at the monastery. Someone runs
around with a wake-up bell. We get up and go to meditation. We sit together
and chant together. We eat together in the meditation hall. We work together
and so forth, always bumping into each other. We get to see where our rough
edges are and someone else's rough edges. After some time when their edges
bump into yours, you get polished up. We have a sense of taking care of each
other and taking care of the community. (2003)

Like Hartman, many of the people we met with noted that much benefit can come from practice done in synchrony with others. This doesn't require actually living in a monastery or other spiritual community. Having a group of like-minded peers that you trust can help you calibrate your experiences. Supportive groups of fellow travelers can take many forms. For example, a supportive group might be any organized or semi-organized group of people that shares your goals, values, or interests—a book club, a travel cohort, a running group, a network of supportive friends and colleagues, or a spiritually minded class or program. Newer on the horizon are Internet- and teleconferencing-based programs like IONS' Shift in Action (www .noetic.org); these venues provide ways for people to discuss their transformative experiences with like-minded others who are (hopefully!) open and nonjudgmental. Finding the right community for you can help support you on your transformative journey.

Indeed, being part of a like-minded community may actually even allow you to learn more from the transformative process. In his learning theory of social development, psychologist Lev Vygotsky posited that social interaction profoundly influences cognitive development (1934). Vygotsky sees development as a lifelong process too complex to be divided into stages. He refers to the distance separating your current level of development (problems you can solve on your own) from your potential level of development (problems you can solve only with guidance from either more developed individuals or peers) as the *zone of proximal development*. For Vygotsky, this zone is where learning occurs. He observes, moreover, that it's the social interactions that take place in this zone—with guides and peers—that define the degree to which someone can learn or internalize new information.

Thus, for Vygotsky, development happens in the context of shared experience and connections with others. He argues that children learn best in environments with older children who can provide what he calls "scaffolding" for learning experiences—not solving problems for the younger children, but providing a supportive structure for them to reach solutions for themselves. Vygotsky also recommends *reciprocal teaching* as a learning method. In reciprocal teaching, students are given the task of leading small groups in the very subjects they're currently learning themselves. Finally, Vygotsky believes that the optimal learning environment is small groups of mixed developmental levels, in which more experienced students are aware of the beginning learners' level and are careful not to dominate interactions.

These elements can all be great criteria for choosing who you want to support you on your transformative journey. Look for a like-minded community consisting of people in a range of developmental levels; a community with guides who don't just hand out solutions but help you discover them for yourself, and leaders who don't dominate all interactions; a community where those who are learning are also given the opportunity to teach. Not surprisingly, many transformative traditions around the world have already built these optimal learning environments into their forms of practice.

CULTS AND UNSUPPORTIVE COMMUNITIES

As Zen teacher Zenkei Blanche Hartman told us with her rock-tumbling metaphor, relationships within transformative communities aren't always easy (2003). While being part of a like-minded community can be a real blessing, just because the members of the community are focused on common goals doesn't mean that personalities, reactivity, and conflict resolution won't be problematic. Indeed, in a transformative community, these challenges can even be more intense than in a more superficial situation like a workplace.

It's important to differentiate between like-minded practice communities that can help your transformation and those that will impact you negatively because they're cults or simply unsupportive. Cults are defined by a set of key criteria: cults discourage questioning of doctrine, leaders, or teachers; require you to either donate more than you can reasonably afford or give up your possessions or residence; use tactics such as humiliation or criticism; encourage you to keep the group's doctrine or practices secret; or urge you to break off all contact with family and friends. If you find yourself participating in a group that follows any of these precepts, you have reason for concern.

Lack of a supportive community can stifle the transformative process. If others completely reject—or simply fail to understand—your experience, it can be harder to integrate your experiences and realizations into your life. As cross-cultural psychologist Stanley Krippner told us:

> One thing that inhibits the integration of these teachings is social pressure. Some people will talk about an epiphany and their friends will make fun of them. Some people will go to an indigenous healer and they will have a sudden healing of some long-standing problem—say a sore throat or an aching muscle—and when they come back, their friends make fun of them. Then back comes the symptom. In my opinion, for a lot of these anchorings to really stick, to really hold and take place, you've got to have social support. (2002)

Indeed, Krippner's point is similar to Tiso's observation earlier—that our dominant culture does not always support the kind of consciousness transformation that emphasizes meaning over material possessions (2002). Transpersonal psychologist James Fadiman agrees that an unsupportive community can undo a lot of good transformative work. He explained to us that an unresponsive social world can substantially inhibit the integration of transformative experiences and new ways of seeing the world:

If everybody says you are crazy, at some point you are off the cultural norm and by definition you are crazy. And if you find yourself lonely and seem to be crazy, it's hard to maintain your shift in perception. There's a little Sufi story called "When the Water Was Changed." It's about a town in which, if you drank the water, you would behave in a bizarre manner. Everyone but this one guy drank the water. He hoarded the old water—he could see that everyone was behaving in this bizarre way… But finally this guy said, "I give up, I'm going to drink the water." And everyone else said, "Oh, he's cured, he's healthy again, he's sane. He was so bizarre, but now he's one of us again." Unless there's some kind of support system—it can even be a book—some kind of external verification and validation, it can be very hard to maintain these changes. (2003)

There are many advantages to pursuing your transformative path with the aid of a community. Having a like-minded cohort can give you the opportunity to connect, share, and celebrate what's working—and repair what's not. Remember, not everyone in your community needs to agree with everything you say. Sometimes a voice of dissent can help us to refine and revise our sense of what's right and true. However, as Gangaji told us, if a like-minded group prevents you from finding your authentic self, it can be the worst thing, rather than the best (2002).

Simple Reminders

Reminders of what you intend for your life—reminders done over and over, and in many different ways—can help you integrate your transformative practice into everyday actions. Sometimes even very simple reminders can help. Such basic acts as reading an inspiring book, listening to an inspirational tape, going to an educational lecture, chatting with friends around a fire, watching a great movie snuggled up with your kids, or even taking a leisurely bath can help transform mundane actions into deeply meaningful practices. And when steps are simple and easy, they become a joy rather than a burden.

Simple reminders can also include objects, symbols, music, or jewelry—anything that has meaning for you. Although the items themselves may be trivial—like the bobble-head Buddha on the dashboard—they can be very helpful in keeping you in the flow of your own personal growth. It's important to rotate reminders so they'll continue to hold your attention, rather than fade into an unnoticed background. And it helps if you get reminders in as many forms as possible, through all of your senses.

These types of reminders serve as *cues*, defined by psychologists as stimuli that, when perceived either consciously or unconsciously, elicit a behavior. Even something as simple as a string of beads—as used in Buddhism and Yogic traditions (the mala) and Catholicism (the rosary)—can signal you on both conscious and unconscious levels to behave in a way consistent with your values and commitments.

With his wrist mala in hand, spiritual teacher and author Ram Dass explained to us how the practice of mantra repetition reminds him to see everyone as souls:

> *I use this method where I pick a name of god and I say to myself, "Ram, Ram, Ram."—I'm walking in the street—"Ram, Ram, Ram." I'm visiting the supermarket—"Ram, Ram, Ram…"*
>
> *It's amazing how many souls there are in Safeway. They think they're something else, but they're souls… It's just phenomenal, because if you're living… you're the actor, you're the audience, you're the writer. And if you forget, the guru reminds you… "Ram, Ram, Ram…" (2003)*

Neuroscientists have found that cues can be extremely powerful motivators of behavior, both in learning (Dessalegn and Landau 2005) and in less healthy processes, like addiction (Carter and Tiffany 1999). In addiction, environmental cues—such as the sounds, sights, or physical surroundings associated with drinking or using drugs—can trigger the addictive behavior (Zickler 2001). Introducing transformative reminders into your environment can work in a similar fashion, but with a positive goal: triggering the qualities and traits you desire to bring fully into your life. For Brother David Steindl-Rast, this takes the form of simple physical reminders, such as yellow Post-it notes that he puts around his house to remind him of his own gratitude. For you, this might be a good fortune from a Chinese cookie or a particularly inspiring quote stuck on your refrigerator. Even very little things can remind you of who and what you are at the core of your being.

Time-Outs

Another simple but very important way to integrate transformative practices and realizations into your everyday life is to schedule quiet time to be alone. Taking a walk in nature or sitting quietly with some soothing music can be very helpful if done with intention and attention.

While daydreaming may be a luxury most of us feel we don't have time for, it is in fact a way of integrating information. Eric Klinger, author of *Daydreaming* (1990), has devoted over thirty years to the study of daydreaming. Klinger writes, "Daydreaming is one of the ways in which you keep your life organized, a way to milk experiences for the lessons they hold, and a way of rehearsing for the future" (1990, 3). Making time for unstructured silence and solitude—for daydreaming—actually makes your life more efficient, because it allows you to cognitively integrate what you've learned. Daydreaming can also help you generalize your realizations by imagining how they might apply to other parts of your life and the future.

Taking quiet time can be quite difficult—you may feel you can't carve out the necessary space for yourself, and you may find silence or solitude uncomfortable once you've managed to make the time. Being in silence and solitude is like most things in that you may not fully engage in the process unless you can find joy in it. Don't worry if silence and solitude are currently strangers to you—there are many ways to change your relationship so you can become trusted friends.

Don Hanlon Johnson, a leader in the field of somatic psychology and a professor at the California Institute of Integral Studies, brings silence into his family setting:

> *I get up at six a.m. and do my things. My son has to get up at about twenty*
> *to eight to get ready for school. I get him his breakfast and my wife takes him*
> *to school on her way to her office: that's kind of our ritual. Every morning*
> *he gets up. He sits on a stair, and I sit with him. Since he's been an infant,*

145

there's been a period of about ten minutes when he is absolutely quiet. It's the most profound meditation, sitting with him. We don't have cable TV, so he's been raised in a kind of quiet. That seems very profound to me. A lot of our interactions have that same quality. (2002)

Just ten minutes of silence a day can make all the difference. Sitting quietly with loved ones, engaging with life and being aware of its sacred nature, can imbue your experiences of silence with delight and deep satisfaction. This can allow you to engage with your daily tasks in a way that makes them conscious, thus helping you bring your transformative practice into your daily routines.

Taking Action

According to many of the teachers we interviewed, one of the best ways to bring the new perspectives you've gained through transformative experiences into your life is to consciously put them into action. Action can take many forms. It can be creative expression, putting your realizations—which can often be difficult to describe—into poetry, drawing, painting, sculpture, or dance. It can be creating new ways of being and spending time with your loved ones. It can be implementing new projects at work—or new elements of existing projects—that are in greater alignment with your emerging values and sensibilities. It can be volunteering in your local community or in broader social or ecological action groups. The bottom line here is bringing your new perspective into the world in some form.

Many of the teachers we interviewed told us that bringing practice into action not only enhances your practice, it enriches all of your life experiences. In other words, consciously bringing transformative realizations into life makes life experiences themselves more transformative. Pagan teacher Starhawk explained it this way:

If you actually take your ideals and put them into practice through action, then the actions that you take create very powerful experiences that you learn from. These open you up to other kinds of shifts.

Probably the most powerful transformative experience of my life has been going to the West Bank and the occupied territories with the international solidarity movement. I walked into a situation with people who I was raised to think of as my enemies—who I feared would hate me and would be dangerous—and I was in solidarity with them, sharing some of the risks and dangers that they face every day. The profound welcome that I've received, the ways in which people have opened and taken us in, have been incredible. For years I led people in trances in which they faced their deepest fear. And that was all very nice, but walking into Nablus when it was locked down and under siege—walking into a refugee camp, past tanks that were shooting at us, and then going into a Palestinian home and sitting and being with these people—that was transformation on a whole different level.

When I faced that fear, it really made me much less fearful. I'm just not afraid anywhere anymore. People will be walking around saying, "It's such a dangerous area!" and I'll be like, "I don't really think so."... It's led me to look at people and expect friendship and expect connection. The real world teaches you a lot if you open yourself to its experiences. (2006)

Of course, action may not be the same as activism. Indeed, it can be as simple as bringing loving kindness to a difficult relationship or even slowing down when your find your busy life taking over.

ANCHORS IN A STORM

As we saw in chapters 4 and 5, our research suggests that engaging in a daily practice of some form or another will help you integrate transformative experiences into your everyday life. Indeed, engaging in a daily practice can aid you in ways fundamental to your sense of balance and emotional stability. Transpersonal psychologist Charles Tart summed this idea up eloquently, describing transformative practice as a form of spirituality: "In general, if you have any kind of even moderately strong spiritual practice, that practice gives you an anchor in turbulent times. It gives you something to keep you more steady when the winds of change are buffeting you" (2003).

Catholic priest Father Francis Tiso reminded us how practice can help you stay on an even keel during what can be a turbulent journey:

Committing oneself to the spiritual path, although we may be seeking peace, actually … seems to put us into huge fluctuations of anguish and ecstasy. You can see there is peace, there is mystical absorption, there are all kinds of wonderful samadhis and states. But there is also this huge fluctuation of emotion and feeling and intensity.

Many spiritual practices—like penitential practices, the practice of humility, the practice of self-abnegation—although they sound like they are contrary to a self-esteem ideology, are actually designed to keep you on an even keel when you are going through those things. Because you are going to go through them. If you do yoga, for example, you're sensitizing your whole body-mind complex so that your pleasures become much greater, as well as your pains. You can become quite attached, even to the physical pleasure of yoga. That's why you have to learn to keep on an even keel.

We need to be more courageous in embracing the suffering aspect of the transformative process. Happiness is not found in evading the rough patches of the journey, and cannot be identified with little surges of happy hormones in the brain. That is not happiness, it is addiction!

Thomas Merton … talks about the fact that Cistercian-Trappist liturgy—the chanting and so forth—is designed to not let you go too high or too low, but to keep you in the middle. It gives you the kind of psycho-physical stability that you need to cope with the fact that you are going to have highs and lows. You can get trapped in either heaven or hell; this [stability] *brings you back, keeps you human.*

There are many anecdotes about [the importance of stability, of staying in the middle] *and we don't appreciate it enough perhaps, when we are hungry for peace and hungry for ecstasy. We don't appreciate why we're being told, "Come back down to Earth." But in fact, there is wisdom in this practice and attitude.* (2002)

Many transformative practice traditions have built-in ways of helping you keep a relatively even keel during the transformative process. Transformative practices such as prayer, meditation, ritual, and many others have been designed in part to help you deal with the kinds of fluctuations Tiso describes. Having guides, a supportive community, a daily mind/body practice—all of these are engineered to both transform you and help you tolerate the challenges of the transformative journey.

Likewise, Stanley Krippner, another transpersonal psychologist, used the metaphor of an anchor this way:

I like the saying "By their fruits, you shall know them." If the person is a better worker, a more loving, happy, joyous person to be with, sure, that's good enough for me. Psychotherapists use the term "anchoring"—you take the epiphany and you anchor it into your everyday experience. You find ways that you can put it to work in your daily life. Many people go to church, or temple, or synagogue, or whatever. They go one day a week and it's completely divorced from the flow of their life. They make a big show of their religious piety, but it's not anchored to anything… This is something you have to work on. You take these insights from these epiphanies and you find something in your daily life that you can hook them onto and you pull the rest of your life along. (2002)

As both Tart and Krippner suggest, transformative practices can help ground you in the face of new ways of being in the world. As you journey along the transformative path, it's often helpful to have practices that can help you integrate new ways of being into your everyday life.

As we also saw in chapter 4, studies on brain plasticity tell us that the more you practice something, the stronger new neural pathways become—and the easier it becomes for them to be stimulated. Whether your practice is daily meditation, periodic fasting, journaling, attending worship services, positive affirmations, walking in nature, or praying, practices foster the integration of transformative experiences. Practice serves as a reminder of a larger set of possibilities than you may experience on a routine basis. Practice connects you repeatedly to the sacred, numinous, or divine. And practice also stimulates further growth and transformation.

Daily practice can provide a strong scaffolding for the transformative process. As Michael Murphy (2002), cofounder of the Esalen Institute, put it, practice acts like the stake that supports the growing vine—you! Andriette Earl, reverend of the East Bay Church of Religious Science, considers daily practice akin to keeping your foot on the gas pedal as you drive uphill (2006). Practice thus fuels your transformative journey, supporting you as you seek to grow and blossom.

BRINGING MEANING INTO LIFE

As you bring your transformative practice more and more into your life, you become an actor rather than a reactor. You become able to use conscious intention to propel yourself forward. Life is yours to give meaning to—you choose the story you want to tell. Yoruba priestess Luisah Teish echoed this sentiment:

> One of the things that I see as fundamental to personal empowerment is coming out of feeling like "I'm a victim of my life" into "I am working with nature, community, and spirit to design and shape our lives." You know, you go from a "me" to an "us." You go from a victim to an actor or an initiator. You go from feeling devalued to valuing what's already really around you. (2003)

Transformation, then, not only shifts how you view the world, but also how you relate to the world. In every situation, ask yourself, "Am I being an actor or a victim? Am I valuing or devaluing? Am I focused on me or on us?" As humans, we are meaning-making creatures. We can create any meaning we want. Why not create a life-enhancing set of possibilities, rather than an endless refrain of victimization and suffering?

Life as Service

Manifesting your transformation in the world is what makes it substantial. For many, transformative realizations are grounded through service to others. Such selflessness to others is a cornerstone of most religions and many spiritual and transformative paths. In English, the word "service" shares its root with the Old English *serfise*, or ceremony. To this day, "service" is used to mean both a religious ceremony and an act of generosity to another. Offering service to others can be a rite that both expresses your intention to grow and transform, and anchors your realizations in everyday reality.

Physician Rachel Naomi Remen has devoted herself to the welfare of others for nearly four decades. As she told us:

> *Service is my practice. Service is one of the most powerful of the practices. As you watch someone being taken unaware by something like cancer, they go through a process of healing. It's a process of the evolution of the self towards wholeness. There are steps in the process, and people go through them in different ways. I believe the final step is service.*
>
> *People who are able to use and experience crisis, suffering, and loss in a way that evolves their unique being will, in the end, use that unique being in service to others, because service has become natural to them. The experience they've just been through—of suffering and loss—is, in some sense, the universal experience. It's the human condition. Having been through it, they don't hold themselves separate from the suffering of other people. They don't protect themselves in the way that most people do.*
>
> *Often they stay in the lives they've been in. They're a CEO or they're a real estate agent, or whatever, but they do it now from a different place and for a different purpose. They do it from a place of deep connection to others. And for me, that's the sign of true practice. I think that a lot of people speak of the web of connection as an intellectual thing. That's very different from knowing it in every cell of your body as the ground of being. (2003)*

Gerald Jampolsky—another physician whose work has helped thousands, perhaps even millions, of ill and dying patients and their family members deal with the crises they face—put it this way:

> Not everyone is called to a life of service—at least not in the most obvious
> sense of becoming a social worker or volunteering in a soup kitchen. Indeed,
> many who take that path soon realize how even these activities can become
> divorced from the rest of your life. Service, defined broadly, can be how
> you interact with each person and in each situation, no matter what the
> circumstances are. (2002)

Bringing service into your life can be a simple process. It can involve the way you interact with your coworkers, talk with your children, share your day with your spouse, or check in with an ailing parent. It can be volunteering at a local school or running a marathon to raise money to help fight cancer. Service as a transformative practice is all about the state of consciousness you bring to these little acts of kindness.

Living the Art of Transformation

An interesting thing happens when we begin to creatively manifest what we've learned through the transformative process: a sort of reversal takes place. Where previously your transformative activities fed your life, now your life feeds your transformation. As Anna Halprin, dancer, choreographer, and cancer survivor, told us:

> One has to commit oneself to looking at whatever comes up without
> knowing what the outcome is going to be and dealing with that outcome
> creatively. What comes up may be very difficult, may be very challenging,
> may be very dark and uncomfortable…
>
> I've always been an artist. But I'd never connected art closely to life
> experience until I was stricken with cancer in 1972. That was a big shift

for me, because I began to ask all kinds of questions: What am I doing?
Who am I doing this for? Why am I dancing? What difference does it make
anyway? Up until that time I essentially used my life to create my art; and
then, by asking all those various questions… I began to shift to using art
to create my life. Making that shift required a lot of different questions and
searching for new answers. (2002)

As Reverend David Parks-Ramage similarly acknowledged, your own personal experiences become "the koans of life" (2006). Used in Zen Buddhist practice, a *koan* is an unanswerable question that, when contemplated at length, can lead to realizations that are paradoxical or even completely nonverbal—truths that are ungraspable by logical reasoning and cannot be taught by means of traditional pedagogy. Life's experiences—many of which similarly resist reason or logical understanding—can have the same effect when approached with openness and curiosity.

Although the peak or aha! moments experienced during retreats or practice can be very powerful, the challenge becomes bringing these moments into the mundane or difficult elements of everyday life. Parks-Ramage expanded on this idea:

[In transformative practice] *you have a "blast" or an "aha!" Enough of us*
have been to retreats to know that blasts happen all the time, allowing the
universe and God to pervade and move through your life while also allowing
you to see the possibilities available to you.

But it's those other 452 koans afterward *that bring the experience*
more permanence. Anybody who has ever gone on a retreat and smelled the
sweet fragrance of the love of God and then gone home and fought with their
family or something knows what I am talking about… (2006)

As Parks-Ramage suggests, these moments of everyday life can stimulate the transformative process just as much as the aha! moments.

Daring to Transform

Consciously engaging in transformation is not for the faint of heart. Adyashanti, author of *Emptiness Dancing* (2004a), told us during our interview that integrating great realizations can require taking risks:

> I don't think that you have to get all your inner stuff together and totally integrated before you can actually be what you've realized. You're going to wait forever if you wait for that. Just start being what you know now. That's a scary thing for people, because all of a sudden we come out of hiding—and then everything comes out of hiding. Even for people who've had an authentic awakening and realized truth, it can be scary. Maybe they've had a relationship that really hasn't had truth in it. There are a lot of things that have not been discussed that are put away in the corners. Now we have an awakening and those things we've pushed into the corners are just glaring at us. Are we going to keep pushing them into the corners? If you keep pretending that things aren't there that you know are there, you'll slip right out of that awakened state.
>
> It might be frightening to totally come out of hiding, because who knows what's going to happen now? Am I going to keep my relationship? Am I going to keep my job? Are my friends going to like me? There will be certain areas where it feels very risky, like there's quite a lot at stake. But there must be an absolute willingness to be totally truthful with yourself and with everybody. (2004b)

Indeed, it takes bravery, courage, and commitment to show up every day and be who you really are. And at the same time, as transpersonal psychologist and Sufi teacher Robert Frager reminded us, being authentic also takes love:

> My old Sufi master, an extraordinary teacher, said to me, "I don't know much about Sufism. The little I know is what I have lived and loved for over forty years." And for me that captures it. In Sufism, the first stage of initiation is that of a muhibb, which literally translates as "lover." You can't learn

anything unless you love it—at least, you can't learn it at any depth. So
loving the practice, loving the discipline, is critical. There has to be love, but
this doesn't mean romantic love. It means the love someone holds for their
vocation. Anybody successful at any vocation will tell you the more successful
people love what they are doing more than people who are less successful.
And it's that love that gets them to go deeper and be better at it. So it's about
loving your practice and then living it. That's what makes it work. (2002)

Loving your practice and daring to embrace your life as a transformative crucible will not only help you integrate realizations into your daily life, it will also help your authentic self to shine through every day.

Embodying Practice

Many of our teachers—and others, such as transpersonal developmental theorist Michael Washburn (2003)—use the word "embodiment" to talk about how the realizations you receive can be integrated into your everyday consciousness. Embodiment involves giving concrete form to an abstract concept (e.g., love or unity or belonging). When you embody something, you take what you've learned—the insights you've gained through your direct experience—and you give it form. For example, you can give something form in the way you are and the spirit you bring to each encounter. Thus, your practice and the truths that are important to you become less of what you do and more of who you are as an embodied human being. As Adyashanti told us:

Some people awaken and basically the bottom drops out and never gets put
back underneath them. But this is extraordinarily rare. What most people
find is they have this great experience, this great awakening, and after
they come back from the honeymoon—which can be anywhere from five
minutes to five months to a couple years—they encounter their unresolved
stuff, the parts of them that aren't awakened, that the light didn't penetrate.
They're really going to need to look at that. And that, for most people, is a
gradual process.

155

*One needs to ask, "At any moment, am I actually being what I know
to be true?" It's another one of those things that sounds very simple. Where
the spiritual rubber hits the road is in relationship: Am I actually being what
I know myself to be? When a situation gets difficult or intense, am I actually
expressing and being what's true? Or am I coming from reactivity? When
people start to get the simplicity of this, what I call embodiment starts to
happen much, much more quickly. They take one or two simple concepts,
and actually apply them, actually work them.* (2004b)

Drawing on another perspective, Catholic priest Francis Tiso speaks of
embodiment in terms of resurrection:

*Christian spirituality is very much about embodiment. One of the
criticisms of Evagrius* [an influential fourth-century ascetic Christian
philosopher], *for example, is that he seems to just be talking about a
disembodied soul. But actually what he should be talking about is the whole
human person. Body, soul, everything is participating in those experiences
and will open out into full consciousness. That's what we mean by the
resurrection of the body, which isn't just about flesh being reconstituted
around bones in the grave—it's about coming to life again in the wholeness
of what you are. Your body, your mind, your virtues, your deeds, everything
you've learned, everyone that you've touched—all of that is part of that
resurrection of the body.* (2002)

Although Adyashanti, Tiso, and Frager (in the previous section)
come from very different traditions, they all emphasize the importance of
embodying transformation. This means living in a way that integrates body,
mind, spirit, environment, and society.

MAKING YOUR PRACTICE YOUR OWN

Many teachers noted that their lives became their practice after they stopped looking for what worked for others and found what worked for them. George Leonard, a pioneer of the transformative practice movement, told us:

> One of the things that I used to demand was reassurance that somehow my life was the correct spiritual life to be living. I know that's not a question for me anymore because I have to live my life—I can't live the life of some teacher. I'm never going to get there the way somebody else did. They didn't get there the way somebody else did either... I would venture to say that the best thing that's happened to me is that I now have a fundamental respect for my own way of doing it, and I don't expect myself to follow some teacher and get there the same way. Now, I am more secure and less demanding.
> (2002)

The essence of living deeply is bringing awareness to the simple ways you can make your life and practice a more seamless and graceful partnership. And as Leonard tells us, it is only by staying true to your own authentic methods of self-exploration that you can make your practice your own.

SUMMARY

In this chapter, we've seen that life and practice are fundamentally a seamless whole. This idea is as revolutionary as it is ancient. Living deeply doesn't require retreating to a mountaintop or embarking on a hero's journey; rather, the convergence of life and practice is about the hero's return—in which you bring the fruits of your journey of self-discovery back home, into your life, your family, and your community. Embodying transformation is a process of continual exploration. It can be a simple act of compassion, or a moment when you stopped and felt gratitude. By finding ways to remind yourself to be aware, you can begin to live transformation in every thought and deed. As both Benedictine monk David Steindl-Rast, who continuously looks for ways to practice gratefulness, and Anna Halprin, who has made dance her form of devotion, show us, there are many ways to live more fully and more deeply. As we see in the next chapter, part of this involves a fundamental shift in your sense of identity—moving from "I" to a more engaging sense of the "we."

For now, stop and consider the ways practice takes form in your daily life.

Experiencing Transformation: Living Practice

One way to look at how practice is currently being integrated into your own life is to explore the extent to which practice has permeated the different domains of your everyday experience (you may discover that a domain has even become a practice, without you realizing it!).

Make a chart with three columns. On the left, list the domains of your life; in the center, list the ways that you're presently integrating practice into these individual domains; on the right, list the ways you'd like to either integrate practice more fully into a specific domain, or recognize a domain more explicitly as a practice. Examples of domains might be work, family, social, health, finances, etc. A sample chart follows.

Domain	Integration of Practice	How I Want to Grow
My work as a teacher.	I've begun to ring a small bell at the beginning and end of each class period, not only to signify the beginning and end, but also to remind myself of my mindfulness practice as a teacher.	I'd like to bring more of my physical practice into my work. I will incorporate five minutes of gentle stretching with my students. Working with a child who is having difficulty with a task is really a loving-kindness practice for me—I'd like to recognize it more consciously as such.
My eating habits.	I've begun to offer thanks for the food I eat.	I want to eat more mindfully and cook more for others.

CHAPTER SEVEN:

From "I" to "We"

Whatever put us here—me, the ocean, the sand—we are all one. We say "I"
or "you" so we can communicate, but ... there is no I, there is no difference
between I and you. I am you, you are me; there is only that.
—SHAYKH YASSIR CHADLY (2006)

As a young man, Yassir Chadly—now a charismatic Sufi teacher—was a
member of the Moroccan national swimming team. One day, he went to the
ocean to bodysurf. It was a particularly calm day, so rather than surfing the
waves of the Atlantic, he decided to float on its flat surface. It was then that
a mystical sense of unity came to him:

> *My eyes were closed. I was on my back and feeling little waves, so small,*
> *under my body... Involuntarily, all of a sudden, I could feel my body*
> *growing out of its limits. I couldn't stop it. It was like yeast rising—it was*
> *growing and growing and growing. I couldn't retrieve it. I couldn't make*
> *it small. It was just growing and growing, until the ocean and I were one. I*

could feel the ocean moving on the Earth, and me within it. I was one with

the whole ocean. I could hear inside my head the verse from the Qur'an

that says, "Say that God is one." And I understood what it means, because I

experienced that oneness. I said, "Yes, all is one." (2006)

Over our decadelong research program, we've found that one of the most common elements of consciousness transformation is an experience of the *transpersonal*: an experience, like Chadly's, in which consciousness or self-awareness extends beyond the boundaries of the individual personality. As we discussed in chapter 2, this kind of experience can result in a consciousness shift—and stimulate a lifelong journey to understand the experience. But "transpersonal" doesn't only refer to isolated experiences. It also refers to a worldview in which you see yourself as not just a separate, individual ego, but as part of a greater whole.

Throughout the course of our lives, we pass through many different developmental stages. *Transpersonal development* refers to those that go beyond the typical stages of the adult. Ken Wilber, one of the leading theorists of transpersonal development, posits ten common stages of development, six of which are stages most of us are familiar with—the development from the immaturity of infancy to mature adulthood (2000). However, Wilber and others—such as Abraham Maslow, Carl Jung, Stan Grof, Michael Washburn, and Sri Aurobindo—have proposed that beyond these six stages are higher stages of development that are transpersonal, in which people experience themselves as not only connected to others both in and out of their tribe, but connected to all that is.

In Wilber's view, during any of the ten stages one can have an experience of a higher stage. However, "the ways in which these altered states will (and can) be *experienced* depends predominantly on the *structures* (stages) of consciousness that have developed in the individual" (2000, 1). Says Wilber, "Overall or *integral development* is thus a continuous process of converting temporary states into permanent traits or structures, and in that integral development, no structures or levels can be bypassed, or the development is not, by definition, integral" (3).

Across traditions, many of our research participants reported experiencing an ever-present sense of unity and connection, with both others and

161

the broader world—a sense of connection, moreover, that grows stronger and stronger the more they engage in transformative practice. As this sense of connection grows stronger and more reliable, it becomes more a permanent part of each person's sense of self, rather than an isolated event or peak experience.

Participants in our studies articulated this experience of a deep, transpersonal connection in many ways. We heard such phrases as "a realization of the interconnectedness of all beings," "a dissolving of the boundary between self and other," "an abiding personal relationship with God—the same God in all the world," "a sense of community at a global level," and "a gradual realization that there isn't any separation." Though people didn't always use the same words to describe this experience, descriptions common across people and traditions included a growing sense of unity, shared identity, and belonging; and an awareness of a divinity universal to all people and all life (Vieten, Cohen, and Schlitz 2008; Vieten, Amorok, and Schlitz 2006).

We asked our study participants to help us understand what changes result from such experiences. How do these experiences of deep connection impact who we are and how we view the world, at a core level?

NOT JUST ME

Discussions of shifting from "I" to "we" can make some of us feel a bit uncomfortable, especially those of us raised in the individualistic West. Fears of socialism, communism, and the Borg mentality (for all you *Star Trek* fans out there) are part of our cultural inheritance and can feel woven into the very fabric of our being. You may instinctively recoil from just the idea of oneness or interconnection. Moreover, some of us have spent years trying to build a solid sense of self; it can seem as if now we're being asked to let it all go.

As briefly discussed in chapter 5, in Western society, healthy psychological development has focused on separation-individuation, creation of a solid sense of self, forming healthy boundaries, and building a strong ego. Here, we're suggesting a model of transformation that includes transcendence of the ego, dissolution of boundaries, and less attachment to a separate solid sense of self. What gives?

Interestingly, it appears that both models are valid—and not necessarily contradictory. Our research suggests that as you let go of self-interest and begin to feel a greater sense of belonging and interdependence, you simultaneously experience a stronger and deeper sense of your own authentic self. As religion scholar Jeff Kripal explained to us, this movement from "I" to "we" is typically—and paradoxically—accompanied by a corresponding movement from "we" to "me" (2006). The more you feel your connection to others, the more you are able to be authentic and appreciate your unique role in each set of circumstances.

We heard this expressed in many ways. One survey respondent noted that individuals experiencing transformation "at once realize that they are a heart connected to many hearts" (Vieten, Cohen, and Schlitz 2008). As another respondent described it, "we are strengthened and deepened when our personal story merges into the larger story." It is clear that transformation doesn't happen in a vacuum. Research participants told us things like, "One of my greatest awakenings was discovering that *my* transformation isn't really *mine* at all, but has more to do with our collective transformation." Gangaji, one of the teachers representing a non-dual tradition, brought this home when she told us:

> *What facilitates the integration of a transformative experience is to recognize that it isn't happening to you. What hinders the integration are the thoughts, "This is my transformation, this is me getting enlightened." In the depths of being, no one gets enlightened. No one transforms. A transformative experience is simply the recognition of what is inherent, meaning "always here" or natural to everyone—the peace of being. If you simply inquire, if you turn your attention to the word "I"—"I" am doing this, "I" am suffering, "I" am happy—you will see there is nothing there. In self-inquiry there is a natural insight, a kind of natural wisdom, inherent to the intelligence of every being. Just stop. Just be still. Turn your attention to who has stopped, who is still, who am I really? (2002)*

Many of the teachers we interviewed expressed this theme in a number of different ways. Not everyone articulated such a clear "no-self" orientation. But most agreed that the transformation we're talking about isn't just "my" or "your" transformation, it is "our" transformation. Gangaji continued:

> By accepting the invitation to stop, what you are really stopping in that moment is your individual concern, and this opens the doorway to discovering the limitless presence of yourself as everything, as all being. When you make a prayer that "all beings be awakened" or "all beings be happy," you are speaking of yourself beyond the individual, yet not excluding the individual. You are including all beings, which to me is the whole point. Otherwise, it is just another narcissistic exercise in feeling good. The prayer is about all being—may all being awaken to itself; may all being know itself, in truth, as all being. (2002)

From many of our teachers' descriptions it's clear that what you perceive as the personal and separate "I" becomes less central as consciousness transforms. Through direct experiences of interconnection you move away from being the only protagonist of every story and to a new sense of belonging. This may come as a simple realization—"Hey, we're all in this together and everyone is pretty much doing their best!"—that leads to a feeling of camaraderie. Or it can be a sensation of literally lacking all separation from others, a perception of your self as no longer a separate being. Or it can be experienced as an ability to see beyond normal perceptions to the Christ light, Buddha nature, Allah, true self, or divine spark that exists in all beings and all of creation.

A DIFFERENT KIND OF LOVE

Our research suggests that the movement from "I" to "we" leads to love. But not just any love—a different kind of love, one that extends out from yourself to your larger community and beyond. And it is in this love, as so many of our research and survey participants told us, that we can rest with deep contentment and clear purpose and begin to truly live deeply. As Vladimir Solovyov, the Russian philosopher of love, states:

> The meaning and worth of love, as a feeling, is that it really forces us, with all our being, to acknowledge for another the same absolute central significance which, because of the power of our egoism, we are conscious of only in our own selves. Love is important not as one of our feelings, but as the transfer of all our interest in life from ourselves to another, as the shifting of the very center of our personal lives. (1894, 43)

As we mentioned, paradoxically, at the same time that people feel connected to a broader humanity, they also typically experience an enhanced appreciation for their own unique gifts and talents. As part of a larger whole you may begin to understand your own significance as an individual—and feel moved to use your individual talents, skills, and gifts to benefit the whole. Making this internal shift begins by taking steps, however tentative, to move yourself out of center stage and into the river of shared identity. When you see yourself as a member of a transforming community rather than as a single individual swimming upstream, you'll worry less about threats to your sense of self—and find yourself naturally being more kind and compassionate to both yourself and others.

As we saw in chapter 2, transpersonal experiences can be profoundly transformative at a core level. As people experience an expanded view of reality and their place in it, they're often (though not always) led to greater intimacy and interrelatedness with the people in their lives, and even strangers. One survey respondent told us that as a result of her transformative experiences she can now make eye contact with strangers and speak from a place of openness and authenticity with everyone with whom she interacts throughout the day, from the person in the tollbooth to her husband. Another survey respondent said, "This practice has opened my heart so I can deal with people—any people" (Vieten, Cohen, and Schlitz 2008). Psychologist Frances Vaughan similarly affirmed that "the more we know each other, the more we love each other. This is the common ground of our humanity" (2002).

For current IONS president, James O'Dea, formerly of Amnesty International, "The transformative path is not a series of steps… The path is the path of love" (2003). He continued:

> I think in my own life the transformational themes revolve around love, essence, and beauty… In my experience, the path of service points towards beauty, it points towards the manifest world, the possibility that the purpose of existence is for us to express some form of beauty and love amongst each other and on planet Earth.

Transpersonal experiences result in a sense of interconnectedness that breaks down the walls between us and others. Drawing from a rich appreciation for different spiritual and religious traditions, Protestant reverend David Parks-Ramage described his understanding of what's revealed through transformative experiences:

> Transformation is openheartedness, intimacy. That's a Zen piece and a Christian piece coming together. Transformation is "Holy God, Lord of love and majesty, the whole universe is filled with your glory." This is a paraphrase from Isaiah in which he tells us that the whole universe is filled with God's glory—it's here as we're sitting in this room, it's in the pew, it's in the window, it's in the light, everything is filled with the glory of God. We don't always see that.
>
> As we grow more intimate with things as they are, as we grow more intimate with the people around us, we begin to notice the glory of God in each one. It's the namaste: the God in me greets the God in you.
>
> In my own life, the one place that this was most there for me was when my daughter was born and I looked into her newborn eyes—she had big brown eyes—and I could see straight through into the universe. There was nothing there; all that was there was love, just love.
>
> As we become more openhearted with one another—and as we see the image of God and the love that is present there in each other—we find the boundaries between us are just a little more diffuse. And it's not just

between us, it's between the trees and the grass and all of it. And then I guess
your consciousness has truly been transformed, hasn't it? (2006)

This dissolution of the boundaries between you and others—a loved
one, a teacher, or even someone perceived as an adversary—boundaries that
some traditions say are illusory, is a hallmark of many transformative experiences. Zenkei Blanche Hartman told us the story of the most transformative moment in her life. It took place during a riot in 1968, and ultimately
led Hartman to become a monk in the Zen tradition of Suzuki Roshi:

During the Vietnam War, I was a political activist. I fought for peace. There
was some contradiction: There wasn't any peace in me. I hated the people
who disagreed with me. That was kind of a war within myself. In 1968,
I was just beginning to look at the way in which I was vigorously clinging
to my opinions about things and denigrating others who had different
opinions, when there was a strike at San Francisco State University…

   The police came with their masks and clubs, started poking people.
And without thinking, I ducked under the hands of people to get between
the police and students. I met this riot squad policeman face-to-face with
his mask on and everything. He was close enough to touch. I met this
policeman's eyes straight on, and I had this overwhelming experience of
identification, of shared identity.

   This was the most transformative moment of my life—having this
experience of shared identity with the riot squad policeman. It was a gift.
Nothing had prepared me for it. I didn't have any conceptual basis for
understanding it. The total experience was real and incontrovertible.

   My life as a political activist ended with that encounter, because there
was no longer anything to fight against. The way I described it to my friends
was the policeman was trying to protect what he thought was right and good
from all of the other people who were trying to destroy it—and I was doing
the same thing.

   Since I had no basis for understanding the experience of shared
identity with someone whom I had considered completely "other" (i.e., the

riot squad policeman), and because the experience had been so real and so
powerful, I began to search for someone who would understand it. How
could a riot squad policeman and I be identical? In my search, I met Suzuki
Roshi. The way he looked at me, I knew he understood. That's how I got
here. (2003)

Like Hartman, respondents from almost every tradition told us that their transpersonal experiences naturally led to less conflict with others. Many teachers also spoke of increased sensitivity to the suffering of others. This sensitivity takes different forms, including compassionate love, empathy, kindness, and a greater orientation toward helping those in need.

Compassionate Love

Experiences of oneness and interconnection play a part in cultivating a particular kind of love—one that isn't limited to close friends and relatives, but includes those who are different from you, even those you've never met! For many of the people in our studies, this sense of belonging and connection was felt in every situation and for people from every walk of life.

Most religious and spiritual traditions—and most modern transformative practice movements, too—include prescriptions for living that involve the cultivation of compassion and altruism. In Sikh- and Hindu-derived traditions, the Sanskrit *seva* refers to being of selfless service to others. In Christian and other Western spiritual traditions, the Greek word *agape* (in Latin, *caritas*) refers to the human manifestation of God's pure love, or the intentional and unconditional love for others—including your enemies. In Buddhist traditions, *metta* in Pali and *maitri* in Sanskrit are both used to refer to the quality and practice of unconditional and unattached loving-kindness, or the strong intention for the happiness of all beings. In Tibetan Buddhist practice, *tonglen* refers to the practice of taking in suffering and giving out love or blessings. As you can see, methods for cultivating compassionate love abound.

Stephen Post, bioethicist and founder of the Institute for Unlimited Love at Case Western Reserve, points out in his book *Unlimited Love* (2003) that you can find rough equivalents of the ideal of divine love across the major spiritual and religious traditions. His analysis points to the importance of transpersonal experiences. He writes, "It may be that the most exemplary altruism is often associated with the agent's personal experience of the utter enormity of the Transcendent, including a sense of overwhelming awe. Overawed, the deeply humbled self is transformed through something like an ego-death to a new self of profound humility, empathy, and regard for all human and other life" (63). Likewise, scholar Gregory Fricchione notes that: "Religious experience … of awe and oneness and heightened perception of the spiritual may be among the most powerful motivators of extraordinary love" (2002, 31). Of course, not all transformative experiences take religious form, but they do seem to lead to similar territories.

The Altruistic Perspective

Kristin R. Monroe, sociologist and author of *The Heart of Altruism: Perceptions of a Common Humanity* (1996), studies the motivations of those who devote their lives to serving others with no reward to themselves. Monroe proposes that the psychological explanation for altruism like this is having an *altruistic perspective*. In other words, in situations where other people might see a stranger, these individuals see a fellow human being. Her research participants "saw themselves as strongly linked to others through a shared humanity" (2002, 109), and this perspective naturally led to spontaneous altruistic acts. Her participants reported, moreover, a sense of having *no choice* but to react altruistically. Monroe suggests these individuals act from this connected sense of self rather than religious obligation.

Similarly, our respondents saw compassion and altruism as naturally growing from their new sense of self in relation to others. This new sense of self—which results from these transpersonal experiences of interconnection, interdependence, and recognition of the inherent sacredness or divinity in all things—is typically both expansive and inclusive.

What motivates some people to engage in altruism but not others? Psychologist Daniel Batson at the University of Kansas has researched altruistic behavior for decades (1991, 2002). In particular, he has studied the effects of religion and spirituality on the development of empathy and altruism. His research suggests that differences in our capacity for empathy are related to four key factors: First is whether or not you've personally experienced the same situation as the individual who is in pain. Second is your perception of the *proximity* of the situation, or how close to home the situation feels. Third is your perception of your relationship to the person whose welfare is in question. Finally, the fourth factor is your dispositional tendency toward feeling emotion, and empathy in particular (1991, 2002).

Although having a transpersonal experience doesn't place you in the same situations as those experienced by the individuals in pain you may encounter, developing a worldview of interconnectedness or shared divinity can bring the situation closer to home. Having an enlarged worldview can make you feel a kinship with the person in need, despite your differences. Moreover, with continuing practice, your overall tendency toward compassion and empathy appear to increase.

Love with Teeth

Many of our respondents told us that as you develop a more transpersonal worldview, you become more sensitive to the awe, beauty, and wonder of the world. At the same time, however, you also become more sensitive to suffering and injustice. As your sense of connection to the suffering of others increases, it can be very difficult to attend to that suffering without being overwhelmed. It can be tough not to feel immobilized and powerless to act. Alternatively, you can fall into a sort of pity or charity—doing *for* others rather than helping them to do for themselves—that in the end may not be the wisest form of action.

Starhawk, a leader in the pagan tradition, spoke eloquently to us of the challenge of being both supportive and empowering at the same time:

> *You know, we have real values—taking care of people who are depressed,*
> *healing, relieving suffering—but these can sometimes lead to … a bias*
> *toward the victim. All someone has to do is define themselves as a victim and*
> *people will flood them with attention. But that isn't always the most effective*
> *thing to do for healing—or the most effective thing to do for building a*

community of real empowerment. Learning how to empower people to
create and do and take leadership, to take risks and face obstacles, is a real
challenge. [It's important to] empower strength, not just empower people
to complain. (2006)

Psychologist Stanley Krippner described this kind of compassion as "love with teeth" (2002). This is active compassion—a kind of love that calls you to act in ways that help remedy suffering, in all its various forms. Although you may still feel distressed by the suffering you encounter, you also feel the desire and intention to ease this suffering. For Krippner, active compassion requires "a love that actually gives people something to eat, something to wear, a place to live, self-esteem, self-empowerment" (2002). Similarly, researchers Jocelyn Sze and Margaret Kemeny define compassion as "a state *beyond* sadness or sympathy, where one is not only feeling sorrow or concern for the suffering of another but, more critically, feels energized and enabled to combat that suffering" (2004, 14).

Again, this is why consistent engagement in some form of community, daily mind/body practice, silence, solitude, and renewal is often built into transformative traditions and can be built into your transformative journey. Engaging in transformative practices such as regular prayer, meditation, movement, ritual, consulting with a trusted guide, and continuing study—not to mention gardening, a walk in nature, or a deep conversation with a trusted friend—can provide you with the internal skills necessary to regulate the distress that can accompany increasing awareness. A daily mind/body practice, a supportive community, and a felt connection to a deeper wellspring of shared consciousness can all help keep you from being overwhelmed and immobilized by your personal distress, or falling into the easier stance of pity; they can also help teach you how to manifest compassion in action.

Prosocial Behavior

As you become more capable of handling the distress of another's suffering, you also become more able to take action. Developmental psychologist Nancy Eisenberg has studied the roots of *prosocial behavior*—

voluntary actions intended to help another—for more than twenty-five years. Eisenberg's research explores the role of emotion regulation in social behavior as well as the motives that lie behind empathy and helping behaviors. Through careful assessment of facial expressions and autonomic monitoring of individuals exposed to compelling images of others in distress (for example, a child trapped in her room during a house fire), Eisenberg has attempted to untangle the fine lines between distress, sympathy, empathy, and altruistic motivations. Her findings (2002) suggest that the better you're able to regulate your own personal distress, the more capable you are of true empathy and altruism.

Let's explore this a bit further. When you encounter the suffering of another, you may be so personally disturbed by it that your primary motive for taking action is to ease *your own* distress. Although this may stimulate helping behavior, because this behavior is engaged in order to remove the problem and thereby alleviate your own distress, it may not be as helpful as it could be. You can become quite attached to the outcome, because you've got a personal stake in it.

Another common way to relieve this personal distress is to ignore or block out the suffering—a response that we're all likely to have either experienced at one point or another or seen in others. Encounters with suffering can paralyze you—particularly when the suffering seems so out of your control that you feel helpless to do anything about it.

In a somewhat paradoxical way, it's actually through your ability to fully experience—and yet also contain and regulate—the distress you feel on encountering the suffering of another that allows you the freedom to help. Indeed, Eisenberg's work has shown that personal distress leads to low levels of helping, whereas sympathetic reactions—which may include non-overwhelming emotion *combined* with cognitive concern—lead to altruistic behavior.

Expanding Your Tribe

Many studies point to the fact that, somewhat contrary to popular belief, we're just as hardwired for compassion and altruism as we are for survival of the fittest, fight or flight, or self-interest (Post et al. 2002; Fehr and

Fischbacher 2003; Lewis, Amini, and Lannon 2000). We clearly possess inherent drives toward cooperation and affiliation that go beyond simple self-interest (doing things because they will benefit you), or even enlightened self-interest (doing things that are good for others because you know doing good for others will benefit you as well).

This phenomenon of loving those outside our tribe is just beginning to be explored by scientists. By this point in the book, you won't be surprised to learn that transformative practice traditions have long incorporated many of the factors that science is just now starting to uncover—factors that nurture compassion, not only for those we love, but even for those whom we perceive to be different from us.

Researchers Phil Shaver at the University of California, Davis, and Mario Mikulincer in Israel study how we relate to people we know and love as opposed to strangers we perceive as outside our kinship circle (Mikulincer and Shaver 2005). Their work is based in *attachment theory*. Developed primarily by psychiatrist John Bowlby, attachment theory proposes that our relationships with the primary caregivers of our early life determine our *attachment style*, or pattern of relating to ourselves and others—a pattern that is carried into our adulthood (1988). Empirical research on attachment theory by Mary Ainsworth and colleagues (1978) and Mary Main (1996) found, moreover, that attachment styles are often transmitted intergenerationally, with a mother's attachment style predicting the attachment style of her child.

Typically, someone with attachment difficulties due to faulty attunement or lack of responsiveness from their caregivers will show patterns of insecurity, avoidance, or anxiety in their relationships later in life. Mikulincer and Shaver's recent research (2005) has revealed that individuals with chronic attachment insecurity score lower on measures of many of the self-transcendent values—such as love, compassion, and generosity—that we've described in this book. They're more likely to feel threatened by out-group members (people who seem different) and more likely to react to them with hostility. On the other hand, individuals with secure attachment styles tend to show greater kindness and openness to other people.

Even if your attachment pattern is insecure or anxious, your pattern isn't necessarily set in stone. As we're learning, consciousness is malleable and transformation is always possible. When security of attachment is manipulated in the laboratory—for example, by asking someone to do something as simple as think of a caring loved one, or even just subliminally (outside of conscious awareness) exposing an individual to the name of a caring loved one—reactions to others, even out-group members, are significantly more positive. Being reminded of a safe and loving figure was found to actually increase compassion, even toward strangers (Mikulincer et al. 2005). Here again, we see that it is often your perspective rather than the situation at hand that determines your thoughts, feelings, and behavior.

Shaver and Mikulincer hypothesize that priming a person's consciousness with the memory of a caring and safe person temporarily activates the person's *secure base schema*, or their thoughts and feelings of being comforted, safe, and reassured. It also increases their scores on the self-transcendent values mentioned earlier, in this case benevolence and *universalism* (a measure of the values of fairness and egalitarianism). This kind of research could go a long way toward helping us understand the internal and external conditions needed to foster an altruistic and compassionate love that transcends kinship circles. Many elements of transformative practice may promote the development of a more secure adult attachment style. For many, a congregation, synagogue, *sangha*, or other transformative practice community is a secure base. For some, a guru becomes a secure attachment figure. For others, God or a sense of an unchanging ground of being or universal energy is a secure starting point from which to explore the world.

SUMMARY

Across our focus groups, interviews, and survey studies, we've repeatedly heard that profound transpersonal experiences of oneness or interconnection can lead to significant shifts in your perspective. As a result, your ideas about yourself, your place in the universe, and your relationship to others may change. Transformative practices can help you integrate those changes into your everyday life and way of being.

In this chapter, we focused on how these experiences and practices can lead you to deep and long-lasting changes, moving you into transpersonal stages of development. Rather than simply having occasional experiences of connection, you begin to hold a permanent worldview that assumes interconnections between yourself, others, and the world itself. For many people, this triggers a natural emergence of compassion and altruism. As Trappist monk Thomas Merton said, "The whole idea of compassion is based on a keen awareness of the interdependence of all these living beings, which are all part of one another, and all involved in one another" (Fox 1983, 25). Think of this as coming home to yourself and your own true nature. As Albert Einstein described:

> A human being is a part of a whole, called by us "universe," a part limited in time and space. He experiences himself, his thoughts and feelings as something separated from the rest ... a kind of optical delusion of his consciousness. This delusion is a kind of prison for us, restricting us to our personal desires and to affection for a few persons nearest to us. Our task must be to free ourselves from this prison by widening our circle of compassion to embrace all living creatures and the whole of nature in its beauty. (1977, 60)

In the next chapter, we'll explore this idea more fully as we consider another theme that emerged from our research: in the course of positive consciousness transformation, life becomes filled with meaning and everything becomes sacred, from the soil to our souls.

For now, take a few moments to consider the art and practice of compassion.

Experiencing Transformation: Cultivating Compassion

In this exercise, we draw on the tonglen method, a compassion practice that originated in Tibetan Buddhism but is now practiced all over the world. Tonglen aims to awaken the compassion that is inherent in all of us, no matter how isolated or detached we might seem to be. It's a natural inclination to avoid that which is painful or unpleasant—to turn aside and say, "Not me," or "Not now." Tonglen can help us see from a new perspective, one where suffering and joy aren't in opposition, but are rather parts of a single whole. From the Tibetan Buddhist perspective, disease and suffering can be transformed if experienced from a sacred place inside yourself.

Tonglen Instructions

In order to have compassion for others, you must have compassion for yourself. So we begin with our own pain, both in body and in mind:

Place yourself in a comfortable position. Imagine something that causes you suffering. Let each in-breath draw this something to the center of your chest. Continue breathing with deep, gentle breaths. Feel the discomfort in the area of your heart. Do not withdraw from it or push it away. Hold it gently. As you cease your struggle against the knots of suffering, notice that they begin to lose their hard edges, that the pain begins to dissolve. Feel compassion for yourself, knowing that every human being deserves acceptance, forgiveness, and love.

Imagine a feeling of great peace flowing through your body, a soft golden light. With ease and endless compassion this light shines into the darkest parts of yourself, touching even the harshest stones or pebbles you hide inside. Feel these stones begin to dissolve in the warmth of the light. Just as the breath is warmed by your body, so are these old sorrows warmed by your heart. With their inner beauty now revealed, let them flow out with the breath, healed and whole, a gift to the world.

This compassionate meditation can be extended to others: First, see yourself as tapping into a great energy or essence not limited to your personal self. Now, imagine someone who is in pain or is ill. Visualize them or otherwise feel their presence using whatever senses work best for you. Imagine their suffering as a heaviness, a thick, tangible darkness. With calm, clear compassionate intent breathe this darkness in.

Continue to breathe calmly and slowly. Begin to bring this suffering into your heart. This darkness cannot hurt you, it's here, at your request, to be transformed. Allow the personal and the universal energy of compassion to fill the chamber of your heart with a soft yet powerful light.

Next, extend this practice to all who suffer and cry out for aid or comfort. Breathe in the sorrows of the entire world and then breathe out— just a single breath, one simple loving breath. And if one loving breath seems too little in the face of the sorrows of the world, remember that you contain within yourself the same essential beingness, the same essence that powers suns and spins planets. It is enough.

When you're ready, return your attention to yourself and your breath. Slowly allow yourself to become aware of the space around you—the temperature of the air, the sounds around you, the presence of the clothes on your body. When you're ready, open your eyes. Spend some time journaling about what you experienced.

CHAPTER EIGHT:

Everything Is Sacred

This integral transformation, the transformation of everything, is
the next great human frontier! St. Paul said, "There are treasures
in heaven. Things the eye hath not seen nor the ear has not heard."
These ecstasies are beyond our present ability to comprehend. Yet, we
get little glimmers. I say: it's peeking up everywhere!
—MICHAEL MURPHY (2002)

Seeing the patterns that connect is a part of the transformative process. For pagan priestess Starhawk, this happened as her life and practice fused. Initially, her practice was all about meditation, trance, and a focus on internal imagery that happened with her eyes closed. Over time, this began to shift. She found herself sitting more purposefully in nature, with her eyes open, observing the world around her. In this process, she gained a deeper understanding of the sacred connections inherent in all of life. "I try to still the inner dialogue and the internal imagery so I can actually listen to the birds and notice and be present in my natural surroundings," she explains.

It's been a very profound transformative shift in understanding,
appreciating, and linking with all the other beings on the planet and the
natural world. If you follow a practice of spending time in nature, sitting,
listening and opening, then over time you begin to notice and see and hear
and sense more. You become aware of patterns. For example, the pattern
of sound changes throughout the day and throughout the year and by the
weather. You start to receive information through those patterns. The world
really comes alive and starts speaking to you. (2006)

Over and over again, across traditions and individual stories of transformation, respondents spoke of moving from catching occasional glimpses of the divine, the numinous, or the transpersonal to more constantly perceiving the underlying sacredness of all things. Respondents described a shift from experiencing moments of epiphany or transcendence to realizing that what they had been seeking was already there, and always had been. All the great metaphors of transformation—the caterpillar becoming the butterfly, darkness shifting to light, deep sleep ending in new awakening—speak to this clearly. Embedded in all of these is the idea that the great change we call transformation isn't really a change at all, but an unveiling, a reorganization, a deepening into who you are and what already is. This is why transformation is often called *integral*: it is embedded in—and touches—every aspect of your life.

Almost invariably, the teachers we interviewed told us that what you're seeking you already implicitly are. What you're longing for is immanent in the world around you, simply awaiting recognition. Herein lies a beautiful paradox: transformation changes everything and it changes nothing.

In this chapter we'll discuss this simple but profound turning of attention—and the paradigm-shifting aha! moment that it brings—as we consider the possibility that *everything is sacred*. We'll discuss, too, the reports of many who have gone through the transformative process—reports of being not only able to see glimmers of numinosity shining through even the most mundane of circumstances, but to also experience themselves as being a part of that light, part of the web of life all around them. And finally, we'll explore the deep connection with the natural world this experience of everything as sacred is linked to—and the deep commitment many of our respondents described to the protection and preservation of the Earth for the future generations of all species.

A LIGHT AND LOVE THAT FILL THE WORLD

What exactly do we mean by everything being "sacred"? Many teachers described the experience of sacredness as recognizing that the world is literally filled with light, grace, the presence of the divine, God, or the mystery of being—and that you are held in this light and love all the time, whether you know it or not. Overall, the teachers we spoke with agreed that the greatest, most extraordinary human transformations—regardless of age, culture, tradition, or land of origin—come from being receptive to the splendor of every day in its most simple, phenomenal presence.

Gay Luce, founder of the Nine Gates Mystery School, told us that her transformation entailed seeing and feeling that the basic substance of the universe "looks like light and feels like love" (2002). Psychiatrist Gerald Jampolsky noted, "If we change our concept of God to one of energy … no one is apart … either I can walk into this light and love and become a part of it, or I can analyze it" (2002). Lakota elder and holy man Gilbert Walking Bull described the sacredness of all things with matter-of-fact clarity. He spoke to us of how "Grandfather" or "the Great Spirit" gives human beings the ability to see and honor the sacred energy inherent in all of creation. In his words:

> *Everything is sacred. Our eyes are given to us by the Great Spirit to see creation. The Great Spirit said the Earth is burning, it is full of an energy that glows. Science knows this now. The Lakota have always known this. Grandfather gave powers to mankind. When you respect everything he created, that's sacred love. The knowledge of who we are gives us the responsibility to walk in a sacred manner upon the Earth.*
>
> *Being out of balance comes from living in a society that values gold, money, oil, nuclear power above all other sacred things. Great Spirit says*

there will come a time they will stop this exploitation and abuse. When you
live the sacred principles, the Great Spirit may come down and touch you,
use you to heal others. It is up to us to stay in balance. (2006)

For Gilbert Walking Bull, recognizing that everything is sacred comes with the responsibility to live in balance with nature. At the same time, recognizing that everything is sacred doesn't mean that you suddenly inhabit a realm of magic and mystery, far removed from everyday life. Quite the contrary! As psychologist Jon Kabat-Zinn, a pioneer in the integration of mindfulness meditation into mainstream medicine, reminded us:

[We are here to] *actually see what's here to be seen. Hear what's here to be*
heard. Taste what's here to be tasted. Smell what's here to be smelled. Touch
what's here to be touched. And know what's here to be known—which is
a classical formulation by the Buddha himself about what mindfulness is
actually about. There's no great mystery to it. There's nothing magical or
mysterious or airy-fairy or even spiritual about it in the way that people
usually use the word "spiritual"—except everything. (2004)

Many of our respondents pointed out that transformative practice is simply a way of staying awake and aware. And when we are awake and aware, we can attune to the divine presence in all things. Some described encountering the sacredness of life as having veils lifted to reveal what was always underneath and at the center of things.

Many described the transformative shift as moving from searching to finding, from trying to know through the intellect to directly knowing through the heart. Others described it as a merging of what's inside and outside of you that makes boundaries that were once opaque transparent. We were told that when you realize who you are most deeply, this new awareness is reflected in everyone and everything. An enormously intimate feeling of love for creation is released; this can change every detail of your life. When you experience the sacredness of everything, this world we share becomes worthy of being treated with reverence—and all of life becomes something to cherish and preserve.

NO SEPARATION

Our research participants not only described a growing ability to perceive this sacredness in everyday life, they also told us that they felt a part of this sacredness. Adyashanti, a teacher in the non-dual tradition, shared with us his favorite quote from the twentieth-century Indian saint Nisargadatta Maharaj: "When I see that I'm everything, that's love" (2004b). Catholic priest Father Francis Tiso told us that "the goal of transformation is living in continuous, conscious, loving union with God, and every moment is a revelation of divine love" (2002).

As you add more depth to your life, what you perceive as inside and outside of you merges. Boundaries between you, others, animals, nature, and the world now become permeable. In fact, as we saw in chapter 7, holding a view of interconnectedness can become a cornerstone of your practice and way of being in the world. Vietnamese Buddhist monk and champion of engaged Buddhism Thich Nhat Hanh writes of perceiving *interbeing*—multidimensional relationships literally inherent in every-thing, so that a piece of paper is also the tree it came from; the soil, water, and sun that made the tree; and the humans that transformed the tree into paper. He noted, "The feeling of respect for all species will help us recognize the noblest nature in ourselves" (1999, 85).

Similarly, Ram Dass spoke to us of a person's inner and outer reali-ties being one and the same. He took this idea of "no separation" one step further, describing how once a person finds inner peace, that person will also be able to discover and create peace in the outer world. As he told us, "You better go inside and find your peace of mind. That's the best thing you can do for all of us. That's the edge where the inner world and outer world come together" (2003). Likewise, dancer Anna Halprin noted:

> It's not enough for me, anymore, to just deal with the inner landscape,
> my so-called "inner consciousness," because that is so affected by the outer
> landscape. I have spent thirty years exploring the natural environment, and,
> simultaneously, exploring community. And the two, for me, go together in
> many ways because, in both instances, both community and nature take me
> to a place that's much bigger than I am alone… (2002)

This felt experience of inner and outer interconnectedness is deeply subjective. However, a growing body of theory and evidence from physics, psychology, and biology is uncovering physical manifestations of interconnectedness that can be predicted and observed scientifically.

Dean Radin has spent more than twenty years studying remarkable yet quite common phenomena such as psychic ability, precognition, and what Einstein called "spooky action at a distance" (Einstein, Podolsky, and Rosen 1935). Radin's theory of what underlies these phenomena is described in *Entangled Minds: Extrasensory Experiences in a Quantum Reality* (2006). In this book Radin writes, "The idea of the universe as an interconnected whole is not new; for millennia it's been one of the core assumptions of Eastern philosophies. What is new is that Western science is slowly beginning to realize that some elements of that ancient lore might be correct" (3). The rapprochement between science and spirituality grows ever stronger if studied within this light.

WAKING UP

Some of the most intensely sweet moments of our focus groups—and the 150 interview hours we spent with our many teachers—were when individuals spoke, sometimes with tears in their eyes, of the feelings of enormous tenderness that arose from their own transformative experiences. Protestant reverend David Parks-Ramage told us:

> [Transformative practice] *helps us begin to tell the story of our life… As we grow more intimate with things as they are, we begin to notice the glory of God in each one. Meditation just makes it easier to remember what God, your self, and all of life are about. Love the Lord your God, your heart, mind, and soul and your neighbor as yourself. It's all right there, there's nothing else really. That's why we are here. That's why we do this practice. Christian, Buddhist, Hindu, Muslim, or whatever, that's why people gather to worship and practice—the abundant life wants to be known! It's the way we need to live together, to weave a tapestry of life that allows the universe to express itself.*

183

Huston Smith told me that we are all enlightened, we just don't necessarily know it. There's nothing mysterious that you are going to give me or that I'm going to give anyone else. It's already all there and it's all been given and we've worked all our lives not to see it but that's how human beings have to do it. It's in the flowers, in the people, in the carpet, in the chair. It's everywhere. (2006)

As Parks-Ramage—and many other participants—told us, when you finally encounter the divinity, sacredness, numinosity (or whatever word works for you) you've been seeking, it's almost as though you realize that it has been here all along, just waiting to be noticed. Shaykh Yassir Chadly shared with us a similar sentiment very succinctly: "God is looking for us like we are looking for God" (2006). Michael Murphy agreed, cheerfully stating, "My metaphysical position is that the divine is latent in all things … and God is waking up!" (2002). And Adyashanti told us, "The awakening state is very ordinary. It is falling in love with the ordinary. It doesn't need to be special. The ordinary is the divine" (2004b). Spiritual pundits through the ages have referred to this irony as "the great cosmic joke."

Andriette Earl, reverend of the East Bay Church of Religious Science, spoke to us of how her own experience had affirmed this truth for her:

You know, I awaken in the mornings with the epiphany of divine knowing and I know I've come home to myself. In these times, I'm letting more light in and I have a greater awareness of who I am and what is possible. To see the presence of God in every situation, regardless of how it feels—this, for me, is to discern God in everything. (2006)

It can be easy to see the sacred spark in all things when we encounter beauty that is aesthetically pleasing—the grandeur of a sunset, the glow in a child's eyes, reflections of light on the water. It can be more difficult when circumstances are not so pleasing, or even horrible. However, our research respondents told us that transformative life events, whether pleasant or distressing, all have the capacity to reveal the sacred. IONS president James O'Dea spoke to us of people he'd met through his previous work at

Amnesty International, individuals who'd been tortured, yet still managed to maintain their awareness of the sacred beauty that infuses the world.

> *What depths of the human spirit are revealed in these places of darkness!*
> *And that seems to suggest that the beauty is what lasts. And somehow, even*
> *in the grossest of places, beauty reveals itself to humanity, and if we can*
> *attune ourselves to that beauty, we may find our way through.* (2003)

The teachers we interviewed reported that when we attune ourselves to the sacred presence—the beauty that resides both within the human and in the world—we can stay awake in even the most sorrowful of places.

Sue Miller, one of the master teachers of Harry Palmer's Avatar course, spoke to us about the importance of choosing to wake up. Avatar is an experiential training program based on the viewpoint that belief precedes experience, so that our beliefs knowingly or unknowingly act as a filter for how we perceive life. Miller said:

> *I love the movie* The Matrix. *You can take the red pill or the blue pill. You*
> *have this choice. But when you choose, you choose it forever. People find some*
> *way to start to awaken to some higher consciousness. There is that moment*
> *of starting to wake up and start questioning anything, looking at some*
> *bigger picture.*
>
> *The ability to take in other viewpoints allows people to appreciate*
> *and have compassion for the differences. Every person who wakes up*
> *benefits, like the hundredth monkey effect. My belief is there's some tipping*
> *point, and as much as it wanders, it is tipping towards a more enlightened,*
> *more aware world. To me the compelling thing is that somehow people*
> *engage with the tools. It doesn't matter if it's Avatar, or another practice,*
> *they go back out into the world more tolerant of divergent viewpoints and*
> *more able to integrate belief systems. They can contribute in some way*
> *to making this world a saner, more peaceful place. Harry [Palmer], the*
> *innovator of Avatar, said, "Love is the willingness to create the space in*
> *which something is allowed to change." (2002)*

As we hear from Miller, shifting our perspective is a choice we can make each and every moment. No matter whether you relate to a spiritual path or one more secular, learning to appreciate the complex nature of different cultures and traditions is a vital skill—one that can open you to the richness of life in all its various forms.

PRACTICE AS A PORTAL TO THE SACRED

Transformative practices have many purposes. So far we've focused primarily on the role of practice in training our minds and our bodies (much like going to a transformative gym), healing old wounds, shedding false skins, cultivating intention and attention, promoting insight, and expanding our capacities. However, the heart of transformative practices—whether ceremonies, rituals, contemplative reflections, altered state inductions, or martial arts—is their ability to bring you into direct contact with the numinous, to wake you up to the sanctity of life. Transformative practices have evolved over millennia (and are still evolving) into precise methods of opening you to the abundant, ever-present, and surprisingly accessible deep meaning that's present in every moment of every day. In this way, as we've said, transformative practice can offer much more than you may have initially bargained for!

For Episcopal priest Lauren Artress, the ancient symbol of the labyrinth is a portal to the sacred. She quoted William Blake to us—"To the imagination, the sacred is self-evident"—and then continued:

> The self-evidence of sacredness to the imagination is something we want to nurture. The labyrinth is a great place to do this because it's a huge symbol. It illuminates the mystery… Another way of describing the experience is that the veil is very thin in the labyrinth—people can see between the worlds where the two worlds meet.
>
> You don't have to be Christian to walk the labyrinth. And actually, in the broad sense, it's an interreligious or interfaith tool, open for everybody. It is used in the Christian tradition as a path—the pilgrimage path to the

New Jerusalem—which the center is called. It became a substitute for the pilgrimage to Jerusalem when the crusades made it dangerous to travel.

Within the labyrinth, because it does have sacred measurement … and … cosmic rhythms, the consciousness is truly transformed. People often get a flash of seeing that opens divine imagination and gives clear, embodied insight. We are starved for sacred beauty, rhythm, and pattern. And the fact that we are starved for beauty sets us up for transformation. When we find beauty and rhythm and pattern and color, we're just so hungry that our consciousness is transformed. (2003)

At the end of the day, many teachers asserted that transformation boils down to embodying virtues, living a good life, and knowing what you care about and then caring for it. Or, as Gilbert Walking Bull told us, to becoming a sacred human being and living a sacred life (2006). For this we have practice to help us. For example, Burmese Buddhist vipassana teacher and professor Rina Sircar told us, "My practice teaches me who am I, what am I, and where am I going" (2003). Johrei healers Lawrence Ammar and Paulo Santos, who practice the Japanese art of intentional hands-on energy healing, told us, "Johrei isn't just a healing technique, it's a means of raising consciousness from self-centeredness to love for others" (2003).

LIVING ECOLOGY FROM THE INSIDE OUT

When we see the sacredness of all life, we naturally want to care for it. It appears that you can't experience a connection to all things or become aware of the inherent sacredness of all things without automatically having your attention drawn to the experiences of the broader world—not only the suffering of other humans, but that of all beings. The current deficit of this awareness is obvious in the brewing ecological crisis. Native American elder and healer Charlie Red Hawk Thom and medicine woman Tela Star Hawk Lake expressed their concern about the endangerment of their people and the Earth—and the need for people to engage in ancient healing practices to restore the "sacred hoop" of creation. Tela said:

> *From the beginning of time all cultures had ceremonies. Our ceremonies still*
> *exist just as they always have; we never changed them. That's why Charlie,*
> *as medicine man for the Karuk, Kiowa, and Hoopa tribes, has so many*
> *people coming to him looking for balance. They're looking because they have*
> *that same philosophy of becoming one with the Earth, and it brings them*
> *back to that circle we all began. Our people still hold that circle; we form the*
> *sacred hoop, as we call it.* (2006)

For many of our respondents, the wholehearted embrace of the realization that everything is sacred led to the unavoidable conclusion that the sustainability of our lives and the lives of those we love dearly is inextricably intertwined with the sustainability of *all* lives, of *all* life.

Our research shows that through the transformative process your personal identity and circle of concern expand to include other people, future generations, and ultimately all of nature. As a result, you may become more concerned about living in a sustainable manner, so that we can collectively create a sane and healthy future. However, actually *living* a practice of ecological sustainability can be very challenging—particularly in the face of resistance. Tela Star Hawk Lake described to us how difficult this challenge can sometimes be:

> *I think the big challenge on walking this medicine path is that Indian people*
> *have to fight for their sacred grounds all of the time. We've got to fight to*
> *save Mt. Shasta. We've got to fight to save the high country. And it's not just*
> *fighting; it's going against the government, the forest service, the lumber*
> *companies, all of these things.*
>
> *Nothing is ever just given to us. It's a constant battle, not over*
> *spirit, but still a battle—because those mountains are where we gain our*
> *knowledge so we may bring that knowledge to the people. Our teachings*
> *come from there. We get over one hurdle and think everything's okay,*
> *and then comes another fight to save our sacred places, to save our sacred*
> *knowledge.*

That's a battle because we have to keep everything in balance. Everything has to be in harmony. Not just for the human beings, but for the animals, for the birds, for the plants, for the fish, for the rocks, for everything. So we're not just keeping human beings in balance, we also have to help our relations in nature to stay in balance.

People don't realize when they change something in the environment that it changes our lives. It hurts us. We fight to save these sacred places for their knowledge, so people can really wake up. (2006)

Native American cosmology includes a core commitment to helping move humanity from a profane way of life in which we degrade our environment to a sacred way of life in which we honor and preserve it. Huston Smith speaks to this in his latest book, *A Seat at the Table* (2006); as he told us during our interview:

I'm going to risk generalization, but the contribution of the indigenous people of the world—of whom the Native Americans are closest and therefore most essential for us in North America to embrace—is namely that all the lines of division we Westerners have ascribed all over creation are really becoming permeated or dimmed... This is great because those divisions ... set us apart and feed our sense of separateness, alienation, and egoism. I think that Native American cosmology is not perfect, but it is certainly wise about the nature of interconnectedness—and this wisdom is essential to carry us into the future. (2006)

Lest this call to cherish and preserve the world begin to overwhelm you, to become yet another thing added to all the many things you must do, remember that through transformative experiences and practices, the motivation and commitment to live ecologically comes quite naturally, from the inside out. It springs from your worldview. As transpersonal psychiatrist Stan Grof told us:

In this worldview, the divine is expressing its endless creativity by moving from the original undifferentiated state of oneness into plurality, into the worlds of immense diversity. In deep self-exploration, we can become aware of the unity underlying all creation. This brings with it compassion for all sentient beings and an increase of tolerance. You see the planet as an organic whole and make a commitment to working towards planetary citizenship and global consciousness, rejecting violence as an acceptable form of solving problems in the world. You begin to see the problems in the world as your problems. With it comes a sense of global responsibility. You no longer feel satisfied with being comfortable yourself while there are serious problems in Iraq, Afghanistan, Africa, India, and other places in the world.

You realize that the roots of the global problems are built into the very structure of human personality, and that to work out problems in the world, we have to start from ourselves, undergo deep psychospiritual transformation. We cannot say anymore, "There is nothing wrong with us, we are okay, but there are some bad guys out there who are the source of all the problems and are spoiling it for us."

Another important dimension, which comes out of transpersonal experiences, is deep ecological awareness and sensitivity. You do not have to teach people ecology after they have had experiences of identifying with what is happening to other species—what it is like to be a fish in the Elbe River, getting all the toxic fallout from German industry. You learn experientially what it is like to be a biological creature that is exposed to industrial pollution. You develop a tremendous craving to have clean water, clean air, clean soil, unspoiled nature, and the rich diversity of species.

(2003)

As Grof's poignant words convey, transpersonal experiences can lead you to connect with something greater than even the human realm. All of the living world, including animals and plants—even rocks and minerals— may be experienced as part of your family. With this noetic understanding, you may deepen your care and concern for other creatures, naturally becoming more likely to act in ways that will bring about as little harm as possible.

As you transcend your small ego-self, many teachers report that you can connect to the world beyond your personal boundaries. The challenges of this connection can be clearly heard in the pained voice of transformative movement pioneer Anna Halprin. While talking to us about the degradation of our environment, she said, "It's like you're destroying yourself." She continued:

> Destroying part of the Earth is a desecration to our children. It really becomes very real and very personal. It goes beyond politics… It goes to the point where you feel so identified that it's like a member of your family is being destroyed before your eyes. Thus, the deepening of your relationship with the environment takes on a social consciousness as well. (2002)

As you move more fully into an integral and interconnected view of life, our research suggests that a more holistic and dynamic model of life takes form. For Yoruba priestess Luisah Teish, transformation leads directly to a richer connection to nature. The effect is like some giant pool of ripples, reaching out from the core of your being to a deeply embedded relationship to the world. As she said to us:

> You come to really understand that you are a part of nature. You come to understand that every time you sit down to eat, every time you wear a piece of clothing, something has sacrificed its life for you. We need to have more gratitude for what we have and what we get. We need to have a feeling of death as a natural part of the life cycle. That's very difficult to do when so many of us are dying because the environment is polluted and because there is so much violence.
>
> Having a consciousness that connects us to nature gives us purpose. If there has been an accident on the corner, rather than run away, we go and we lay flowers. We pay attention to what has happened there. We go from that symbolic act to taking some action to improve the situation. This is an engaged spirituality… It's not about sitting in church and looking for

individual salvation. This is really important if we're going to survive on the
planet. (2003)

For Wink Franklin, a man who spent decades studying individual and global mind change, such realizations are in fact the foundation for progressive social and political movements throughout history. He told us shortly before his death:

Recognizing that we are deeply connected with all life is the basis … for a
true ecological movement, a true appreciation of diversity, and a sense of
community at a global level. Closely related to that is honoring different
ways of knowing that complement and deepen intellectual understanding.
The heart of the transformational path is this deepening into ourselves
while, at the same time, deepening into the universe. It is in that inquiry that
we find the common ground with all humanity, all nature, all life. It is out
of that common ground that we [begin to] transform ourselves and our
society.

If we experience all as one, then we also feel injured every time any
other living creature is injured. It changes everything. We also recognize
that we can learn from all of life. It isn't just that there is knowledge and
wisdom to be gained from plants and animals… As we get deeper into the
transformational path, we understand that knowledge and wisdom can
come from all kinds of places. We are not, as human beings, the pinnacle of
wisdom in the universe. There's both a humility and an openness that comes
from this.

All the major movements during my lifetime—beginning with
the civil rights movement and including the feminist movement, the
environmental movement, the human rights movement, the alternative
health care movement, and the spiritual renaissance in the West—all of
them are grounded in the common core that is at the heart of transformative
inquiry and practice. Without that we are forever fragmented, separate, and
conflicted. It's nothing short of awe and full appreciation for all of life; it's

fundamentally understanding that we are one… It's how we will construct
a global society, and it's how we will come to terms with living a sustainable
life with our environment. It's out of this deep well of understanding that
we'll find our common ground. (2003)

Starhawk, an inspiring teacher and important leader in the American pagan movement, shared her hopes and fears about our planet's future:

Dirt is holy and sacred itself. Without it we would not be alive. The
sacred is in the immanent world. This is my hope, and one of the reasons
that I devoted so much of my life to this path. If we collectively shift our
consciousness to understand the sacredness of the Earth; if we can somehow
heal the mind/body, light/matter, and spirit/Earth split; if we can somehow
embrace the immanence of the sacred, then we'll also learn how to actually
physically heal the Earth. We will stop messing her up. We'll learn how to
make the shift out of the really insane, disconnected, destructive culture that
we live in. It's not enough to sit and meditate, or pray about the problems
in the world today. The world today really demands our action and our
engagement. Whether we can really do that in the time we have left, before
we have irrevocably damaged the Earth's life systems before the point of no
return, I don't know. We may have already passed the point of no return—
many people think we have. (2006)

As Starhawk points out, the sacred is in everything, even dirt. And, there is no reason to seek the divine as an abstraction outside ourselves. It is you and you are it. We heard a similar message from Lawrence Ammar and Paulo Santos, whose Johrei practice includes natural farming:

The fundamental principle of natural farming is to understand that the
soil itself is alive, that the soil itself has consciousness—it's a living entity,
and like all living entities, it responds to our love. You come to realize the
common thread of life force energy and consciousness that strings through
all living things, and everything has its place. Every blade of grass, every tree,

every insect, every stone has its place in the greater harmony. And when each
is growing in its own place, there's a harmony that's created. And when one
steps out of its place, as human beings often do, that's when chaos is created.
Now the world is in a very difficult situation. We really want to encourage
as many people as possible to share as much of the light as possible to help
alleviate the darkness. (2003)

It's clear from our research that you are your own meaning maker. You can choose to sit on the sidelines, or you can choose to engage fully with life. Vital to any transformative practice is becoming the most powerful, creative practitioner that you can be, each and every moment. Every second and every breath can be imbued with purpose and possibility, if you choose to engage deeply with your life.

EMBRACING SORROW AND JOY

Understanding that everything is sacred not only imparts a passionate intimacy, love, and concern for life, it also makes us feel everything more deeply and fully. Over and over again, we were told that this understanding brings with it not only joyful recognition but also deep sorrow over the suffering of the world. Transformation brings you closer to the truth of who you are, but this truth involves the full-hearted recognition of both the suffering and the joy of being.

Unitarian Universalist minister Jeremy Taylor spoke to us with frank honesty about how difficult it is to feel the pain inherent in our interconnectedness:

One of the things that dreamwork tends to do is cultivate both compassion
and an awareness of multiple realities—other people's realities, other ways
of viewing the shared reality. The more I acknowledge alternative realities,
the more the doorways into despondence and despair open up. This is one
of the reasons why people are sometimes forced to abandon the company of
other human beings in the course of their spiritual development: it's painful
to be around folks who are hurting each other and themselves.

Ironically, my sense is that, except for a very small minority of folks, this doesn't work, because nature is red in tooth and claw everywhere you go—even if you retire to the woods and don't see another human being from one end of the year to the next... If you are attuned enough to the voices of nature, you will hear the cries of pain. It's very difficult not to hear the trees complaining about the acid rain. It's very difficult not to hear the birds complaining about the polluted air.

The more one remains open to that awareness of misery, the greater the possibility and likelihood of transcendence. In the middle of all of the misery, the fog will part and there will suddenly be an awareness that all of this doesn't matter, all of this pain is unimportant in comparison to the larger meaning of it all—the interconnection of all life.

It's like being in a rainstorm—you don't have to be sorry for the raindrops when they smash into the ground; you don't have to be sorry for the trees that get their limbs blown off. They survive; it's part of their life. It makes them what they are. The same is true for the rest of us, but it's so much harder to connect with that empathetic acceptance of my own and other creatures' apparently needless pain.

A hurricane is one thing, and bullets and bombs and poisonous industrial waste are something else, but ultimately I believe they are the same—forces that shape our evolution, individually and collectively. It is the archetypal cauldron of change. And to the extent that we are conscious at all, we must participate in this process of change as consciously and responsibly as possible. (2006)

Psychologist Ralph Metzner emphasized the process of bringing "as much consciousness as you can to bear on everything." Go into your despair, he tells us, for your power is there. "Everyone finds a way of being that is appropriate to them" (2002).

Avatar teacher Sue Miller aptly pointed out that attending to the suffering in the world allows you to stay open and move forward on your transformative path:

There's a piece in Avatar that involves the shift to realizing that you're the one who can deliberately create your life. But then you look around and you see the suffering in the world at large. If you don't have a way to help alleviate that suffering, it can be so painful that you can potentially just shut back down. When people have a way to alleviate that suffering, they keep opening up and are willing to become more aware… One of the main things that happens is that at some point people think, "Enough about me and my life and all my stories and my dramas and my whatevers." It's old news. You may wonder, what else is there? To me the "what else is there" is being of service, and the joy people get from that interaction. (2002)

Transformation is a path of deepening into *all* that life offers us. This is why we've titled this book *Living Deeply*. Time and again, you learn that there is no spiritual bypass. You cannot embrace the beauty of life without embracing all that is. And when you do so, your heart is effectively broken open and the world rushes in. As a result, you may find yourself motivated by a new, internally generated moral imperative to make a difference to be of service to others, and to protect the Earth for future generations.

LITTLE GLIMMERS EVERYWHERE

We began this chapter with a quote from Esalen cofounder Michael Murphy, stating that integral transformation—the kind that touches every aspect of our lives—"is waking up or peeking through everywhere!" (2002). In fact, this integral transformation "is the next great human frontier."

Throughout this book, we've discussed how, through the grace of transformative moments, you can glimpse both what is undeniably true and what is possible. Through sincere and determined efforts, you can tend your garden, fertilize the soil, pull the weeds, stake the seedlings, and provide the conditions for the natural, never-ending process of transformation to take place. You can heal old wounds, repair and restore, and as Aldous Huxley put it so perfectly, "cleanse the doors of perception" (1954, 5).

As you continue on your path, you'll become an even better vessel for love, light, and goodwill to shine through. When your life and practice converge, as many people told us during our research, you'll rest ever more deeply into your authentic self. As a result, your worldview can shift from personal to transpersonal. And, as you come to understand the sacredness inherent in all things, you can move from self-centeredness to working for the good of all.

Swami Nityananda shared with us some wisdom he'd learned from his own guru, noting that inner experience determines our view of the world and everyone in it:

> *Whenever people asked Swami Muktananda what the heart of his teaching was he would say, "Meditate on yourself, honor yourself, worship yourself. God dwells within you as you." That is really the crux of the path—teaching us what we should meditate upon. Unless I know myself, all of myself, unless I worship myself and see God within me, there is no point in going anywhere, because what I have here within me is what I am going to see in everyone else. If I am able to honor, respect, and worship myself, I will see the divine here and everywhere, because wherever I go, I go. So if I carry that experience of contentment with me, in my mind, in my being, then that's what I'm going to see, that's what I'm going to experience, and that is what I'm going to give to everybody.* (2006)

Indeed, through practice you can cultivate the capacity to see beauty in all things.

Demonstrating the courage inherent in hope, expressive arts dancer and teacher Anna Halprin shared with us a quote she attributes to Martin Luther King: "Even if I was certain that the Earth would end tomorrow, I would plant a tree today." Anna, with eyes twinkling, then said to us, "It's a good quote for our times, don't you think?" (2002).

Each of us can open our eyes wide and meet the world with courage. If your mind is open, your attention trained, your perception clear and broad, and your intention pure and strong, you can follow the flashes of inspiration that appear to you each day. When encountering the sacred, mystical, or numinous in life, transpersonal psychologist Frances Vaughan advises us all to remember that:

> The thing about mystical experiences is that they're always temporary and transitory, yet they are also a gift and an inspiration. When you come back to your ordinary daily life, you realize that it's possible to see the world differently. So how do you learn to shift your perception? It doesn't work to try to hang on to those mystical experiences, and it doesn't work to try to re-create them either. You need to accept what is given and bring your life into alignment with what you learned from the experience. Now you know it is possible to see the world in a different light. Once you know this you can't pretend that it didn't happen. Once you are awake, you can't go back to sleep. If you try to, if you deny your experience or discount it, this generally creates difficulty and contributes to inner turmoil. (2002)

The goal isn't fireworks or fourth-of-July thrills. It's a deep appreciation for the little glimmers of hope that appear to you, even in the midst of the chaos of everyday life: looking into the frank stare of a newborn baby, experiencing a surprising moment of laughter with a colleague with whom you've never gotten along, enjoying the dancing sunlight of a bright winter's day or the darkened clouds of a spring rain. As spiritual teacher Ram Dass told us,

> Most of our work is about redefining ourselves as a spiritual being, as a soul. And a soul has only one motive: going to the One. When you start to see yourself with only that motive, wow, it gets very simple. And that's the spiritual work. The spiritual work from the soul's point of view is just moving closer and closer and closer to the Beloved. (2003)

SUMMARY

In this chapter you heard many voices telling a common story. It's a story of hope and possibility, grounded in thoughtful reflection. The transformative process can bring you into a more intimate connection with the fullness of life. It doesn't require that you pull yourself away from your friends, family, work, or play (although you might). It requires that you become aware of the beauty in every moment and every exchange, even when they're difficult exchanges. Ultimately, the process of transformation is very simple. As you commit to clear intention, attention, and engagement, you'll find new openings for yourself, the people, and the world that you care deeply about. In the final chapter, we offer a model of transformation that may help ground the various insights we have identified throughout the book. For now, you may wish to take a few minutes to explore your own sense of interconnection.

Experiencing Transformation: The Art of Interdependence

This practice asks you to let your mind drop into your heart and, with all your senses, welcome the world in while you contemplate the sacredness of everything.

First, find a place to sit outside comfortably. This could be in your backyard or favorite park or at a beach, mountain, or stream. Just sit, relax, and let yourself merge into your surroundings.

There you are, and there you belong. Your body made of earth is touching the Earth, as the Earth is touching your body. This is the most vital connection you have—this is interdependence. Ponder the interrelatedness of all you see. With the loving eyes of your heart, see what is before you, beneath you, above you, to the right of you, to the left of you, all around you, and within you. Notice the patterns inherent in the things you gaze upon. Notice the patterns embedded within the patterns. Breathe in this reality, breathe in this dynamic stillness. Feel it in your heart beating, your blood flowing, your mind attending, your eyes seeing, your consciousness as part of the universal consciousness.

Breathe and let this vibrant, dynamic, relational life breathe you. What do you see? Clouds? Birds? Waves? Insects? Flowers? Your hands? Rain? Now pull back further. Make your perspective grow even wider by relaxing more, centering your vision in your heart and letting your breath expand to envelop everything around you. Pretend for a moment that anything is possible. Just be. Just observe. Let it in. Be a part of it.

Now, take some time to journal about this experience and how you felt in this state of consciousness.

CHAPTER NINE:

No More Floating Clouds

The Navajos have a wonderful term for a great realization or
insight that is not sustained: they call it a floating cloud. It's just
there. It's beautiful in its shape and we describe it and we talk about
it—and then it dissipates because it hasn't been mobilized or
grounded or sustained… We're generating lots of floating clouds.
We need to ground our ideas so that they can change the world…
Nothing changes unless it's grounded and it's manifested.
—ANGELES ARRIEN (2002)

Throughout all of our research, our goal has been to learn more about the phenomenon of transformation, whereby people's lives are changed for the better in profound and long-lasting ways. We wanted to find out how, through transformative experiences and practices, people can radically shift their worldview, values, and priorities. And, too, we wanted to discover how it is that many paths lead to one mountain: how apparently widely divergent traditions and practices can all guide us to becoming more open, loving, balanced, authentic, kind, and generous—to living more deeply.

In speaking to many explorers and knowledgeable travelers, we've searched for overlapping commonalities to help us construct a map of the terrain of consciousness transformation. We've also sought to learn more about the sights one might see *off* the beaten path, as told to us by trailblazers who have gone to uncommon lengths—from trips to the moon to living for thirteen years in a cave—to transform their lives. We've shared with you the important themes that have emerged from our research—themes that are woven throughout the tapestry of transformation: no matter where you separate the cloth, the same threads will show themselves.

Now we seek to draw the various threads together. We don't want the information you take from this book to become just another floating cloud in your life—a collection of interesting ideas that are fascinating to consider but never find a place to land. It can be all too easy to forget the insights that come from transformative experiences. As transpersonal psychologist and transformational pioneer Ralph Metzner told us:

> *The potential for awakening enlightenment is within us because we are all cosmic beings of light. But intention is not inherent. We have free will. So you can choose to intend.*
>
> *There's always the inherent tendency to forgetfulness—that's the default position: unconsciousness. Once we incarnate into this world of multiplicity, of time, space, and matter, we can lose ourselves completely. Our senses are constructed to give us stimulation, to give us all this information about the external world. The cost is that we may get hooked, because we find the sense stimuli so fascinating. We have to learn how to get unhooked.*
>
> *There is the story of the prodigal son, or child—which should really be called the prodigal soul—who leaves the heavenly world or the royal palace of the mother and the father and goes on this journey. The prodigal son is supposed to find the treasured pearl that is being guarded by a dragon. And so the child leaves the royal palace, leaves the heavenly world of the mother and father, and goes into the world and gets addicted. He goes to*

Egypt and gets hooked on their drink and food—becomes addicted until he is groveling with the pigs in the field, totally forgetting everything.

And then he remembers. Somebody comes and brings him a letter. "Ah yes. Now I remember. I'm supposed to be doing something here on this planet. Not just living with the pigs"—no disrespect intended to the pigs, in essence they are noble animals! But that's the kind of experience where people suddenly remember.

Sometimes I've heard it referred to as "the return"—the mystical journey where you return from the heroic adventure in the world. You come back to your community. This is also part of the mystical journey: you return home to God from whom you came. Once the prodigal soul recognizes that he is on the return path, he will do everything to help him remember: collaborate with others, find teachers, read books, do practices…

And that is the way I think it is for most of us. We remember, we have good times, and we forget again. We fall off the wagon. We may have longer or shorter periods where we are hopelessly lost and confused and can't figure out if we are coming or going, which way is the right way. If we are fortunate and things work out, we find ways to help us on the way, grateful to grace, the amazing grace. (2002)

For most people, the transformative journey includes a number of twists and turns; sometimes it can be hard to tell if you're still on course. While transformation can be very disorienting, it can also provide the opportunity for a radical reorientation of your life—changing both where you stand in relation to yourself and to the world, and what you stand *for*. In this book we've attempted to present the great paradoxes of the transformative journey responsibly. We've tried to convey the simplicity and universality of teachings without resorting to oversimplified easy answers. We've also tried to point out the potential pitfalls and perils along the way. Obviously, transformation isn't always easy or pleasurable; we've tried to strike a balance between recognizing the upheaval and pain that can accompany shifts in worldview and sharing the liberation and joy that result from the transformative process.

CHARTING A COURSE

We've found that having a cosmology (story of the universe) can help give meaning and language to your transformative process. This can be a particular religious belief system, a set of spiritual principles that you live by, or your own guiding philosophy. Today, as science and religion converge for the first time in nearly four hundred years, you can chart your own course, guided by the power of discernment and your own inner wisdom. Our main goal in this book has been to develop a map of the transformative process that will help you do just that. We offer you a story of how transformation happens that is applicable no matter what spiritual, religious, or even atheistic philosophy you already hold. Below, we offer a summary of the transformative process we've unveiled in our research.

The Process of Transformation

As we've seen time and again, transformation is, at its essence, a shift in your perspective on your self, your life, and the world in which you live. Stimulated by a variety of potential catalysts, this worldview change often begins with a glimpse—an aha! moment or epiphany—that alters the steady state or status quo. These moments can result from experiences of awe, wonder, or great beauty. They can also result from great pain, loss, or suffering.

Not all transformative paths start with a dramatic peak experience, but most begin with some kind of noetic experience or deeply felt, unshakable internal realization. This shift can be triggered by something as subtle as reading a book that discusses an idea new to you or by something as dramatic as a near-death experience or a sudden awareness of a physical or perceptual phenomenon that is completely unexplainable in your current belief system. Typically, these moments are characterized by a recognition of some undeniable truth that flies in the face of—or puts the lie to—some fundamental belief you've held, possibly without even knowing it.

As we discussed in chapter 3, at this point in the transformative process you are presented with a choice: you can either assimilate the new realization into your current worldview, explaining it in terms of how you already see the world, or you can shift your worldview to accommodate the new realization. This is a very important crossroads. Failure to shift your worldview in the face of compelling evidence to the contrary can not only lead to a return to your previous status quo, it can also reinforce and rigidify your worldview in an attempt to make it impervious to destabilizing factors. In extreme cases, this reinforced worldview can become like a fortified castle wall, impenetrable to any information that might contradict it; this can lead to fundamentalism and fanaticism. Alternatively, you can either choose to—or feel you have no choice *but* to—shift your worldview in response to this new experience or realization. What makes a worldview shift more likely? Being vulnerable and open—such as when you're in periods of displacement, transition, and loss—can catalyze transformation. These periods create chinks in your armor into which new experiences can wedge themselves, thus cracking your shell open.

Shifting your worldview is also more likely if the experience is dramatic, profound, earthshaking, or carries with it such authority that it's simply undeniable. Take, for example, the Magic Eye posters that were popular in the 1990s. These are the posters that upon first glance appear just a jumble of lines and colors—a fine colored pattern, like static on a television. If you don't have someone, or many people, tell you that there's something to see in the poster, you won't give it a second glance. But if you heed others' advice to look at the poster in a particular way (by broadening your focus—much like the broadening of focus that occurs in many transformative experiences), something previously unseen will leap into your field of vision. When you finally do shift your focus and attend to it in a different way, aha! An airplane, dolphin, or ship emerges. Once you've seen the image, a thousand people can tell you it's not there, and you'll still be certain that it is, because of the veracity of your direct subjective experience: you know what you've seen and you cannot unsee it. You've stretched your worldview to include the possibility that, within seemingly random visual stimuli, a cohesive object can actually be perceived. Similarly, what makes an extraordinary experience transformative is when your worldview is forced to expand to make room for the new information you've encountered in your direct experience.

What else encourages transformation? In addition to direct experiences of moments that are profound or surprising, we're more likely to trust the reliability of our insights when they're repeated. Repetition carries weight: at some point experiences reach a threshold at which they can no longer be ignored or denied. We've all had the experience of the universe presenting something important to us again and again, until we finally take notice. On the other hand, depending on your state of mind, even one event can be enough.

As we saw in chapter 2, having a meaning system that offers a conceptual framework for understanding new experiences or new pieces of information makes it less likely that you'll chalk up a potentially transformative experience as just an inexplicable anomaly. It's almost like having a language and context gives the new experience or information ground to land on and take root. Recall Darwin's story from chapter 1 and how, until he knew about the theory of massive glaciers cutting through stone to create geological features, he *didn't even notice* the evidence that was all around him. Once he became aware of the possibilities of glaciers, this incontrovertible evidence was suddenly obvious to him.

Before we can have experiences that shift our worldview, it helps to know that such shifts are possible. Having a set of teachings or a group of people who can assure us that a worldview shift *is* possible because it has happened to them increases this likelihood. The opposite—refusing to accept that a shift is possible, despite evidence that it is—can be a huge inhibitor of growth. We're reminded of a high-ranking official in the National Institutes of Health who attended a symposium in which the findings of research on distance healing were presented. He commented that he didn't believe any of it. When asked what would convince him, he replied, "There is no evidence that could convince me." This kind of closed-mindedness inhibits new insight and discovery.

You're also more likely to be able to comprehend what's happening to you as you proceed along the transformative path if you have people you can talk to about your experiences, people who can guide you through the stranger parts of the transition. As we've said, transformation is no walk in the park. Our teachers told us that the most important things you can bring to the transformative table are your sense of adventure, an open mind, curiosity, and the intention to attend to potentially transformative moments— even to seek them out. Regular practice and participation in a supportive community can help growth continue to occur and keep you grounded in the midst of change.

For many people, one or a few experiences won't be enough to have a lasting effect, no matter how powerful these experiences are. As we saw in chapter 4, a potential pitfall here can be seeking transformative experiences that are more and more intense without engaging in the more mundane work that's needed to integrate them into everyday life. As author and cofounder of Integral Transformative Practice George Leonard reminded us, you've got to "learn to love the plateau" (2002).

Transformation is something that you grow into. As your path deepens over time, a reciprocal interaction takes place between your inner subjective experiences of contemplation and self-inquiry and your more outward practices and actions. The inner and the outer reinforce one another, helping you integrate transformative realizations into daily life. By training your attention, through practices such as contemplative study, being in loving relationships, reading sacred books, affirmations, rituals, ceremonies, meditation, time in nature, and much more, you can literally lay down new neuropathways in your brain. The subjective and the objective become linked. Psychiatrist and cofounder of the transformative practice of Holotropic Breathwork Stan Grof succinctly explained to us how our subjective and objective realities influence and ultimately determine one another and our life experience. He quoted to us the famed French Jesuit priest, paleontologist, and philosopher Fr. Pierre Teilhard de Chardin, saying, "We are not human beings having a spiritual experience. We are spiritual beings having a human experience." "If that's true," Grof continued,

> ... How come we settle for something less? Alan Watts spoke and wrote about "the taboo against knowing who we are." Our materialistic cultural paradigm does not support our spiritual awakening. In fact it ridicules it and pathologizes it. But the only thing that can stand up to and transform the dominant scientific paradigm, as well as the dogmas of organized religions, is direct spiritual experience.
>
> Spirituality is something that is experiential; it reflects our direct experience of normally hidden dimensions of reality. Through our personal

experiences we discover our own divinity and the numinosity of the cosmos.
For that we do not need a special place or appointed officials. Our body and
nature become our temple. (2003)

As Grof suggests, transformation involves allowing direct experience
to make meaningful, lasting shifts in your attitudes, priorities, motivations, thinking patterns, and behaviors. Why settle for less, he asks us. Why
indeed?

As you become an active participant in the transformative process
and your own evolution, the separation between your practice and the
rest of your life begins to dissolve. You start to see your own transformative journey in the context of the transformation of your community, and
of the world. It's as Lawrence Ammar and Paulo Santos, two teachers of the
healing art of Johrei, told us:

> *If I were to sum it up in this language of Johrei, together each of us is*
> *transforming ourselves, transforming our families, our homes, our*
> *neighborhoods, our communities, our cities, and our states—and then out*
> *into general society. It's like ever-expanding circles—like when you drop a*
> *stone in the pond... So as each of us transforms and we begin to connect*
> *with the others close that we love, we can really begin to make a real paradise*
> *on Earth. A real world of health and peace and prosperity.* (2003)

You may experience a greater sense of belonging and a greater capacity
for compassion. It is also possible that you will experience a call to service.
And more and more often, you may have a sense of deep love—of the sacred,
of the mystery and beauty that permeates even the simplest moments.

If this model holds true, eventually these new ways of thinking and
behaving—this new way of *being*—will become the norm for you. Still, vigilance is required to prevent even this new improved worldview from becoming rigid and closed to new information. It's helpful to constantly cultivate a
sense of curiosity that will not only keep you open to new information, but
will encourage you to consistently seek it out. By staying curious and intentionally paying attention to what lies outside of your expectations, you can
become both a dynamic explorer and the cocreator of your life.

SHIFTING WORLDVIEWS

We need only look to the extraordinary changes of the last few decades in the areas of civil rights, social and ecological justice, medical and psychological advancements, health and healing, and peace and reconciliation to see that we're learning more every day about how to positively transform our personal and collective consciousnesses. And we need only glance at the morning news or the front page of the paper to see how far we still have to go.

We've been asked, isn't transformative work primarily philosophical—the lucky pursuit of privileged people with the luxury to contemplate the further reaches of human potential? We think not. Our firm belief is that most of the unnecessary suffering on this planet—as well as much of our environmental decline and the rapid rate of species extinction—finds its root cause in the limited consciousness of a strictly materialistic culture that accepts the objective world outside ourselves as the only useful reality. Indeed, the greatest achievements of our species' relatively short time on Earth have taken place as a result of quantum leaps in consciousness—great shifts that started with one or a few individuals changing their perspective and doing things differently.

Learning how people can change their consciousness to become more balanced, compassionate, altruistic, tolerant of difference, able to hold complexity, and motivated to promote peace and sustainability is one of the most fundamental tasks before us.

A quote often attributed to Albert Einstein states, "No problem can be solved from the same level of consciousness that created it." George Leonard, whose writing on consciousness transformation from the 1960s to today has paved the way for the human potential movement and positive psychology, spoke to us of the importance of developing a grounded metaphysics that recognizes both the opportunities and the challenges before us. When we embrace our divine essence, we are incapable, Leonard notes, of engaging in violence, hatred, or injustice:

> *I believe that our failure to develop our potential is one of the most dangerous*
> *tendencies on the planet. Crime and war can be attributed to our failure to*

develop the potential of the vast majority of people. The main aim, shall we say, of all this work is to make it possible to develop your divine, God-given, universal potential. You've got no time to study war if you're developing your potential. You'll be too busy to get into that kind of trouble.

If you have a path of practice, you won't be as insecure. For some, this insecurity says: blow up the world. That's a problem. If you are on a path of practice, you will see yourself as part of all life. You will understand the spiritual in all its parts. And you won't need to dominate others.

Ultimately I feel that everything is spiritual. What we call matter is just one manifestation of spirit. I think that the heart of the atom just blazes with spirit. The heart of every atom and every subatomic particle is spiritual. I don't see a mind/body split or a body/spirit split. So much evil has occurred because we fail to see that. (2002)

Blind optimism and new age reductionism—in which overly simple solutions are sought for complex problems—aren't what's needed. With pragmatic optimism, we see the potential for what author Malcolm Gladwell calls *tipping point*. As Gladwell notes in *The Tipping Point* (2002), ideas can be contagious, just like viruses. If you look at human history you can find many examples of major and rapid changes in the way we collectively hold reality. Epidemics of ideas can spread. Collective worldviews can shift in a moment, as a critical mass of people begin to share a similar way of thinking. Perhaps it's time for an epidemic of consciousness transformation. Each of us can be a catalyst for this positive epidemic.

Many of the teachers we spoke to expressed the need for such a shift in our collective worldview. World religions scholar Huston Smith told us:

Positive, affirmative transformation is not just self-contained or self-centered. It improves the individual but it also improves all the individual's relations, including the community as a whole. Someone once asked Mahatma Gandhi, "Wouldn't it be wonderful if goodness were as contagious as the common cold?" and Gandhi said, "When will we ever learn that goodness is as contagious as the common cold?" Any personal transformation is contagious for others.

To summarize the importance of personal and global
transformation, there is a little familiar quatrain in the song "Swinging
on a Star"… "Would you like to swing on a star, carry moonbeams
home in a jar, be better off than you are, or would you rather be a mule…"
I think it puts its finger on the lure of transformation. Transformative
practice is to overcome our narrow ego, so to expand it into the universal
Self. There is a better dream than the collective nightmare of separation,
domination, and destruction we are living out right now—it is liberty and
equality for all. Not just for Americans, but for all people, for all beings. We
must follow our own conscience; follow the light where it leads us. It is true:
"seek and thee shall find." (2006)

Consciousness transformation holds the potential to course-correct social and ecological wrongs created by humanity's short-term thinking. As Native American elder Charlie Red Hawk Thom told us in sobering tones: "It is about time we wake people up. There have been difficult times for the last few hundred years. People in North America have wasted a good amount of energy" (2006).

At a 2006 meeting of the Pachamama Alliance, founder Lynne Twist delivered a message from the indigenous elders the alliance collaborates with in South America in a quest to preserve the rainforest and indigenous culture. She recounted, "Last year when we met, the elders told us to tell people in the north that it is the eleventh hour. Now they tell us to relay the message to our brothers and sisters in the north that this *is* the hour." It's time for us to make use of *all* our intelligences—including the intellectual, social, emotional, intuitive, spiritual, and ecological dimensions—to wake up to who we are and what we are capable of becoming.

A NEW STORY

Cosmologists Brian Swimme and Thomas Berry have suggested that we are a culture that is presently in between stories (1992), between worldviews. Both science and spirituality have a stake in the story that is being created. Each alone has only partial answers to the questions of who we are and what we are capable of becoming. Indeed, as twenty-first-century life unfolds, it is becoming increasingly clear that each of us has a voice in the answers to these questions. Through transformations in consciousness, each of us is empowered to help craft a new story—one that is more just, compassionate, and sustainable, now and for future generations.

We've shared with you what we consider to be the most important elements we learned about transformation—and suggested some ways these elements might apply to your own life. We invite you to become the practitioner, the scientist, and the wisdom keeper as you blaze your own trail to living deeply.

Take-Home Messages

- *Notice* catalysts, windows of opportunity, and moments pregnant with transformative potential, large and small.

- *Recognize* what you can—and do—bring to the table.

- *Discern* what is right and true for *you*, based both on your subjective experience and your observations.

- *Practice* holding intention, cultivating attention, repeating life-enhancing actions, and seeking both internal and external guidance.

- *Integrate* your transformative practice into your life.

- *Expand* your practice and your transformation beyond the personal.

- *Connect* with the mystery, the sacred ground of all being.

- *Live* deeply, in every way you can.

Resource Guide

THE INSTITUTE OF NOETIC SCIENCES

Since 1973, the Institute of Noetic Sciences (IONS) has been at the forefront of research and education in consciousness and human potential. Founded by Apollo 14 astronaut Edgar Mitchell, the institute seeks to explore the frontiers of consciousness to advance individual, social, and global transformation. The word "noetic" is derived from the Greek word *nous*, which refers to direct and immediate access to knowledge beyond what is available to our normal senses and powers of reason. Today, IONS is an international nonprofit organization with nearly 20,000 members; a quarterly magazine, *Shift: At the Frontiers of Consciousness;* a unique membership program featuring an annual book, quarterly CDs, weekly teleseminars with gobal leaders from a wide range of fields, and an active online community (www.shiftinaction.com); ongoing research and educational programs; a stunning retreat center on 200 acres; and 220 self-organizing community groups throughout the world, all working together to foster a global shift in consciousness. In 2007, IONS began publishing *The Shift Report* (www.shiftreport.org), an annual document that charts the transition that appears to be underway worldwide from a rigid, mechanistic, and materialistic worldview to one that is built on a foundation of interconnectedness, cooperation, and the intersection of science and spirituality. Through research, education, and community networking, IONS fosters linkages between apparently divergent ideas and disciplines, exploring familiar territory with a new perspective on what is possible for ourselves and the world at large. For more information, to become a member, or to make a contribution to the Institute of Noetic Sciences, please call us toll free at (877) 769-4667 or visit www.noetic.org.

THE COMPANION DVD

Living Deeply: Transformative Practices from the World's Wisdom Traditions, by Marilyn Mandala Schlitz, Tina Amorok, and Cassandra Vieten. This DVD contains nine guided experiential practices by teachers from the world's wisdom traditions, suitable for use by individuals and groups. Published by New Harbinger Publications/Noetic Books, January 2008. To order, visit www.amazon.com, www.livingdeeply.org, www.newharbinger .com, or your local bookstore.

THE E-LEARNING COURSES

Explore the nature of transformation through a self-guided e-learning course that is based on the research findings from *Living Deeply*. The program combines readings, video, and audio downloads that feature teachers, researchers, and average householders, each describing the nature of living deeply. To enroll, go to www.livingdeeply.org.

CONSULTING AND LECTURING

The principles of *Living Deeply* have been adapted for use in business, medicine, and education. Visit www.livingdeeply.org or www.marilynschlitz .com to learn more.

Teachers of Transformation

RESEARCH INTERVIEWEES

Adyashanti is a spiritual teacher, author, and founder of Open Gate Sangha. He offers nondual teachings via live Internet radio and silent retreats for meditation and self-inquiry. www.adyashanti.org

Lawrence Ammar is a Johrei teacher and practitioner. Johrei is a spiritual practice that was developed in Japan by Mokichi Okada, a contemporary of Mikao Usui. newyork@izunome.org

Angeles Arrien, Ph.D., is a teacher, an author, a cultural anthropologist, and a consultant. She is the founder of the Four-Fold Way Program, and founder and president of the Foundation for Cross-Cultural Education and Research. www.angelesarrien.com

Lauren Artress, D.Min., is an Episcopal priest and a psychotherapist. Author of *Walking a Sacred Path*, she currently serves as the canon for special ministries at San Francisco's Grace Cathedral. She is also the creator of the Labyrinth Project; in 1996 she founded Veriditas: The Voice of the Labyrinth Movement. www.veriditas.net and www.LaurenArtress.com

Sylvia Boorstein, Ph.D., is a psychologist and an author. She is also a cofounding teacher of the Spirit Rock Meditation Center. www.spiritrock.org

Shaykh Yassir Chadly is a professor, a teacher, and a musician; since 1993 he has been the imam at the Masjid-Al Iman (a multicultural mosque) in Oakland. He is currently an associate professor at the Graduate Theological Union in Berkeley. www.yassirchadly.com

Andrew Cohen is a spiritual teacher and the founder of the international organization EnlightenNext. www.andrewcohen.org

Andriette Earl is a reverend and a teacher of transformative spiritual principles, as well as an assistant minister at the East Bay Church of Religious Science. She is the author of *Embracing Wholeness: Living in Spiritual Congruence.* www.ebcrs.org

James Fadiman, Ph.D., is a professor, a consultant, and a teacher in the Sufi tradition, as well as a founder of the Institute of Transpersonal Psychology (ITP). www.jamesfadiman.com

Robert Frager, Ph.D., is a transpersonal psychologist, a professor, a Sufi teacher, an aikido master, and an author. The founder and past president of the Institute of Transpersonal Psychology (ITP), he currently serves as the director of the Spiritual Guidance Program at ITP. www.itp.edu/academics /faculty/frager.cfm

Winston (Wink) Franklin was a past president of the Institute of Noetic Sciences (IONS) and a trustee of the Fetzer Institute. Wink passed away in the fall of 2004. www.noetic.org

Gangaji is a spiritual teacher in the lineage of H. W. L. Poonja and Sri Ramana Maharshi and an author. She is also the founder of the Gangaji Foundation. www.gangaji.org

Stan Grof, MD, Ph.D., is a psychiatrist, a professor, and an author. One of the founders and chief theoreticians of the field of transpersonal psychology, he is also a cofounder of Holotropic Breathwork. www .holotropic.com

Anna Halprin is an expressive arts originator, a choreographer, a dancer, and a teacher. She is also the founder of the Tamalpa Institute for expressive arts education and therapy. www.annahalprin.org

Zenkei Blanche Hartman is a Zen teacher, a priest, and an author. Formerly the abbess of the San Francisco Zen Center, she currently teaches at the Monastic Interreligious Dialogue (MID) and the San Francisco Zen Center. www.monasticdialog.org

Gerald Jampolsky, M.D., is a psychiatrist, a teacher, and an author, as well as a cofounder of the Center for Attitudinal Healing. www.jerryjampolsky anddianecirincione.com and www.attitudinalhealing.org

Don Hanlon Johnson, Ph.D., is a philosopher, a professor, and an author, as well as the founder of the Somatic Psychology program at the California Institute of Integral Studies. www.donhanlonjohnson.com

Dennis Kenny, D.Min., Ph.D., is a reverend and a therapist. The author of *Promise of the Soul,* he currently serves as the director of Pastoral Care at the Cleveland Clinic in Ohio. www.clevelandclinic.org/pastoralcare

Shakti Parwha Kaur Khalsa is an author and a teacher of kundalini yoga; she is known as the Mother of 3HO (a kundalini yoga teaching institute). www.3ho.org

Stanley Krippner, Ph.D., is a professor of psychology at Saybrook Graduate School, San Francisco. www.stanleykrippner.com

George Leonard is a pioneer in the field of human potential, an aikido master, and a cofounder of Integral Transformative Practice. www.george leonard.com

Noah Levine is a Buddhist teacher, an author, and a counselor. He is also a cofounder of the Mind Body Awareness Project, a nonprofit organization dedicated to serving incarcerated youths. www.dharmapunx.com

Gay Luce, Ph.D., is a transpersonal psychologist, a teacher, and an author. She is also the founder of Nine Gates Mystery School. www.ninegates.org/council.html

Ralph Metzner, Ph.D., is an ecological psychologist, a professor, and an author. He is also cofounder and president of the Green Earth Foundation. www.greenearthfound.org

Sue Miller, MSW, has been involved with Star's Edge International and the Avatar courses as a teacher and as a trainer since 1992. www.avatarepc.com

Edgar D. Mitchell, Sc.D.; Captain, U.S. Navy (retired), is a former Apollo astronaut and the sixth man to walk on the moon. In 1973 he founded the Institute of Noetic Sciences. www.edmitchellapollo14.com

Mary Mohs, LVN, MA, MAC, holds a master's in transpersonal counseling psychology. She is a cofounder of Awakening: A Center for Exploring Living and Dying, where she currently serves as a director. www.awakeningonline.com

Michael Murphy is an author and a teacher. He is a cofounder of both the Esalen Institute—where he also serves as chairman—and Integral Transformative Practice. www.esalen.com and www.itp-life.com

Mahamandaleshwar Swami Nityananda Paramahamsa is a disciple of Baba Muktananda; in July 1981 he was chosen to succeed Baba and carry on the work of educating and inspiring people to practice meditation and the yoga of self-knowledge. He is the founder of Shanti Mandir. www.shanti mandir.com

James O'Dea is the current president of the Institute of Noetic Sciences (IONS). www.noetic.org

Jonathan Omer-Man is a rabbi, a kabbalist, a meditation teacher, and an author. He is the founder of the Metivta Center for Contemplative Judaism and past publisher and editor of the *Shefa Quarterly*. www.omer-man.net

David Parks-Ramage, M.Div., STM, is a United Church of Christ minister at the First Congregational United Church of Christ in Santa Rosa, California. www.fccsr.org

Lewis Ray Rambo, M.Div., Ph.D., is a minister, a professor, an author, and a counselor. Since 1978 he has been a Tully Professor of Psychology and Religion and a faculty member at the Graduate Theological Union in San Francisco. www.sfts.edu/rambo/rambo.cfm

Ram Dass, Ph.D., is a transpersonal psychologist, a spiritual teacher, a yogi, and an author. www.ramdass.org

Charles Red Hawk Thom, Sr., whose Karuk name translation is "Walking Back into the Future," is a full-blooded Native American elder, spiritual leader, and medicine man from northern California. He is a member of the council of elders of the Karuk Nation of the upper Klamath River of northern California, and he is a ceremonial leader who has revived the practice of many traditional ceremonies and dances among the Karuk neighboring tribes. www.earthcircle.org/redhawk

Rachel Naomi Remen, MD, is a professor at UC San Francisco, an author, and a teacher. One of the earliest pioneers of the mind/body holistic health movement, she is a cofounder of the Commonweal Cancer Help Program in California. www.rachelremen.com

Peter Russell is a futurist, an author, and a teacher; he focuses on integrating Eastern and Western understandings of the mind. www.peterrussell.com

Sharon Salzberg is a teacher and an author. She is also a cofounder of the Insight Meditation Society (IMS), where she continues to serve as a guiding teacher. www.sharonsalzberg.com

Paulo Santos is a Johrei teacher and practitioner. Johrei is a spiritual practice that was developed in Japan by Mokichi Okada, a contemporary of Mikao Usui. losangeles@izunome.org

Pa Auk Sayadaw is the founder and main teacher of the Pa Auk Forest Monastery in southern Burma. www.paauk.org

Rina Sircar, Ph.D., is a professor of Buddhist studies at the California Institute of Integral Studies (CIIS), where she holds the World Peace Buddhist chair. She is also a cofounder and resident meditation teacher of Taungpulu Kaba-Aye Monastery and its San Francisco center. www.ciis.edu/faculty/sircar.html

Huston Smith, Ph.D., is the Thomas J. Watson Professor of Religion at Syracuse University, where he is also an emeritus professor of philosophy. www.hustonsmith.net

Starhawk is a cofounder of Reclaiming, an activist branch of modern pagan religion, as well as a cofounder of Root Activist Network of Trainers (RANT); she is also the author or coauthor of ten books. www.starhawk.org

Tela Star Hawk Lake is a traditional native healer, teacher, and author. She is of Yurok, Hupa, and Chilula heritage and is one of the last female shaman-doctors of the Yurok tribe.

Charles Tart, Ph.D., is a transpersonal psychologist, a professor, and an author, as well as a core faculty member of the Institute of Transpersonal Psychology. www.paradigm-sys.com

Jeremy Taylor, D.Min., is an ordained Unitarian Universalist minister and founding member and past president of the International Association for the Study of Dreams; he teaches at the Graduate Theological Union in Berkeley. www.jeremytaylor.com

Luisah Teish holds a chieftaincy title in the Fatunmise lineage as head Oshun priest in the United States, within the Orisha tradition of southwestern Nigeria. She is the founding mother of Ile Orunmila Oshun, the School of Ancient Mysteries and Sacred Arts Center. An internationally known storyteller, playwright, and director, she has been on the faculty at several San Francisco Bay Area institutions. www.ileorunmilaoshun.org/

Francis Tiso, Ph.D., is an ordained Roman Catholic priest of the Diocese of Isernia-Venafro. Father Tiso currently serves as the associate director for interreligious relations at the Secretariat for Ecumenical and Interreligious Affairs of the U.S. Conference of Catholic Bishops. www.usccb.org/seia/

Ron Valle, Ph.D., is a psychologist and an author. He is also a cofounder and director of Awakening: A Center for Exploring Living and Dying. www.awakeningonline.com

Frances Vaughan, Ph.D., is a pioneer of transpersonal psychology, a psychologist, a teacher, an author, and a trustee of the Fetzer Institute. www.francesvaughan.com

Gilbert Walking Bull was a Lakota elder and holy man of distinguished Sioux ancestry. In 2000 he founded Tatanka Mani Camp with his wife Diane Marie and Marilynn Bradley. Gilbert passed away in the spring of 2007. www.tatankamani.org

ADDITIONAL TEACHER INTERVIEWEES

Zorigtbaatar Banzar, Ph.D., is a Mongolian chief shaman and the director of the Center of Shaman and Eternal Heavenly Sophistication Mongolia.

Jon Kabat-Zinn, Ph.D., is a scientist and a meditation teacher. The founder of the Center for Mindfulness in Medicine, Health Care, and Society, he is also the author of several books, including *Coming to Our Senses* and *Wherever You Go, There You Are.* www.umassmed.edu/behavmed/faculty/kabat-zinn.cfm

Satish Kumar, Ph.D., is a professor, a lecturer, and an author, as well as the editor of *Resurgence* magazine. He currently serves as the director of Schumacher College. www.schumachercollege.org.uk/prospect/homepage.html

Marion Rosen is the inventor of Rosen Method bodywork and a pioneer in the field of therapeutic touch. www.rosenmethod.org

Brother David Steindl-Rast, Ph.D., is a Benedictine monk, an author, and a teacher. He currently serves on the board of directors for the worldwide Network for Grateful Living, through www.gratefulness.org, an international interactive website. www.gratefulness.org/brotherdavid

Mahamandaleshwar Swami Veda Bharati, Ph.D., is a teacher and an author. A disciple of Swami Rama of the Himalayas, he has spent the past sixty years traveling internationally to promulgate yogic and vedic knowledge. www.swamiveda.org

B. Alan Wallace, Ph.D., is a Tibetan Buddhist monk ordained by H. H. the Dalai Lama and one of the most prolific writers and translators of Tibetan Buddhism in the West. www.alanwallace.org

References

Adyashanti. 2004a. *Emptiness Dancing*. Boulder, CO: Sounds True.

———. 2004b. Interview by C. Vieten and T. Amorok. Video recording. December 8. San Jose, CA.

Ainsworth, M., M. Blehar, E. Waters, and S. Wall. 1978. *Patterns of Attachment*. Hillsdale, NJ: Erlbaum.

Ammar, L., and P. Santos. 2003. Interview by C. Vieten. Video recording. February 21. Institute of Noetic Sciences, Petaluma, CA.

Arrien, A. 2002. Interview by T. Amorok and C. Vieten. Video recording. November 11. The Four-Fold Way, Sausalito, CA.

Artress, L. 2003. Interview by C. Vieten and T. Amorok. Video recording. February 12. Grace Cathedral, San Francisco, CA.

Astin, J. A., S. L. Shapiro, D. M. Eisenberg, and K. L. Forys. 2003. Mind-body medicine: State of the science, implications for practice. *Journal of the American Board of Family Practice* 16:131-147.

Banzar, Z. 2006. Interview by T. Amorok and M. Schlitz. Video recording. September 5. Institute of Noetic Sciences, Petaluma, CA.

Barna. 2006. Half of Americans say faith has "greatly transformed" their life: *The Barna Update*. The Barna Group, Ltd. http://www.barna.org/FlexPage.aspx?Page=BarnaUpdateNarrow&BarnaUpdateID=240 (accessed June 6, 2006).

Batson, C. D. 1991. *The Altruism Question: Toward a Social-Psychological Answer*. Hillsdale, NJ: Lawrence Erlbaum.

———. 2002. Addressing the altruism question experimentally. In *Altruism and Altruistic Love: Science, Philosophy and Religion in Dialogue*, edited by S. G. Post, L. G. Underwood, J. P. Schloss, and W. B. Hurlbut. New York: Oxford University Press.

Boorstein, S. 2005. Interview by C. Vieten. Video recording. January 21. Institute of Noetic Sciences, Petaluma, CA.

———. 2007. *Happiness Is an Inside Job: Practicing for a Joyful Life*. New York: Ballantine Books.

Bowlby, J. 1988. *A Secure Base: Parent-Child Attachment and Healthy Human Development*. New York: Basic Books.

Carlson, L. E., M. Speca, K. D. Patel, and E. Goodey. 2003. Mindfulness-based stress reduction in relation to quality of life, mood, symptoms of stress, and immune parameters in breast and prostrate cancer outpatients. *Psychosomatic Medicine* 65(4):571-581.

Carter, B. L., and S. T. Tiffany. 1999. Meta-analysis of cue-reactivity in addiction research. *Addiction* 94:327-340. http://www.blackwell-synergy.com (accessed July 6, 2007).

Castillo-Richmond, A., R. H. Schneider, C. N. Alexander, R. Cook, H. Myers, S. Nidich, C. Haney, M. Rainforth, and J. Salerno. 2000. Effects of stress reduction on carotid atherosclerosis in hypertensive African Americans. *Stroke* 31:568.

Chadly, Y. 2006. Interview by C. Vieten. Video recording. April 2. Richmond, CA.

Cohen, A. 2003. Interview by C. Vieten. Video recording. September 22. Emeryville, CA.

Darwin, C. 1887. *The Autobiography of Charles Darwin*. http://www.darwinliterature.com/The_Autobiography_of_Charles_Darwin (accessed June 14, 2007).

Davidson, R. J., J. Kabat-Zinn, J. Schumacher, M. Rosenkranz, D. Muller, S. F. Santorelli, F. Urbanowski, A. Harrington, K. Bonus, and J. F. Sheridan. 2003. Alterations in brain and immune function produced by mindfulness meditation. *Psychosomatic Medicine* 65(4):564-570.

Dessalegn, B., and B. Landau. 2005. Relational language helps children bind visual properties of objects. Paper presented at the 17th annual meeting of the American Psychological Society, Los Angeles.

Earl, A. 2006. Interview by M. Schlitz and T. Amorok. Video recording. February 22. East Bay Church of Religious Science, Oakland, CA.

Eck, D. 2006. *The Pluralism Project at Harvard University.* Pluralism Project, Harvard University. http://www.pluralism.org/research/articles/index .php (accessed July 6, 2007).

Einstein, A. 1977. Letter dated 1950. In *Mathematical Circles Adieu: A Fourth Collection of Mathematical Stories and Anecdotes,* edited by H. W. Eves. Boston: Prindle, Weber & Schmidt.

Einstein, A., B. Podolsky, and N. Rosen. 1935. Can the quantum mechanical description of physical reality be considered complete? *Physics Review* 47:777.

Eisenberg, N. 2002. Empathy-related emotional responses, altruism, and their socialization. In *Visions of Compassion: Western Scientists and Tibetan Buddhists Examine Human Nature,* edited by R. J. Davidson and A. Harrington. New York: Oxford University Press.

Erikson, E. 1982. *The Life Cycle Completed: A Review.* Revised by J. Erikson, New York: Norton, 1997.

Fadiman, J. 2003. Interview by C. Vieten and C. Farrell. Video recording. January 21. Menlo Park, CA.

Fehr, E., and U. Fischbacher. 2003. The nature of human altruism. *Nature* 425:785–791.

Fox, M. 1983. *Original Blessings.* Santa Fe, NM: Bear.

Frager, R. 2002. Interview by T. Amorok and C. Vieten. Video recording. February 18. Institute of Transpersonal Psychology, Los Altos, CA.

Franklin, W. 2003. Interview by T. Amorok. Video recording. February 28. Institute of Noetic Sciences, Petaluma, CA.

Fricchione, G. 2002. Human development and unlimited love. The Institute for Unlimited Love. http://www.unlimitedloveinstitute.org/publica tions/pdf/whitepapers/Human_Development.pdf (accessed July 13, 2007).

Frisina, P. G., J. C. Borod, and S. J. Lepore. 2004. A meta-analysis of the effects of written emotional disclosure on the health outcomes of clinical populations. *Journal of Nervous and Mental Disease* 192(9):629-634.

Gangaji. 2002. Interview by C. Vieten and T. Amorok. Video recording. November 20. San Anselmo, CA.

Gladwell, M. 2002. *The Tipping Point: How Little Things Can Make a Big Difference.* Boston: Little, Brown.

Griffiths, R. R., W. A. Richards, U. McCann, and R. Jesse. 2006. Psilocybin can occasion mystical-type experiences having substantial and sustained personal meaning and spiritual significance. *Psychopharmacology* 187(3):268–83.

Grob, C. 2005. Interview by M. Schlitz. Phone interview. October 8. Petaluma, CA.

Grof, S. 2003. Interview by C. Vieten and T. Amorok. Video recording. January 10. Mill Valley, CA.

Halprin, A. 2002. Interview by T. Amorok. Video recording. February 4. Mountain Home Studio, Kentfield, CA.

Hanh, T. N. 1999. *Going Home: Jesus and Buddha as Brothers.* New York: Riverhead Books.

Harman, W. 1994. Personal communication with M. Schlitz, Sausalito, CA.

Hartman, Z. B. 2003. Interview by C. Vieten and T. Amorok. Video recording. February 25. City Zen Center, San Francisco, CA.

Huxley, A. 1945. *The Perennial Philosophy.* Repr., New York: HarperCollins, 2004.

———. 1954. *The Doors of Perception and Heaven and Hell.* Repr., New York: HarperCollins, 2004.

Idler, E. L., M. A. Musick, C. G. Ellison, L. K. George, N. Krause, M. G. Ory, K. I. Pargament, L. H. Powell, L. G. Underwood, and D. R. William. 2003. Measuring multiple dimensions of religion and spirituality for health research: Conceptual background and findings from the 1998 General Social Survey. *Journal of Research on Aging* 25:327-365.

Inhelder, B., and J. Piaget. 1958. *The Growth of Logical Thinking from Childhood to Adolescence: An Essay on the Construction of Formal Operational Structures*. New York: Basic Books.

James, W. 1902. *The Varieties of Religious Experience*. Repr., Cambridge, MA: Harvard University Press, 1985.

Jampolsky, G. 2002. Interview by C. Vieten and T. Amorok. Video recording. January 25. Sausalito, CA.

Johnson, D. H. 2002. Interview by C. Vieten and T. Amorok. Video recording. November 19. Marin, CA.

Jung, C. G. 1972. *The Structure and Dynamics of the Psyche*. Princeton, NJ: Princeton University Press.

Kabat-Zinn, J. 2004. Interview by M. Schlitz. Video recording. February 10. Institute of Noetic Sciences, Petaluma, CA.

Keltner, D., and A. Cohen. 2003. Berkeley social interaction laboratory. BSI Lab, Department of Psychology, University of California at Berkeley. http://socrates.berkeley.edu/~keltner/ (accessed July 6, 2007).

Keltner, D., and J. Haidt. 2003. Approaching awe: A moral, spiritual, and aesthetic emotion. *Cognition & Emotion* 17(2):297-314.

Kenny, D. 2006. Interview by T. Amorok. Video recording. May 10. Institute of Noetic Sciences, Petaluma, CA.

Khalsa, S. P. K. 2002. Interview by T. Amorok. Video recording. January 22. The Kundalini Yoga Teaching Institute, 3HO, Los Angeles, CA.

Klinger, E. 1990. *Daydreaming*. Los Angeles: Jeremy P. Tarcher.

Kounios, J., J. L. Frymiare, E. M. Bowden, J. I. Fleck, K. Subramaniam, T. B. Parrish, and M. Jung-Beeman. 2006. The prepared mind: Neural activity prior to problem presentation predicts subsequent solution by sudden insight. *Psychological Science* 17(10):882-890.

Kripal, J. 2006. Interview by M. Schlitz, T. Amorok, and C. Vieten. Phone interview. August 30. Petaluma, CA.

Krippner, S. 2002. Interview by T. Amorok and C. Vieten. Video recording. February 7. Saybrook Institute, San Francisco, CA.

Kumar, S. 2005. Interview by Kelly Durkin. Video recording. July 18. IONS conference, Arlington, VA.

Larkin, M. 2000. Meditation may reduce heart attack and stroke risk. *Lancet* 355(9206):812.

Lazar, S. W., C. E. Kerr, R. H. Wasserman, J. R. Gray, D. N. Greve, M. T. Treadway, M. McGarvey, B. T. Quinn, J. A. Dusek, H. Benson, S. L. Rauch, C. I. Moore, and B. Fisch. 2005. Meditation experience is associated with increased cortical thickness. *Neuroreport* 16(17):1893-1897.

Leonard, G. 1992. *Mastery*. New York: Plume.

———. 2002. Interview by T. Amorok and C. Vieten. Video recording. November 20. Mill Valley, CA.

Levine, N. 2003. *Dharma Punx*. San Francisco, CA: Harper.

———. 2005. Interview by T. Amorok and C. Vieten. Video recording. November 18. San Rafael, CA.

———. 2007. *Against the Stream: A Buddhist Manual for Spiritual Revolutionaries*. San Francisco, CA: Harper.

Lewis, T., F. Amini, and R. Lannon. 2000. *A General Theory of Love*. New York: Random House.

Linehan, M. M. 1995. *Understanding Borderline Personality Disorder: The Dialectic Approach Program Manual*. New York: Guilford Press.

Luce, G. 2002. Interview by C. Vieten and T. Amorok. Video recording. December 2. Corte Madera, CA.

Lukoff, D. 1998. From spiritual emergency to spiritual problem: The transpersonal roots of the new DSM-IV category. *Journal of Humanistic Psychology* 38(2):21-50.

Lutz, A., L. L. Greischar, N. B. Rawlings, M. Ricard, and R. J. Davidson. 2004. Long-term meditators self-induce high-amplitude gamma synchrony during mental practice. *Proceedings of the National Academy of Sciences* 101(46):16369-16373.

Mack, A., and I. Rock. 1998. *Inattentional Blindness*. Cambridge, MA: MIT Press.

Main, M. 1996. Introduction to the special section on attachment and psychopathology: 2. Overview of the field of attachment. *Journal of Consulting and Clinical Psychology* 64:237-243.

Markham, J. A., and T. Greenough. 2004. Experience-driven brain plasticity: Beyond the synapse. *Neuron Glia Biology* 1(4):351-363.

Maslow, A. H. 1954. *Motivation and Personality.* New York: Harper & Row.

―――. 1970. *Religions, Values, and Peak Experiences.* Repr., New York: Penguin, 1994.

Metzner, R. 2002. Interview by C. Vieten and T. Amorok. Video recording. November 26. Institute of Noetic Sciences, Petaluma, CA.

Mikulincer, M., and P. R. Shaver. 2005. Attachment security, compassion, and altruism. *Current Directions in Psychological Science* 14:34-38. http://www.blackwell-synergy.com (accessed July 6, 2007).

Mikulincer, M., P. R. Shaver, O. Gillath, and R. A. Nitzberg. 2005. Attachment, caregiving, and altruism: Boosting attachment security increases compassion and helping. *Journal of Personality and Social Psychology* 89:917-939.

Miller, S. 2002. Interview by T. Amorok and C. Vieten. Video recording. February 5. Institute of Noetic Sciences, Petaluma, CA.

Miller, W. R., and J. C'de Baca. 2001. *Quantum Change: When Epiphanies and Sudden Insights Transform Ordinary Lives.* New York: Guilford Press.

Mitchell, E. 2002. Interview by C. Vieten and T. Amorok. Video recording. December 23. Institute of Noetic Sciences, Petaluma, CA.

Monroe, K. R. 1996. *The Heart of Altruism: Perceptions of a Common Humanity.* Princeton, NJ: Princeton University Press.

―――. 2002. Explicating altruism. In *Altruism and Altruistic Love: Science, Philosophy, and Religion in Dialogue,* edited by S. G. Post, L. G. Underwood, J. P. Schloss, and W. B. Hurlbut. New York: Oxford University Press.

Murphy, M. 1972. *Golf in the Kingdom.* New York: Viking.

―――. 1992. *The Future of the Body.* Los Angeles: Jeremy P. Tarcher, Inc.

―――. 2002. Interview by C. Vieten and T. Amorok. Video recording. December 11. Sausalito, CA.

NCCAM. 2006. Backgrounder: Meditation for health purposes. Publication No. D308. February 2006, updated June 2007. http://nccam.nih.gov/health/meditation/(accessed July 13, 2007).

Nityananda, S. 2006. Interview by T. Amorok. Video recording. June 8. Petaluma, CA.

O'Dea, J. 2003. Interview by T. Amorok. Video recording. May 7. Institute of Noetic Sciences, Petaluma, CA.

Omer-Man, J. 2006. Interview by T. Amorok and C. Vieten. Video recording. October 22. Berkeley, CA.

Ornish, D. 2005. Opening your heart: Anatomically, emotionally, and spiritually. In *Consciousness and Healing: Integral Approaches in Mind-Body Medicine*, edited by M. Schlitz, T. Amorok, and M. Micozzi. St. Louis, MO: Churchill Livingstone/Elsevier.

Parks-Ramage, D. 2006. Interview by T. Amorok. Video recording. May 23. First Congregational Church of Christ, Santa Rosa, CA.

Pennebaker, J. W. 1990. *Opening Up: The Healing Power of Confiding in Others*. New York: W. Morrow.

Post, S. G. 2003. *Unlimited Love: Altruism, Compassion, and Service*. Philadelphia: Templeton Foundation Press.

Post, S. G., L. G. Underwood, J. S. Schloss, and W. B. Hurlbut, eds. 2002. *Altruism and Altruistic Love: Science, Philosophy, and Religion in Dialogue*. New York: Oxford University Press.

Radin, D. I. 2006. *Entangled Minds: Extrasensory Experiences in a Quantum Reality*. New York: Simon & Schuster.

Rambo, L. 2006. Interview by C. Vieten. Video recording. May 16. Institute of Noetic Sciences, Petaluma, CA.

Ram Dass. 2003. Interview by T. Amorok and C. Vieten. Video recording. January 4. San Anselmo, CA.

Red Hawk Thom, C., Sr., and T. Star Hawk Lake. 2006. Interview by T. Amorok. Video recording. May 20. Institute of Noetic Sciences, Petaluma, CA.

Remen, R. N. 1996. *Kitchen Table Wisdom: Stories That Heal*. New York: Riverhead.

———. 2003. Interview by C. Vieten and M. Schlitz. Video recording. May 12. Mill Valley, CA.

Rosen, M. 2005. Interview by C. Vieten and K. Durkin. Video recording. November 22. Berkeley, CA.

Russell, P. 2002. Interview by C. Vieten and T. Amorok. Video recording. December 3. Sausalito, CA.

———. 2004. *From Science to God: A Physicist's Journey into the Mystery of Consciousness*. Novato, CA: New World Library.

Salzberg, S. 2002. Interview by C. Vieten and T. Amorok. Video recording. December 12. Berkeley, CA.

Sayadaw, P. A. 2003. Interview by C. Vieten. Video recording. January 15. Daly City, CA.

Schlitz, M., T. Amorok, and M. Micozzi. 2005. *Consciousness and Healing: Integral Approaches to Mind-Body Medicine*. St. Louis, MO: Churchill Livingston/Elsevier.

Siegel, D. J. 2001. Toward an interpersonal neurobiology of the developing mind: Attachment relationships, mindsight, and neural integration. *Infant Mental Health Journal* 22(1-2):67-94.

Simons, D. J., and C. F. Chabris. 1999. Gorillas in our midst: Sustained inattentional blindness for dynamic events. *Perception* 28(9):1059-1074.

Sircar, R. 2003. Interview by T. Amorok. Video recording. March 7. Taungpulu Kaba-Aye Center, San Francisco, CA.

Smith, H. 2006. Interview by M. Schlitz and T. Amorok. Video recording. July 18. Berkeley, CA.

Smith, H., P. Cousineau, and G. Rhine. 2006. *A Seat at the Table: Huston Smith in Conversation with Native Americans on Religious Freedom*. Berkeley, CA: University of California Press.

Solovyov, V. 1894. *The Meaning of Love*. New trans. by T. R. Beyer, Herndon, VA: Lindisfarne Books, 1985.

Speca, M., L. E. Carlson, E. Goodey, and M. Angen. 2000. A randomized, wait-list controlled clinical trial: The effect of a mindfulness meditation-based stress reduction program on mood and symptoms of stress in cancer outpatients. *Psychosomatic Medicine* 62:613-622.

Starhawk. 2006. Interview by T. Amorok. Video recording. April 25. Institute of Noetic Sciences, Petaluma, CA.

Steindl-Rast, D. 1984. *Gratefulness, the Heart of Prayer: An Approach to Life in Fullness*. New York: Paulist Press.

———. 2006. Interview by M. Schlitz. Video recording. September 17. Institute of Noetic Sciences, Petaluma, CA.

Steuco, A. 1540. *De Perenni Philosophia Libri X*. Repr., New York: Johnson Reprint Corp., 1972.

Sundararajan, L. 2002. Religious awe: Potential contributions of negative theology to psychology, "positive" or otherwise. *Journal of Theoretical and Philosophical Psychology* 22(2):174-197.

Swimme, B., and T. Berry. 1992. *The Universe Story: From the Primordial Flaring Forth to Ecozoic Era Celebration of the Unfolding of the Cosmos*. New York: HarperCollins.

Sze, J., and M. Kemeny. 2004. Compassion: A literature review and concept analysis. Unpublished manuscript, University of California at Berkeley and San Francisco.

Targ, E., M. Schlitz, and H. Irwin. 2000. Psi-related experiences. In *Varieties of Anomalous Experience: Examining the Scientific Evidence*, edited by E. Cardena, S. J. Lynn, and S. Krippner. Washington, DC: American Psychological Association.

Tart, C. 1975. Science, states of consciousness, and spiritual experiences: The need for state-specific sciences. In *Transpersonal Psychologies*, edited by C. T. Tart. New York: Harper & Row.

———. 1990. *Altered States of Consciousness*. San Francisco: Harper.

———. 2003. Interview by C. Vieten and C. Farrell. Video recording. January 23. Berkeley, CA.

Taylor, J. 2006. Interview by C. Farrell and T. Amorok. Video recording. April 3. Fairfield, CA.

Teish, L. 1998. IONS Focus Group. Moderated by M. Schlitz and M. Killoran. Video recording. November 20. Mill Valley, CA.

———. 2003. Interview by C. Vieten and T. Amorok. Video recording. December 6. Oakland, CA.

Tiso, F. 2002. Interview by T. Amorok and C. Vieten. Video recording. December 4. Church of St. Thomas Moore, San Francisco, CA.

Valle, R., and M. Mohs. 2002. Interview by T. Amorok and C. Vieten. Video recording. December 20. Awakening: A Center for Exploring Living and Dying, Brentwood, CA.

Vaughan, F. 2002. Interview by C. Vieten and T. Amorok. Video recording. December 10. Mill Valley, CA.

Veda Bharati. 2002. Interview by C. Vieten and T. Amorok. Video recording. November 24. Mill Valley, CA.

Vieten, C., T. Amorok, and M. Schlitz. 2006. I to we: The role of consciousness transformation in compassion and altruism. *Zygon: Journal of Religion and Science* 41(4):917–33.

Vieten, C., A. B. Cohen, and M. Schlitz. 2008. Correlates of transformative experiences and practices: Results of a cross-sectional survey. Manuscript in preparation, Institute of Noetic Sciences, Petaluma, CA.

Vygotsky, L. S., and A. Kozulin. 1934. *Thought and Language*. New trans. by E. Hanfmann and G. Vakar, Cambridge, MA: MIT Press, 1962.

Walking Bull, G., and D. Marie. 2006. Interview by T. Amorok. Video recording. March 27. Wildlife Associates, Half Moon Bay, CA.

Wallace, B. A. 2003. Interview by M. Schlitz. Video recording. September 7. Institute of Noetic Sciences, Petaluma, CA.

———. 2007. *Contemplative Science: Where Buddhism and Neuroscience Converge*. New York: Columbia University Press.

Washburn, M. 2003. *Embodied Spirituality in a Sacred World*. Albany, NY: State University of New York Press.

White, R. A. 1994. *Exceptional Human Experience: Background Papers*. Dix Hills, NY: Exceptional Human Experience Network.

Wilber, K. 2000. *Waves, Streams, States, and Self: A Summary of My Psychological Model (Or, Outline of An Integral Psychology)*. Shambhala Publications. http://wilber.shambhala.com/html/books/psych_model /psych_model1.cfm/ (accessed July 6, 2007).

Wilson, D. S. 2003. *Darwin's Cathedral: Evolution, Religion, and the Nature of Society*. Chicago: University of Chicago Press.

Wolfe, W. B. 1932. *How to Be Happy Though Human*. Repr., London: Routledge, 1999.

Zickler, P. 2001. Cue-induced craving linked to brain regions involved in decision making and behavior. *NIDA Notes* 15(6). http://www.drugabuse .gov/NIDA_Notes/NNVol15N6/Cue.html (accessed July 13, 2007).

Marilyn Mandala Schlitz, Ph.D., is a clinical research scientist, medical anthropologist, writer, speaker, thought leader, and change consultant. Her work over the past three decades explores the interface of consciousness, science, and healing. She is vice president for research and education at the Institute of Noetic Sciences and senior scientist at the Research Institute at California Pacific Medical Center. She has published hundreds of articles on consciousness studies, lectured widely on a number of topics, including talks at the United Nations, the Smithsonian Institution, and the Explorers Club, has taught at Trinity, Stanford, and Harvard Medical Centers, and is the coeditor of *Consciousness and Healing: Integral Approaches to Mind-Body Medicine* (Churchill Livingston/Elsevier, 2005).

Cassandra Vieten, Ph.D., is a licensed clinical psychologist, research psychologist at the Institute of Noetic Sciences, and an associate scientist and codirector of the Mind-Body Medicine Research Group at California Pacific Medical Center Research Institute in San Francisco, and vice president of the Institute for Spirituality and Psychology. Her research over the last twelve years, funded by the National Institutes of Health, the state of California, and several private foundations, has focused on how biology, psychology, and emotion are involved in addiction and recovery, mindfulness-based approaches to cultivating health and well-being, the role of compassionate intent and belief in healing, and factors, experiences, and practices involved in psychospiritual transformation. She has published several academic articles and chapters as well as conducting numerous presentations at international scientific conferences.

Tina Amorok, Psy.D., is a clinical psychologist and research psychologist at the Institute of Noetic Sciences where she coedited the anthology *Consciousness and Healing: Integral Approaches to Mind-Body Medicine* (Churchill Livingston/Elsevier, 2005). With a background in integral health and healing, clinical psychology, and change management, Amorok designs and delivers programs for professional, university, corporate, and lay sectors on personal and social wellness and transformation. Her current research, *The Eco-Trauma and Eco-Recovery of Being*, examines how to heal and transform the primal wound of human alienation from nature from which destructive ecological behaviors, violence, and unhealthy lifestyles arise.

Foreword writer **Robert A. F. Thurman, Ph.D.,** is the Jey Tsong Khapa Professor of Indo-Tibetan Buddhist Studies in the Department of Religion at Columbia University. He also serves as the president of the Tibet House U.S., a nonprofit organization dedicated to the preservation and promotion of Tibetan civilization, and as the president of the American Institute of Buddhist Studies.

Preface writer **Richard Gunther** is a noted businessman from Los Angeles.

About the Institute of Noetic Sciences (IONS)

Noetic Books is an imprint of the Institute of Noetic Sciences, which was founded in 1973 by Apollo 14 astronaut Edgar Mitchell. IONS is a 501(c)(3) nonprofit research, education, and membership organization whose mission is advancing the science of consciousness and human experience to serve individual and collective transformation. "Noetic" comes from the Greek word *nous*, which means "intuitive mind" or "inner knowing." Noetic sciences further the explorations of conventional science through rigorous inquiry into those aspects of reality—such as mind, consciousness, and spirit—that include but go beyond physical phenomena. Our primary program areas include integral health and healing, extended human capacities, and emerging worldviews. The specific work of the institute includes the following:

- Sponsorship of and participation in research

- Publication of the quarterly magazine *Shift: At the Frontiers of Consciousness*

- The monthly membership program, Shift in Action, and its associated website, www.shiftinaction.com

- Presentation and cosponsorship of regional and international workshops and conferences

- The hosting of residential seminars and workshops at its on-campus retreat facility, located on 200 acres forty-five minutes north of San Francisco

- The support of a global volunteer network of community groups

Other titles from Noetic Books, copublished with New Harbinger Publications, include *The Untethered Soul* and the *Living Deeply* DVD companion.

For more information on the institute and its activities and programs, please contact:

Institute of Noetic Sciences
101 San Antonio Road
Petaluma, CA 94952-9524
707-775-3500 / fax: 707-781-7420
www.noetic.org

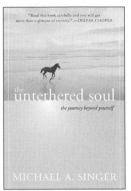